Hoasca

The Sacrament of the União do Vegetal

Science, Society and Environment

A Publication of CEBUDV-USA

Novato, California

Hoasca
The Sacrament of the União do Vegetal
Science, Society and Environment©

Editor - Portuguese
Joaze Bernardino-Costa

English Version Project Coordination
Jeffrey Bronfman
Celina Bennett

Publication Management
Celina Bennett

Translation
Celina Bennett

Portuguese-English Revision
Satara Bixby

Proofreading
Tama Jones Lombardo
Donna Thomson

Cover and Book Layout
Sue Lion

Cover Photos
Renata Cassis Law

Divider Page Photos
Augusto Pessoa

Back Cover Graphics
Judy Haas

Copyright ©2013 – CEBUDV USA

All Rights Reserved

Printed in the United States of America – 1st edition 2013

ISBN: 978-0-9910658-1-3

For further information please contact:
http://udvusa.org/

Edited by Joaze Bernardino-Costa
Translation by Celina Bennett
Portuguese-English Revision by Satara Bixby
Cover Design and Interior Layout by Sue Lion
Cover Photos by Renata Cassis Law
Divider Page Photos by Augusto Pessoa
Back Cover Graphics by Judy Haas

Printed at CreateSpace
4900 LaCross Road
North Charleston, SC 29406
USA

Published originally in Portuguese as *Hoasca, Ciencia, Sociedade e Meio Ambiente* by Mercado de Letras, Campinas, São Paulo, Brazil, 2011.

Library of Congress Cataloguing-in-Publication Data

Hoasca: The Sacrament of the União do Vegetal
Science, Society and Environment. Edited by Joaze Bernardino-Costa

Includes bibliographical references.
ISBN: 978-0-9910658-1-3

1. Anthropology   2. Ayahuasca   3. Centro Espírita Beneficente União do Vegetal (CEBUDV)
4. Beneficent Spiritist Center União do Vegetal   5. Science   6. Environment   7. Psychopharmacology
8. Religion   9. Rituals   10. Hoasca   11. Hoasca Societies   12. Religious Societies.

Hoasca

The Sacrament of the

União do Vegetal

Science, Society and Environment

Contents

	Gratitude	1
1	Foreword to English Publication *Marlene Dobkin de Rios*	5
2	Preface *Joaze Bernardino-Costa, Jose Roberto Campos de Souza*	13
3	Introduction *Joaze Bernardino-Costa, Flávio Mesquita da Silva*	21

Opening Speeches at the Second International Hoasca Congress

4	The Strength of Example: UDV, Memory and Mission *Raimundo Monteiro de Souza*	43
5	The Expansion of the UDV and its Achievements *James Allen Paranayba*	47
6	Citizenship of the Forest: The Heritage of a Sacred Right *Perpétua Almeida*	56

PART I – Hoasca and Science

The Constitution of DEMEC and the Scientific Commission

7	The Formation of the Medical and Scientific Department and the Scientific Commission *Lucia R.B. Gentil, Edison Saraiva Neves*	61
8	Objectives and Procedures of the Scientific Commission of the UDV *Luiz Fernando Milanez*	69

Hoasca Project 15 Years Later and the Study on Adolescents

9	Hoasca Project: Personal Opinion of the Hoasca Project *J.C. Callaway, Ph.D.*	75
10	Hoasca in Adolescence: A Study on the Health and Behavior of Adolescent Users of Hoasca in a Ritual Context *Otávio Castello de Campos Pereira*	83

11 Ayahuasca in Adolescence: A Neuropsychological Assessment   97
    *Evelyn Doering-Silveira, Enrique Lopez, Charles S Grob,
    Marlene Dobkin de Rios, Luisa B. Nunes Alonso, Cristiane Tacla,
    Itiro Shirakawa, Paulo H. Bertolucci, Dartiu Xavier Da Silveira*

12 Ayahuasca in Adolescence: A Preliminary Psychiatric Assessment   109
    *Dartiu Xavier da SilveiraCharles S. Grob, Marlene Dobkin de Rios,
    Enrique Lopez, Luisa K. Alonso, Cristiane Tacla, Evelyn Doering-Silveira*

13 Report on Psychoactive Drug Use Among Adolescents   117
    Using Ayahuasca Within a Religious Context
    *Evelyn Doering-Silveira, Charles S. Grob, Marlene Dobkin de Rios,
    Enrique Lopez, Luisa K. Alonso, Cristiane Tacla, Dartiu Xavier da Silveira*

14 Ayahuasca in Adolescence: Qualitative Results   125
    *Marlene Dobkin de Rios, Charles S. Grob, Enrique Lopez,
    Dartiu Xavier da Silveira, Luisa K. Alonso, Evelyn Doering-Silveira*

15 Methodology in the Study of the Use of Hoasca tea by Adolescents   133
    Luiza B. Nunes Alonso

16 Adult Life Narratives of Experiences with Religious Orientation   143
    in Childhood and Adolescence
    *Julia Maria Casulari Motta, Edison Saraiva Neves,
    Erica Monteiro de Almeida, Janine Rodrigues*

PART II – Hoasca and Society

The UDV in Brazil

17 Objectives of the União do Vegetal as a Brazilian   159
    and International Religious Group
    Edson Lodi Campos Soares, Cristina Patriota de Moura

18 The Legalization of the Hoasca Tea with the CONFEN   173
    Luís Felipe Belmonte dos Santos

19 The UDV Action Before CONFEN and CONAD   181
    Marisa Mendes Machado

The UDV Overseas

20 The Struggle for the Religious Freedom of the UDV   189
    in the United States of America
    Jeffrey Bronfman

21 The Legal Victory of the UDV in the United States Supreme Court: 195
    A Personal Statement
    John Boyd

22	Legal recognition of the UDV in Spain and brief considerations on legal recognition in other European countries *José Vicente Marín Prades, Patricia Lúcia Cantuária Marín*	203

Historic Hoasca Institutions

23	The UDV and the Historic Hoasca Institutions *Edson Lodi Campos Soares*	221
24	The Dialogue Between the Government Authorities and the Ayahuasca Religions: the Offering of a Treasure *Antônio Alves*	227
25	The Mission of Mestre Daniel *Francisco Hipólito de Araújo Neto*	235
26	Ayahuasca: from the Sacred to the Mundane The Conversion of Ayahuasca into a Psychoactive *Jair Araújo Facundes*	243

PART III – Hoasca and the Environment

Caring for the Mariri and the Chacrona

27	Ecology: Caring for the Mariri and Chacrona and The Preservation and Improvement of the Landscape and the Environment *Paulo Afonso Amato Condé*	251
28	Distribution, Cultivation, Sustainability and Conservation of the Species Used in the Preparation of the Hoasca Tea *Maria Alice Corrêa*	253
29	Genetic Conservation of the Mariri (Banisteriopsis sp) and Chacrona (Psychotria sp) – Germplasm Bank *José Henrique Cattânio, José Beethoven Figueiredo Barbosa, Maria Alice Corrêa*	269
30	Agroforestry Systems in Plantation Areas *Maurício Hoffman*	277
31	Environmental Work in the UDV *Flavio Gordon, Iára Reinke Soares Castro, Sara da Silva Abes*	281
	About the Authors	299

Gratitude

The elaboration of any book requires the effort of many people; it could be no different with *Hoasca: Science, Society and Environment*. This book came to be as a result of the Second International Hoasca Congress in May 2008 and the two-and-a-half years we spent polishing the lectures that were presented. During this period, a strong sense of unity was present among the people who worked on this project, which made all the necessary work lighter. We are grateful to everyone who contributed toward the realization of the congress and the compilation of this book.

We thank:

The members of the Council of the Recordation of the Teachings of Mestre Gabriel: Mestres Raimunda Ferreira Da Costa (Mestre Pequenina), Raimundo Monteiro de Souza, José Luiz de Oliveira, Raimundo Carneiro Braga, Francisco Herculano de Oliveria, Raimundo Pereira da Paixão, Jair Gabriel da Costa, Roberto Evangelista and Roberto Souto Maior. They all graciously contributed, enriching the Congress with historical information regarding the Beneficent Spiritist Center União do Vegetal.

Peregrina Gomes Serra (madrinha Peregrina), of *CICLU-Alto Santo,* for her willingness to appear on film side by side with Mestre Pequenina.

Antonio Alves, of *CICLU-Alto Santo;* Franscisco Hipólito de Araújo Neto, of *Barquinha;* and Jair Araújo Facundes, Federal Judge from the State of Acre, for enriching the Congress with their respective experiences.

James Allen Paranayba, President of the General Directorate of the UDV at the time of this project; for his trust in the organization of the Congress and of this book.

Renata Maria Guedes Neves, the executive secretary for the Congress, who was fundamentally important to its organization.

The staff of the General Directorate, for their dedication above and beyond their duty.

Jace Callaway, Charles Grob and Dennis McKenna, the strongholds of scientific research on Hoasca.

The musicians Juraildes da Cruz, Mambembricantes, Marcos Mesquita, Paulo Matricó, Xangai, Coral da Amizade, and the childrens musical trio from Belém do

Pará, composed of Daniel, Ariel, and Clarissa, for bringing their joy to the entire Congress. The sound recording team: Marco Lazarin, Cássio, Robinho, Claudinele and Renata from Nucleo Rei Inca (Goiania); Eric Botassine from Nucleo Apuí (Salvador); Angela Barreto from Nucleo Purpuramanta (Rio de Janeiro); Katia Shardong from Nucleo Senhora Santana (Campo Grande); Elaine Sardinha, Barbara and Flavio Pelacio from Nucleo Estrela Matutina (Brasilia); Alvaro from Nucleo Gaspar (Brasilia); and Suelene from Nucleo Canario Verde (Brasilia).

Cristina da Luz, for the revision of some of the recorded lectures and for her helpful conversations.

Luiz Claudio Pinho, for his support during certain phases of the book.

Alexandre Retamal and Iura Menão, secretaries of the General Directorate, for providing administrative information on the Center.

Bruno Wider, Director of the Legal Department, for his prompt attention to several requests for legal clarification.

Glacus de Souza Brito, for his ongoing contributions and living memory of the organization of the Medical and Scientific Department.

Friends Yuugi Makiuchi and Ivone Menão, for the numerous resources they made available and for the constant and detailed clarifications on the history of our Center.

Thiago Beraldo, Pablo Alejandro, Tuco and Renato Palet for their graphic design work in some parts of the book.

Terry Chambers, chief editor of the Journal of Psychoactive Drugs, for the permission to publish four articles published originally in English on the Hoasca in Adolescence study.

Bia Labate and Jeffrey Bronfman, for obtaining permission from the *Journal of Psychoactive Drugs* to publish the study on adolescents in Portuguese.

Professor Otavio Velho, for his collaboration with this work.

All the lecturers who participated in the Second Hoasca Congress and the collaborators of this book, for their patience in the dialogue to improve the lectures as well as the articles in the book.

Lastly, but not less important, Maria Elisa, editor of *Mercado de Letras*, for her effort and patience in the work of preparing this book.

For the English version, we express gratitude to:

Luís Felipe Belmonte dos Santos, for his generous support of the translation project and for all the years he has dedicated to dialoguing with government authorities to legalize the UDV's sacramental use of Hoasca tea in Brazil and overseas.

Jeffrey Bronfman, for his support coordinating this publication and his steadfast dedication to the legalization of the UDV's religious use of Hoasca tea in the USA. His admirable generosity and contributions to this effort have meaningfully assisted the UDV becoming recognized for its beneficent works, in the United States and in the world.

Dr. Marlene Dobkin de Rios (in memoriam), for the prologue she wrote to this English version. Dr. Dobkin de Rios's academic dedication to the study of the ayahuasca tea has been an asset to this field of study. We are deeply grateful for her collaboration and contributions to this book and to this field of research. She is a friend who will be dearly missed.

The Journal of Psychoactive Drugs for permission to publish the study on adolescents articles in this English version.

Mercado de Letras, the Brazilian publishing company, for permission to publish the English version of this book.

The translation team:

Celina Bennett, for her resolute leadership of this publication project and for her many years of translation support.

Satara Bixby, for her committed attention to detail and admirable skills in the Portuguese-English revision.

Tama Jones Lombardo and Donna Thomson, for their meticulous editing and final proofreading.

1: Foreword to the English Version

Hoasca: Science, Society and Environment

Marlene Dobkin de Rios, Ph. D.[1]

When I reflect on my career as a medical anthropologist, since 1967 it seems that I have been studying Hoasca tea (also known as Ayahuasca) non-stop. It was a great privilege and honor to be given a free hand to study Hoasca in its Brazilian context in 2001, focusing on the use of this important plant in the religious milieu of the União do Vegetal and its effects on adolescents, as well as from an anthropological perspective. The organization is formally known as the Beneficent Spiritist Center União do Vegetal. My work for many years since 1967 has been about plant hallucinogens as used by tribal, Mestizo and urban populations throughout Latin America, and urban use in the United States, Brazil, and worldwide. Recognized as a key researcher in this area by the 2nd National Commission on marihuana and Drug Abuse in 1970, I gathered data on a global basis to understand the role of plant hallucinogens in general across the ages and in different types of societies. I used my cultural-scientific training in this endeavor to understand how the use of such powerful mind-altering substances contributes to and has contributed to the survival of human beings across the world. Recognizing that these plants are likened to a double-edge sword that can be used for the good of humankind or not, the social scientist examining this data must search carefully to understand its impact and to what degree its use signals positive contributions to humankind.

In this brief prologue to the book, Hoasca: Science, Society and Environment I look at the key focus of my research: namely how these powerful substances have been utilized as a sacrament within a religious community to aid in the advancement of moral, intellectual and spiritual values. The UDV, as I shall refer to this Brazilian-based new religion, is not the only spiritually oriented group using Hoasca as a sacrament in their rituals and prayers. After a very difficult pair of decades, this group has realized the importance to show its face, so to speak, and to alert scientists, the public

---

[1] Associate Clinical Professor of Psychiatry & Human Behavior (retired), University of California, Irvine, USA.

and even its own adherents of its goal—to bring peace to humankind.

To help understand the realization of this goal, I will share with the reader the knowledge we have accumulated regarding the ancient use of Ayahuasca by tribes of the Upper Amazon for countless centuries. I will look at the context of Ayahuasca use by Mestizo farmers along the edges of major river systems in lowland South America, including groups similar to the UDV which was founded by Mestre Gabriel in Brazil in 1961. I will then examine my fieldwork in the Peruvian Amazon in 1968-9 among farmers in cities who have incorporated Ayahuasca into healing activities. Finally, in recent years, a nasty turn for the worse has spread throughout Latin America, as American, Europeans and others become tourists in a phenomenon we now label "Drug Tourism." Individuals, foreign to the spiritual role of Ayahuasca over time and space, have commoditized this substance, seeking out the substance for hedonistic purposes. There are large numbers of men and women hawking their wares in Amazon cities and towns.

What a welcome surprise in 2001 to have the opportunity to work with physicians and social scientists on a partially-funded study by the Heffter Foundation to examine the role of Hoasca among Brazilian youth, members of the UDV, along with a matched group. In the first instance, the Brazilian youth were members of the UDV Church and imbibed Hoasca ritually twice a month. This contrasted with the matched group who differed from the first only in their lack of participation in Church rituals and ingestion of the tea. A number of chapters in this volume detail the efforts and results of this interdisciplinary scientific activity.

Time and space will not allow me to examine all aspects of the materials assembled for the reader in this encyclopedic volume, but I will return to the evolutionary issue of what is the contribution of this sacrament in human development. I think we shall be pleased with the findings.

Part I – Ayahuasca Use in Tribal Societies of the Amazon

The Hoasca tea has been known by many names such as ayahuasca, natema, yaje among others, in the rain forests of western South America, which are drained by the upper Amazon tributaries and include parts of modern-day Ecuador, Colombia, Brazil, and Peru. The tea is a decoction of a plant hallucinogen, generally of the Banisteriopsis species, mixed with another plant, *Psychotria viridis*, and called chacruna in Spanish, among traditional horticultural groups. These tribal peoples live in thatched houses, use hammocks, dugout canoes and make pottery. They subsist on fish and other animal life in the forests and cultivate root crops such as manioc and yucca. Their culture is characterized by simple village type societies which lack any occupational specialization or social differentiation.

Ayahuasca has been incorporated into the culture of the rain forest for magical and supernatural rituals to allow the denizens of the forest to receive divine guidance and communication with the spirits that are believed to animate the plants. Men drink a potion that is a "union" of two plants, to receive a special protective spirit. For purposes of divination, the state created by drinking this potion tells if strangers are coming, and enables those drinking it to prophesy the future clearly. Also noted was its use in witchcraft to cause illness to another through psychic means and to use as a preventative agent against the malice of others. Ayahuasca was also incorporated into the health care system to determine the cause of and affect a cure for disease often thought to be caused by witchcraft. Finally, ayahuasca provided pleasurable or aphrodisiacal states, helped individuals to achieve ecstasy and facilitated social interaction among people.

Major transformations occurred since the Second World War, with large migrations of both civilizing tribal peoples (called Cholos in Peru), as well as the spread of the Mestizo populations to urban centers. Christian missionaries added to the changes. Healing with ayahuasca has undergone some major transformations. In the rain forest secluded Indian tribes took ayahuasca in ritual feasts or else limited its use to shamanic healers whom anthropologists called technicians of ecstasy. This has virtually disappeared in the spread of the plant use to cities like Iquitos, Pucallpa and other rain forest areas of lowland South America. Rather, we see Mestizo healers (called mestres in Portuguese) with both European and Native American heritage using the visionary vine to determine the magical cause of illness and to neutralize or deflect evil that their clients believe is responsible for their sickness. Also important to note are some of the roots of the União do Vegetal organization, which can be traced to the transformations of ayahuasca use and beliefs as the result of Christian proselytization in the post World War II years.

Part II – Mestizo Healing in Urban Centers of Latin America

My research with the sacred plants occurred from 1968-9, and 1979 in the cities of Iquitos and Pucallpa, where I studied urban healing with the plant that Peruvians called ayahuasca. I also worked closely with one ayahuasca healer in Pucallpa, Don Hilde and his patient population of almost 100 men, women and children. In Iquitos, with a population of 120,000 people, many of whom lived in squatter settlements such as Belen, ayahuasca use was either known to all the adults I interacted with or taken personally during illnesses or misfortune. The urban poor comprised the major clientele of shamanic healers, who administered the ayahuasca potion 2-3 times a week to anxious clients. In my book, Visionary Vine, (1972) I liken the beliefs and value systems of Belen to the culture of poverty found throughout overpopulated Third World centers. Witchcraft beliefs are regnant and reflect the high stress of individuals trying to survive in a very difficult world. The ayahuasca visions are used by the healers to ascertain the cause of the illness, often thought to be due to witchcraft hexes. Then the healer must return the evil willing to the perpetrator before he calls upon his pharmacopeia of plant remedies to heal.

In addition to my research in Peru, I visited Brazil on two different occasions as the guest of the UDV, and spoke to several hundred congregants; I observed three Hoasca ceremonies and interacted with individuals in 11 different temples in 4 major cities, including São Paulo, Rio de Janeiro, Manaus and Brasilia.

On return visits to Iquitos in 1979 and 2007, populations had grown tremendously, perhaps doubling in that 38 year period. Also now present was a tremendous growth of interest in the ayahuasca tea, attracting what I have labeled "drug tourism" from the U.S., Europe and Latin America, at the same time that religious groups such as the União do Vegetal and other Brazilian religions had incorporated elements of the ayahuasca culture into their own rituals and beliefs. Let us turn now to the development of Hoasca use within the UDV, noting the dramatic difference between the casual hedonistic use of the plant within a world of commodification of the plant, and the spiritual and institutional focus of its religious focus by the UDV in Brazil and the United States.

Part III – The UDV: Some General Remarks

In this preface, I have chosen not to examine the belief systems of the UDV church, as this area of activity is quietly preserved by congregants and participants; Rather, I will talk about the setting in which our inter-disciplinary team of scholars examined the impact of the use of Hoasca as a sacrament on adolescents in Brazil who had imbibed the drink twice a month. This compares with a matched group of students who had no actual contact with the Church. This is one of the very few studies that match two groups as we have done with the ability to generalize based on hard data due to experimental instruments, psychological tests and participant observation.

The report of this research can originally be found in the Journal of Psychoactive Drugs, (2005) titled "Ayahuasca Use in Cross-cultural Perspective." Additionally, we should note the important contribution of the UDV church in scientific studies and interest, its complex administrative structure, and its defense of religious freedom—themes with many adherents in a modern world.

In the research conducted by our international research team from Brazil and the United States, we see the way that Hoasca has been used as a religious sacrament taken by adolescents as well as adults. In our study of adolescent Hoasca use, the findings showed that when hallucinogen-induced managed altered states of consciousness were used under optimal conditions, positive and salutary outcomes resulted. This data is well presented in the Hoasca volume, and contrasts historically with Euro-American culture, where altered states of consciousness have been associated with negative and antisocial behaviors. From a sociological perspective, such states world-wide were synonymous with alienation, excessive introspection, rebelliousness as well as illegal behaviors. In our study of the UDV, this powerful hallucinogen was incorporated into ritual and ceremonial events of the UDV church. This sacrament attempts to offer spiritual, emotional and ethical support to those who ingest the tea. As the individual drinks the tea, he or she becomes part of a religious congregation and part of a religious event that has as its major goal the development of spirituality in adherents. People who drink the tea participate as family units and include their adolescent children.

As the result of my visits to Brazil and interviews with congregants, I spoke with nine mestres of the UDV in Manaus. With Dr. Charles Grob and Dr. John Baker, we published a paper on "Hallucinogens as Redemption," (2002) which examined the role of Hoasca in changing behavior as manifested by the concept that "good drugs may cast out bad ones." All the mestres spoken to had major life changes that were positive as the result of their work with the UDV and commitment to the community. The actual sociological rubric for what I observed in Manaus is called drug substitution, however, in this case set within the concept of redemption. This is a key element in the UDV setting. The redemptive model posits that the proper use of one psychoactive substance within a spiritual or clinical context helps to free an individual from the adverse effects of their addiction to another substance and thus restores them as functioning members of their community or group.

Unlike the redemptive use of Hoasca by individual members of the church and the mestres referred to above, the activities labeled drug tourism give the scholar cause for concern. Throughout Latin America, tourists are attracted to so-called "healing centers" by poorly prepared individuals who advertise on the internet and collect hefty fees for their service. The clients are given powerful hallucinogenic drinks including witchcraft plants of the nightshade spp. along with the ayahuasca, and left to their own devices to find their way home to a hotel in the middle of the night. There have been occasional deaths and mental illness resulting from this fly-by-night activity that Rumrrill and I have documented in our book, An Hallucinogenic Tea Laced with Controversy (2008), and which I have argued can be traced in some degree to social scientists simply describing and analyzing a social phenomenon eventually leading to abuses. The book also examines a new category of false shamans who see the ayahuasca tea simply as a way to enhance their pocketbook. The scholarly literature on ayahuasca is voluminous and dispersed worldwide since the 1960s leading to a tremendous growth of interest in the phenomenon. Mea culpa, mea culpa.

Part IV – The Book Before Us

It is a privilege to be part of the research team covering an encyclopedic study not only of research elements but interdisciplinary collaboration across three continents and Hoasca use. While this may have resulted in somewhat of a time lag in making the data available to the interested public, the hard work and enthusiasm of the participants cannot be denied.

As the reader will see from the thoroughness of the data in this book, the breaking work with regard to the UDV church in New Mexico, USA is worthy of comment. The victory before the US Supreme Court, allowing the Hoasca to be utilized as a sacrament in the USA, was previously unheard of in the famous and infamous "war on drugs." One of the sections of the book, "The UDV Overseas" written by Jeffrey Bronfman, at the time responsible for the União do Vegetal in the United States, has narrated the enormous legal battle of this religion and its defense of religious freedom that began in 1999, winding its way to the Supreme Court. This battle can be likened to the fight years ago when the Native American Church in the U.S. was able to utilize peyote in its religious rituals as determined by the US Supreme Court.

One of the major effects of indole hallucinogens like Hoasca is what has been referred to as the "lovingness" quality of the effects and how it binds people together. Back in the 1970s, an American anthropologist, Janet Siskind, studied a Christianized tribal group in the Peruvian Amazon, which was matrilineal in its social structure. Simply speaking, when a woman married, her husband left his community of origin and came to live with his wife's relatives. A small group of people under l00 in number included a number of brothers-in-law who had to interact with each other in the hunt to survive. Two or three times a week they came together in the jungle to imbibe the ayahuasca tea, to be of one heart. It is my contention that from an evolutionary perspective, these powerful mind-altering plants have had and continue to have an important role in human evolution. Compared to the dangers of solitary drug use, the example set by the União do Vegetal, two plants to unify society in a ritually controlled setting, with careful screening of participants, "unlocks the secret of the universe" and is worth the wait.

Bibliography

Dobkin de Rios, Marlene. "Visionary Vine: Hallucinogenic Healing in the Peruvian Amazon." Waveland Press: Prospect Hts., Illinois. 1972.

Dobkin de Rios and Charles S. Grob. "Ayahuasca Use in Cross-cultural Perspective." Journal of Psychoactive Drugs. Vol 37, No 2, June 2005.

Dobkin de Rios, Marlene, Charles S. Grob and John R. Baker, Dr. Phil. "Hallucinogens and Redemption." Journal of Psychoactive Drugs. 34:3: July-Sept. 2002.

Dobkin de Rios, Marlene and Roger Rumrrill. "An Hallucinogenic Tea Laced with Controversy." New York: Praeger Press. 2008.

Siskind, Janet. "Preliminary Report of an Investigation of the use of Ayahuasca by a Tribe of the Selva." In Michael Harner, ed. Hallucinogens and Shamanism. N.Y.: Oxford University Press.1972.

2: Preface

Joaze Bernardino-Costa
José Roberto Campos de Souza

For almost 50 years the Beneficent Spiritist Center União do Vegetal (Centro Espírita Beneficente União do Vegetal – CEBUDV) has worked toward its core objective: the development of the human being in the sense of perfecting moral, intellectual and spiritual virtues. Parallel to this essential work, the CEBUDV also has developed multiple charitable initiatives both within the Center and for the public, through its executive and support branches, which are its departments.

Nevertheless, half a century of relevant social works carried out in practically the entire country of Brazil and several locations around the world, has not been sufficient to remove suspicion and diminish the lack of understanding.

We recurrently witness increasing suspicion, making the UDV a target of criticism by those who do not know what it is. Another aspect of this issue is the awareness that even our internal public, our membership, has a limited or incomplete vision of its own institution. Many lack knowledge of the Center's many activities or, at best, have a partial notion of its existence, scope and importance. Based on these findings, it has become evident that it is important for the Center to take a proactive approach to be visible to the authorities and to society as a whole. This same approach is important for our own membership since many of these members are the ones carrying out these activities unaware of their importance, like bricklayers laying bricks and not realizing that they are building a cathedral.

The departments of the CEBUDV are the support branches of the General Directorate of the Center, generally structured with a director, assistant director, regional coordinators, and monitors in each núcleo and authorized distribution of the Vegetal. This organizational structure makes it possible for all the members to participate in the activities of the Center, supporting its growth and strengthening two main areas of action: the spiritual and the institutional. Institutionally we interact with national society and with the state through fields such as legal work, charitable outreach and scientific research.

The Center's founder, José Gabriel da Costa, whom we call Mestre Gabriel, founded the Center with the intention of making it a reference of seriousness and transparency, focused on respect for the laws of the country, as well as for spiritual laws, in order to fulfill his goal: to make peace among men. The five pointed star is used as a symbol for the perfect man, with his feet firmly planted in earthly reality, opening his arms in a gesture of fraternity and elevating his head and mind to the highest. Likewise, the UDV is firmly developing on this earth, steadfastly participating in charitable works and contributing, in a relevant manner, to the development of the human being. The interest of the scientific community, which was awakened two decades ago, has grown exponentially since the benefits of the ritual use of Hoasca in the lives of UDV members have been ascertained. The accumulated knowledge regarding our sacred plants, their cultivation, their active principles, the importance of preservationist activities, and the obvious repercussions within the fields of medicine, anthropology, psychology, sociology, etc., must be preserved, expanded and made available to the public. It is with this intention that we briefly present the accomplishments of the Beneficent Spiritist Center União do Vegetal in this book *Hoasca: Science, Society and Environment*.

This book has its starting point at the Second International Hoasca Congress that took place on May 9-11, 2008, at the Brasil 21 Convention Center in Brasilia, Federal District, Brazil. At that time we came together with an audience of approximately 1,200 participants, who had the opportunity to hear from presenters from several different academic areas and also to broadcast the knowledge we have about Hoasca on the worldwide web. In addition, we had the opportunity to report on the institutional development of this religious society. Many of the papers presented at that Congress, after extensive editing and perfecting, are present in this book; however, this book is not only restricted to the texts and the presenters that originally participated in the Congress.

It is significant that the majority of the articles presented in this book are texts written by the people who have lived, and continue living, parts of this story. They are expressing in these statements their vision as members of this religion: a perspective that is on the frontier between religion and academia, religion and the state, and religion and society. Therefore, to simply describe this book as a native contribution to this field of study would be a mistake; that is, if we understand native contribution to mean not having any knowledge of what academia has written about the so-called Ayahuasca field of study. On the contrary, a good number of the chapters gathered here are in dialogue with pertinent academic and scientific literature.

The book begins with the article Building the *World of Hoasca: The Organization of the União do Vegetal,* which as an introduction, explains the structure and the institutional functioning of the União do Vegetal. At the same time this article indicates the tone of this book: an emphasis not on the psychoactive substance, but on the institutional and material accomplishments that this religious society, the UDV, has been able to achieve through the union among the people, made possible by the enchantments and mysteries of the Hoasca Tea.

Following we have three articles derived from the opening speeches of the Second International Hoasca Congress. The speech given by Raimundo Monteiro de Souza, Mestre Monteiro, who was at that time the General Representative Mestre of the UDV, speaks of his memories of the first moments of the UDV in Porto Velho, and the mission of this religion. Then, James Allen Paranayba, who was at that time the president of the UDV, describes the challenges and the institutional victories of the UDV in its process of growth, relations with the authorities, the scientific community and the general public. In closing, we have the article by Congresswoman Perpétua de Almeida, PCB- Acre, discussing the proposal, of which she was one of the authors, sent in 2008 to the IPHAN (National Institute of Historical and Artistic Heritage) requesting the recognition of Ayahuasca as a Brazilian Intangible Cultural Heritage.

After the opening speeches, the book is divided into three sections. The first, titled Hoasca and Science, focuses on the internal organization of the UDV, both for the stimulation of research on Hoasca and for the interface with the general public and the state. The article by Lúcia Gentil and Edison Saraiva traces the developmental history of the UDV's Medical and Scientific Department (DEMEC), tracking important information presented at prior scientific congresses organized by the UDV. In the next article, Luiz Fernando Milanez discusses the constitution of the Scientific Commission, its objectives, scope of action, and procedures utilized by scientists and the UDV.

Following this, Jace Callaway, a neuro-scientist from the University of Kuopio, Finland, who participated in the Human Pharmacology of Hoasca Project conducted in the mid-1990's, presents a personal account of his experience with Hoasca in a religious context. Callaway's account is enriched by his elucidating narrative of the relationship between the Hoasca Project research group and the UDV during the implementation of that study.

Within this first section we have a subsection titled *The Adolescents Study.* This subsection begins with a presentation by Otavio Castello de Campos Pereira, a doctor affiliated with the UDV, who was responsible for the data collection logistics of that study in 2001. In this article he presents a summary of the results and of the logistical aspects of the *Hoasca in Adolescence* study, which was conducted by researchers who are not affiliated with the UDV. It is important to emphasize that the UDV only participated in the logistics of the study, and did not interfere in the definition of the methodology or the interpretation of the results.

The four articles that follow in the subsection titled *The Adolescents Study* contain the results of the study. The publishing of the original Portuguese edition of this book marks the first time that these articles were made available to the Portuguese speaking public, as they were originally published in English in the Journal of Psychoactive Drugs in 2005. These articles contain the results of several assessments conducted with adolescents who are users of Hoasca in a religious context. The bi-national research team, composed mainly of researchers from UNIFESP (Federal University of São Paulo) and the University of California at Los Angeles and at Irvine, questioned the long-term effects of prolonged use of Hoasca on the physical and mental health of adolescents. More specifically, they sought to evaluate the mental state of the adolescents studied, tracking any psychiatric disorders, including describing any pattern of drug consumption. The cognitive function of the subjects was also studied in multiple aspects, as well as their psycho-social universe, their values, beliefs, and vision of the world. For the implementation of this research, a comparative methodology was chosen, comparing the adolescents who were drinking the Hoasca tea, at least twice a month, in the religious context of the UDV, with adolescents of the same socio-economic and cultural profile, who had never drank the Hoasca tea.

At the conclusion of this subsection, Luiza Alonso, a member of the Adolescents Study research team, presents some methodological observations and the challenges of the qualitative study used with the adolescents (extensive interviews and focus groups). Based on these two research techniques, several topics were examined: family life, relationships with friends and acquaintances, social integration and alienation, sexual experiences, vision of the world, and plans for the future.

The second part of the book, titled *Hoasca and Society,* is divided into three subsections that address the process of the UDV's institutionalization in Brazil and overseas, as well as describe the existing alliance between the UDV and other religious societies who use the Hoasca Tea as a sacrament.

The first subsection titled *The UDV in Brazil,* begins with an article by Edson Lodi Campos Soares and Cristina Patriota de Moura, narrating the main steps taken by the UDV to formally organize and achieve legal recognition in Brazil as well as overseas. The article presents a historical perspective from the very first dealings of the UDV with the public authorities in Porto Velho during the 1960's; through the procedures of the CONFEN (Federal Narcotics Council); to the present CONAD (National Anti-Drug Council), during the 1980's and 1990's; to the study carried out by the Multi-disciplinary Working Group of the National Drug Council, which approved its final report in 2006, and published it in the *Diário Oficial da União* (Official Registry of Brazil) in January of 2010. It is important to emphasize that throughout this long historical trajectory, the União do Vegetal, along with other institutions that use Hoasca as a sacrament, has affirmed it values and principles.

The article by Luis Felipe Belmonte dos Santos, the attorney for the União do Vegetal during the mid-1980's, describes the occasion when the plants used in the preparation of the Hoasca tea (also called Vegetal), and the Hoasca tea itself, were listed on the schedule of narcotic substances in Brazil. Hence, this article deals with the lawsuit filed by the UDV with the Brazilian Federal Narcotics Council and the unfolding of this case until the Hoasca tea was removed from the list of narcotic substances of the Brazilian National Health Surveillance Division and Drug Administration of the Brazilian Ministry of Health.

The next article, written by attorney Marisa Mendes Machado, narrates the actions taken by the União do Vegetal toward the CONFEN (Federal Narcotics Council) and the CONAD (National Anti-Drug Council), during the 1990's, when the CONFEN recommended prohibiting minors from using the Hoasca tea without any justification for such action. After this new lawsuit, filed by the UDV in the name of preserving the right to freedom of religion and the adequate exercise of parental rights, the guarantee of the parental right of children's religious education prevailed.

The second subsection, titled *The UDV Overseas,* contains three articles. In the first one Jeffrey Bronfman, one of the people responsible for the UDV in the United States, narrates in first person the enormous legal battle of this religion in defense of its right to freedom of religion, which started in 1999, when the office of the UDV in the U.S. was invaded by the FBI. The subsequent article, related to Bronfman's, is written by John Boyd, one of the attorneys hired by the UDV to represent the UDV in the United States. Boyd describes in detail the various steps of the legal process in the United States, the victories of the UDV in relation to the United States' government, in the Federal District Court of New Mexico, the Tenth Circuit Court of Appeals, and the United States Supreme Court.

Following, José Vicente Marín Prades and Patricia Lúcia Cantuária Marín relate the process of the legalization of the UDV in Spain and weave in their narrative the landmarks of the legal process in five European countries: United Kingdom, France, Germany, Holland, and Italy. This text has a wealth of information regarding religious laws in the European context.

In the succeeding section, *Historical Hoasca Institutions* starts with a brief introduction by Edson Lodi Campos Soares, the coordinator of Institutional Relations for the UDV, in which he offers a historical perspective of the friendly contacts and good relations Mestre Gabriel had with other Hoasca societies' leaders, with public authorities, and with society in general. The actions of Mestre Gabriel have also guided relations with other Hoasca societies, among them the *Centro de Iluminação Cristã Luz Universal* (CICLU – Alto Santo), or the "Universal Light Center for Christian Illumination (CICLU – High Saint)" and the *Centro Espírita e Culto de Oração "Casa de Jesus – Fonte de Luz" (Barquinha)*, or "Spiritist Center and Prayer Worship "Home of Jesus – Fountain of Light (Little Boat)." In the same tone, the following text is by Antonio Alves, official orator of CICLU – Alto Santo, a religious society founded by Mestre Irineu that today is under the responsibility of his widow, Madrinha Peregrina (Peregrina Gomes Serra). The article by Antonio Alves describes the dialogue between the public authorities with the societies who use the Hoasca tea, specifically the Santo Daime. By recovering information from people who knew Mestre Irineu and from other societies that use Hoasca Tea, this text explains how the intention of the authorities to obstruct the existence of these societies has been dissolved by the love contained in the Hoasca Tea.

Also in this section is an article by Francisco Hipólito de Araújo Neto, the President of the Spiritist Center Prayer Worship "Home of Jesus – Fountain of Light" *(Barquinha)*. In this article the author describes the spiritual mission of Mestre Daniel, the founder of Barquinha, the history of friendly relations between this society and the Santo Daime and the UDV, as well as the challenges faced, since its inception to present day, to the process of reducing society's prejudice in the state of Acre and nationally, in relation to the religious use of the Hoasca tea.

Concluding this subsection is the text of the Federal Judge from the state of Acre, Jair Araújo Facundes, a member of the Multi-disciplinary Working Group of the National Drug Council, responsible for the regulation of the religious use of the Hoasca tea. This regulation was consolidated in the CONAD Resolution no. 1, of January 25, 2010, published in the *Diário Oficial da União* (Official Registry of

Brazil), and based on the agreements between the Hoasca religious societies since the signing of the Letter of Principles in 1991. In this lucid article, Dr. Facundes makes a fundamental distinction for these groups between recreational use and religious use of the Hoasca tea. He explicitly describes what these historical Hoasca societies have in common: the perception of Hoasca as a religious element, an integral part of a social context that is filled with sentiment, belief, ritual, and a cosmology that goes much beyond the simple chemical pharmacology of a substance.

The third section of this book, titled Hoasca and the Environment, encompasses both the advances of the Plantation Department and the ecological work carried out by the UDV through its NGO, *Associação Novo Encanto de Desenvolvimento Ecológico* (The New Enchantment Association for Ecological Development). This section begins with a text by Paulo Afonso Amato Condé, making a brief introduction on the concerns and efforts of the UDV to develop studies for maintaining good quality plant specimens used in the preparation of the Hoasca tea, the Mariri and the Chacrona. He also describes the development of environs that resemble the natural habitat of these species as much as possible. In addition, he addresses the development of an ecological consciousness among the members of the Center through the educational work carried out by The NGO New Enchantment.

The article by Maria Alice Corrêa stems from 20 years of botanical observations regarding the geographical distribution, cultivation, sustainability and preservation of the two species used in the preparation of the Hoasca tea. Claiming no conclusive results, this researcher presents a set of extremely informative data on the status of the botanical research accomplished by the UDV and offers directives for new research.

The article *Genetic Preservation of the Mariri and Chacrona – Nursery of Germplasm* based on findings of a reduction of bio-diversity due to intensive deforestation on the planet, indicates the necessity for research regarding the genetic variability of the Mariri and Chacrona, the systematization of the information acquired, and the preservation of this information through a germplasm bank.

The article by Mauricio Hoffman, an agronomy engineer, describes some experiences implementing a system called agro-forestry, which substitutes the model based on monoculture in the plantations of the UDV. Inspired by the technique developed in the 1980's by Ernest Götsch of Switzerland, the agro-forestry system has demonstrated to be an appropriate technique for reconstituting an eco-system, with results such as: natural soil fertilization, reduced water usage for irrigation and development of an environment that closely resembles the natural habitat of the Mariri and Chacrona.

The last article, *Environmental Work in the UDV,* presents a perspective on the principles of ecology and spirituality linked to the New Enchantment Association for Ecological Development. This NGO, that is legally independent from the UDV, is formed by members who are for the most part also affiliated with the UDV. This subsection presents a brief historical time line of its founding, as well as information on its administrative structure and its accomplishments and ongoing projects. The many efforts of this NGO are carried out by the members of the UDV, such as selective garbage collection, promotion of composting kitchen scraps, development of "green" building approaches, and permaculture workshops at the different locations of the UDV. Different environmental projects that the New Enchantment Association has developed in the community at large are sometimes in partnership with state governments.

These projects include awareness campaigns on the importance of water preservation, on both the national and international level, the development of agro-forestry systems, and sustainable solidarity economy projects with artisans and low-income populations, among others. Both the internal and external initiatives of the New Enchantment Association described in these articles can be read as a gradual effort to develop an ecological consciousness linked to spirituality, weaving together the threads that unite us to nature, to our fellow humans and to ourselves.

Returning to the metaphor of the five pointed star mentioned previously, the texts that are brought together in *Hoasca: Science, Society and Environment,* are examples of how the União do Vegetal, throughout this half a century, via the work of its departments, has firmed its feet on earthly reality through the preservation of its memory and the environment, scientific research, and the defense of freedom of religion, while opening its arms to charitable works and elevating its mind to the heights, seeking spiritual inspiration and motivation to carry out this work.

We hope that this book facilitates a deeper understanding of the current state of the realm of Hoasca tea drinkers, establishing a more symmetric dialogue with academia. Concurrently, we hope to inform society as a whole of the steadiness, seriousness and commitment of the generations and the families who are part of this religious society in order to establish a more respectful dialogue. In conclusion, we want, with this book, to honor all those who have contributed voluntarily to the development of this religious society.

Building the World of Hoasca: The Organizational Development of the União do Vegetal[1]

Joaze Bernardino-Costa
Flávio Mesquita da Silva

Hoasca is the word used in the Centro Espírita Beneficente União do Vegetal (CEBUDV), for the tea produced from the decoction of the *Banisteriopsis caapi* vine and the leaf of *Psychotria viridis*.[2] The communion of the Hoasca tea, also called Vegetal, is a central part of the religious ritual of the União do Vegetal. When we speak of Hoasca – or simply Vegetal – we are not referring to the substance in its chemical dimension. Our point of view stems from the symbolic, cultural and social universe of a specific religion, the União do Vegetal.

As it is well documented in the anthropological, botanical, and pharmacological literature, the beverage we refer to as Hoasca also has several other nomenclatures, such as Ayahuasca, daime, cipó, mariri, yagé, or kamarampi.The term Ayahuasca has been the one most commonly used in academic bibliographies to refer to the tea and the cultural practices related to it, including its religious use by different groups in Brazil and other countries. For this reason, when we use the term Ayahuasca we are referring to the practices and beliefs outside of the UDV or to what this religious group has in common with other institutions. The use of Ayahuasca has drawn the attention of researchers from numerous areas of study: anthropology, sociology, history, science of religion, biology, pharmacology, neurology, psychology, etc., increasing the number of academic-scientific studies on this subject (see Labate, Rose, and Santos 2008). The so-called Ayahuasca universe, even though it has the use of Ayahuasca as a common element, is also a very heterogeneous universe, encompassing a number of different groups (Labate and Araújo 2002; Labate, Rose and Santos 2008).

---

[1] The authors are grateful for the collaboration of Yuugi Makiuchi, Joelson Ferreira da Costa and Ivone Menão for the historical information; Renato Palet for the diagrams and maps; Alexandre Retamal and Iura Menão for the institutional information, and Cristina Patriota de Moura for the careful reading.

[2] The name *Centro Espírita Beneficente União do Vegetal* is most often translated into English as Beneficent Spiritist Center União do Vegetal. "União do Vegetal" is generally left in the original Portuguese, and means Union of the Vegetal, referring to the Union of the two plants that are united to produce the Hoasca Tea, which is also referred to as Vegetal, a word that also means "plant" in Portuguese.

This book brings forth several reports on scientific research, legal victories and alliances formed with other religious societies, as well as on the environment, which will fill in some of the gaps in this field of study. The set of articles included here will also present the positioning of the União do Vegetal (or simply UDV) in each of these fields and before the other groups that use Ayahuasca ritually.

The União do Vegetal, as a religious society, was created on July 22, 1961, on the border between Bolivia and Brazil, by José Gabriel da Costa, or Mestre Gabriel as he is called by his disciples.[3] José Gabriel da Costa was born on February 10, 1922, as the eighth child in a family of 14 children, in the *sertão* (backlands) near *Feira de Santana,* in the state of Bahia, Brazil.[4] Between 1943 and 1944, he enlisted as a rubber soldier and went to work in the Amazon rubber-tapping forests. He was married in Porto Velho in 1947 to Raimunda Ferreira da Costa, Mestre Pequenina, and together they formed their family.[5] He drank the Vegetal for the first time on April 1, 1959, in the heart of the Amazon forest, having received his first cup of Vegetal from another rubber tapper named Chico Lourenço. He drank the Vegetal a few times with Chico Lourenço and began to distribute the Vegetal by his own initiative. Soon thereafter, in mid-1961, while still in the forest, he announced to his disciples the creation of the União do Vegetal. A few years later, at the end of 1964, Mestre Gabriel moved with his family to the city of Porto Velho, then the capital of the Brazilian Federal Territory of Rondônia. Since then the União do Vegetal has worked for the improvement of the human being, developing moral, intellectual and spiritual virtues, and is considered by its members to be a place of equilibrium on Earth.

One of the characteristics of the religious ritual created by Mestre Gabriel is the oral transmission of the teachings, "from mouth to ear." In this transmission the degree of commitment demonstrated by the disciples is considered, as well as the capacity their memory has to receive these teachings. The spiritual teachings are maintained in secret, only revealed in the religious sessions of the Hoasca tea and according to the

---

[3] The word Mestre means "master" or "teacher." In the context of the União do Vegetal outside Brazil this term is left in the original Portuguese and not translated.

[4] The parents of Mestre Gabriel were Manoel Gabriel da Costa and Prima Feliciana da Costa. They had 14 children: João, Dionísio, Prasília, Pedro, Romão, Maria, Maria "Miúda," José (Mestre Gabriel), Silerina (Sinhá), Alfredo, Antônio (member of the UDV, in the Cadre of Mestres), Maximiniano, Albertina and Hipólito. The oldest was born in 1911 and the youngest in 1932.

[5] Mestre Gabriel and Mestre Pequenina had 10 children, all with birth certificates, from oldest to youngest: Getulio (born in 1948), Jair, Jandira, Carmiro, Abomir, José Gabriel da Costa Filho (Róseo), Salomão, Carmemiranda, Vicente and Benvino (born in 1970).

position the disciple occupies in the hierarchy of the UDV.

In addition to this characteristic, the UDV mirrors the life example lived by Mestre Gabriel, a man who despite having little formal education, brought to humanity the most noble values of human relations.He is considered a model example of a father, husband and friend to those who had the opportunity to know him.Mestre Gabriel supported his family with the sweat of his brow and valued fidelity to his home and as a husband and father.As a spiritual leader, he did not receive any remuneration for his religious services.He was a volunteer in his work.The process of registering the UDV as a religion started at the end of 1964 in Porto Velho, as a result of an incident in which Mestre Gabriel was arrested for further investigation and then released.The official registering of the UDV took place in October of 1967 with the name of *Associação Beneficente União do Vegetal* (Beneficent Association União do Vegetal).[6]

Approximately two years after the registration, in 1970, the authorities strongly persecuted the association as the chief of police of the Rondonia Territory endeavored to close it.At that time there was a motion to file suit against the Rondonia Territory Government.This event brought about the transformation of the Association, on June 19, 1971, into the Centro Espírita Beneficente União do Vegetal (Beneficent Spiritist Center União do Vegetal), which is the present denomination of this religious institution.[7]

Just days after this official registering of the Beneficent Spiritist Center União do Vegetal, Mestre Gabriel disincarnated in Brasilia, on September 24, 1971, leaving with his disciples the responsibility to continue his work.To facilitate the continuity of his work he left some fundamental principles for the structuring of the UDV, which have served as a beacon to this day.One of these principles is the precept that all disciples are copartners in the building of his work, independent of their hierarchical degree.

---

[6] At that time, the first directorate of the Beneficent Association União do Vegetal was composed as follows: President: Hilton Pereira Pinho; Vice President: Raimundo Monteiro de Souza; First Secretary: José Luiz de Oliveira; Second Secretary: Antônio Cavalcante de Deus; First Treasurer: Raimundo Carneiro Braga; Second Treasurer: Antonio Domingos Ramos; Official Orator: Modesto Alves de Souza; Social Director: Florêncio Carvalho; General Director: Manuel Emiliano de Lima. The President, Hilton Pereira Pinho, was not able to complete his term to end on January 6, 1971, which was completed by Vice President Raimundo Monteiro de Souza.

[7] At this time the second directorate of the UDV, the first of the Beneficent Spiritist Center União do Vegetal, was composed as follows: President: Francisco Adamir de Lima; Vice President: Messias Paula de Sá; First Secretary: José Luiz de Oliveira; Second Secretary: João Ferreira de Souza; First Treasurer: Raimundo Pereira da Paixão; Second Treasurer: Raimundo Ferreira de Souza; Official Orator: Bartolomeu Pinheiro do Nascimento. The narrative of this event is also the subject of the text by Campos Soares and Patriota de Moura, in this book.

While still incarnated, Mestre Gabriel began to train a Cadre of Mestres, composed of people who would be responsible for caring for the UDV, with the assistance of the other disciples. While he lived in the rubber-tapping forests from 1961 to 1964, he gave the title of Mestre to the disciples Manoel Severino Felix (Mestre Pernambuco), Raimundo Ribeiro das Chagas (Mestre do Bacurau) and Raimunda Ferreira da Costa (Mestre Pequenina).

In 1966 he instituted the first examination for arriving in the Cadre of Mestres of the UDV, in which eight disciples were approved: Waldemar Santos (Mestre Santos), Modesto Alves de Souza (Mestre Modesto), Manoel Nogueira da Silva (Mestre Manuel Nogueira), Hilton Pereira Pinho (Mestre Hilton), Florêncio Siqueira de Carvalho (Mestre Florêncio), Raimundo Carneiro Braga (Mestre Braga), Antônio Domingos Ramos (Mestre Ramos), and José Luiz de Oliveira (Mestre Zé Luiz).

Between 1968 and 1970, several more received the star of Mestre: Raimundo Pereira da Paixão (Mestre Paixão), Raimundo Monteiro de Souza (Mestre Monteiro), Bartolomeu Pinheiro do Nascimento (Mestre Bartolomeu) and Napoleão Victor de Oliveira (Mestre Napoleão).

On March 27, 1971, a historical and commemorated date in the UDV, when Mestre Gabriel returned to Porto Velho after having spent four months in Fortaleza, Ceará, for health reasons, he convoked the following people to the Cadre of Mestres: Francisco Adamir de Lima (Mestre Adamir), João Ferreira de Souza (Mestre Joanico), and Messias de Paula Sá (Mestre Messias). On July 22, 1971, Francisco Herculano de Oliveira (Mestre Herculano) also received the star of mestre. After this date, the second examination for the Cadre of Mestre took place and several more were approved: Roberto Souto Maior (Mestre Roberto Souto), Francisco dos Anjos Feitosa (Mestre Sidon), Raimundo Nonato Marques (Mestre Nonato), Cícero Alexandre Lopes (Mestre Cícero).

A total of 23 disciples received the star of mestre directly from Mestre Gabriel. It is important to note in this work the distribution of knowledge among the disciples. Mestre Gabriel said that he could have entrusted all the knowledge of the União do Vegetal to one single person, but he did not, in order for the disciples to need one another and to unite.[8] Furthermore, Mestre Gabriel valued the different abilities that each of his disciples had, all of which could possibly be of service in the consolidation of his work, according to the moment and the circumstance.

---

[8] Personal statement of José Luiz de Oliveira, Mestre Zé Luiz (see Makiuchi, s/d).

In addition to the Cadre of Mestres, Mestre Gabriel himself also created the Body of Counsel, the Instructive Body and the Cadre of Associates. These hierarchical positions represent the commitment each member has to this religion, their capacity for learning and memorizing the orally transmitted teachings, their capacity to put these teachings into practice, and to conduct themselves according to the teachings of the UDV. It is worth mentioning also that within the Cadre of Mestres there is an internal order. Thus, the hierarchy of the União do Vegetal is established in the following manner:

General Representative Mestre
General Assistant Mestre[9]
Central Mestre
Representative Mestre
Assistant Mestre
Cadre of Mestres
Body of Counsel
Instructive Body
Cadre of Associates

The General Representative Mestre is the highest authority of the UDV, responsible for supervising all the work taking place in Brazil and overseas. To achieve his goals he is assisted by the General Assistant Mestre. The Central Mestre reports directly to the General Representative Mestre and the General Assistant Mestre, and is responsible for the supervision of the núcleos and authorized distributions of the Vegetal in an administrative region of the UDV.[10] Next in the hierarchy is the Representative Mestre, the maximum local authority, assisted by the Assistant Mestre, which is a position that rotates every two months. Following is the Cadre of Mestres, consisting of all the mestres

---

[9] The post of General Assistant Mestre was the only post within this hierarchy that was not created by Mestre Gabriel. It was created on October 12, 1996, when Mestre Manoel Nogueira was elected General Representative Mestre, for the term beginning on January 6, 1997. The reason behind the creation of this post was the growth of the UDV.

[10] Presently there are 17 regions of the UDV in Brazil and two overseas (US and Europe). In the UDV a region is a geographic location where two or more *núcleos* exists, and do not necessarily correspond to the states of a nation. In general, núcleo is the designation given to a location where there is a physical structure in which to drink the Vegetal, a consolidated group of participants, and most importantly a minimum number of mestres to compose the Cadre of Mestres and the Body of Counsel, who are experienced and willing to be responsible for the works. An Authorized Distribution is a location which recently began the works and is still under the supervision of the núcleo where it originated.

of a núcleo, who provide assistance to the authorities of the Center. The Body of Counsel is part of the direction (leadership) of the núcleo, composed of counselors who assist the Cadre of Mestres. The Instructive Body is composed of people who demonstrate a commitment to the União do Vegetal, and also assist the Cadre of Mestres and the Body of Counsel. Lastly, the Cadre of Associates is formed by individuals who have taken their first step within this hierarchy, indicating their commitment to attend sessions.

This hierarchical system has often been misunderstood by hasty and imprecise spectators, who accuse the UDV of being authoritarian.[11] First, it is important to emphasize that none of these posts are occupied on a long-term basis. Elections take place every three years for the posts of General Representative Mestre and Representative Mestres.[12] The General Representative Mestre, once elected, designates the General Assistant Mestre, and proposes, within each region, three names for the post of Central Mestre, who will be chosen by the mestres in the respective regions. The Assistant Mestre of each núcleo holds this post for only two months at a time. The Cadre of Mestres and the Body of Counsel are the Direction of the núcleo and assist as necessary. Holding these positions is not an indication of acquiring an incontestable right. One is subject to being removed if one's conduct is not in alignment with the ascribed decorum expected for these posts.

The hierarchical degrees are positions open to all the members who demonstrate commitment to this religious society, understanding its values and subsequent congruent conduct, as well as the capacity to perpetuate the ritual practices and religious aims. Not only do the associates drink the Vegetal of their free and spontaneous will, they also contribute voluntarily to the goals of this work. They are encouraged to attain greater spiritual capacity, mental concentration, and expansion of their consciousness through seeking and examining the teachings and doctrine. The emphasis in the sessions is personal development and the achievement of independent thinking to be used in acquiring greater personal equilibrium in all aspects of life, including interpersonal relations.

The participatory nature of UDV activities, which uniquely harmonizes with its hierarchical characteristics, is, without a doubt, one of the trademarks of this religious society. Independent of the length of time a person has been a member of the UDV, he/

---

[11] Anthony Henman produced one of the first texts in the area of Human Science regarding the União do Vegetal. His analysis was imprecise, dense and prejudiced, including inferences such as that the União do Vegetal might have used the military regime in its favor (see Henman 1986).

[12] Throughout the institutional history of the UDV the duration of the each term has undergone modifications. Presently, this period is limited to three years.

she is able to contribute voluntarily according to his/her possibility, capacity and means.

The UDV is a religion open to the participation of its disciples, and has strong egalitarian traits, such as: (a) all members have the right to be co-responsible for the work of the UDV; (b) ascension in the hierarchy is independent of economic, political, educational, or social status; (c) a system of checks and balances which prevents the abuse of power by those in the upper tiers of the hierarchy; (d) the example of Mestre Gabriel that everyone is worthy of respect and consideration, whether someone is a long time disciple or recently arrived, and all disciples have the capacity to contribute to the cause of Mestre Gabriel. They only have to be willing.[13]

Mestre Gabriel created and developed the União do Vegetal with a strong participatory character, not only through the convocation of disciples to the Cadre of Mestres or to other important hierarchical positions, but also in many other ways. An example is the construction of the first temple of the UDV from 1968 to 1973, which was done by the entire congregation at that time.[14] Previously, the sessions took place at Mestre Gabriel's home. We can also notice, among countless examples, the participation of the disciples in the elaboration of the laws of the UDV, and in the composition of the *Chamadas* that are part of the rituals.[15]

Mestre Gabriel sought to train leaders that would be capable of continuing the material and spiritual administration of the União do Vegetal after he disincarnated. The unquestionable evidence of this is demonstrated in the fact that he formed a Cadre of Mestres with 23 disciples. Well aware of human fallibility, he established a system of checks and balances to prevent any excessiveness by those who might hold decision-making positions. One of these mechanisms of deterring the abuse of power is the law of the UDV, which states, "Those who know how to give orders must also know how to obey."

Another mechanism of power control is the rotation of those who occupy posts in the hierarchy of the UDV. In 1969 Mestre Gabriel designated Raimundo Carneiro Braga (Mestre Braga) to serve as the Representative Mestre of Mestre Gabriel, equivalent to the present post of General Representative Mestre.[16] On November 5, 1970, when Mestre Gabriel needed to travel to the state of Ceará for health reasons, he left Raimundo Monteiro de Souza (Mestre Monteiro) responsible for the Representation until May of 1971, when Mestre Monteiro passed it to Mestre Gabriel himself.

---

[13] One of the challenges of modern thinking has been the conciliation of hierarchy and equality, as seen in the influential work of Louis Dumont (1992).

[14] The historical headquarters of the UDV located in Porto Velho, Rondonia.

[15] Hymn-like calls sung by individuals during the UDV's religious rituals.

Mestre Gabriel disincarnated on September 24, 1971. From that date until April 1972, the ones responsible for the UDV were those who occupied the post of Assistant Mestre, in a schedule that rotated every two months.[17]

April 1972 was the start of a period when the UDV was directed by the capable members of the Cadre of Mestres, the majority trained by Mestre Gabriel. The ones who were elected to occupy the position of General Representative Mestre are listed below in Table 1.

TABLE 1 – GENERAL REPRESENTATIVE MESTRES SINCE THE DISINCARNATION OF MESTRE GABRIEL (1972 TO PRESENT)

General Representative Mestre	Term
Raimundo Monteiro de Souza (Mestre Monteiro)	Term: April 1972 to 1/6/1974
João Ferreira de Souza (Mestre Joanico)	First Term: 1/6/1974 to 1/6/1977 Second Term: 1/6/1977 to 1/6/1979
Raimundo Carneiro Braga (Mestre Braga)	First Term: 1/6/1979 to 1/6 1981 Second Term: 1/6/1981 to 2/8 or 2/12/1982*
Manoel Nogueira da Silva (Mestre Manoel Nogueira)	Term: 5/12/1982 to 10/16/1982†
Raimundo Monteiro de Souza (Mestre Monteiro)	Term: 10/30/1982 to April/1988
Raimundo Carneiro Braga (Mestre Braga)	First Term: April 1988 to 1/6/1991 Second Term: 1/6/1991 to 4/8/1993
Luis Felipe Belmonte dos Santos (Mestre Felipe)	Term: 4/8/1993 to 1/6/1994
Raimundo Monteiro de Souza (Mestre Monteiro)	Term: 1/6/1994 to 1/6/1997
Manoel Nogueira da Silva (Mestre Manoel Nogueira)	Term: 1/6/1997 to 2/13/1998‡
Raimundo Nonato Marques (Mestre Nonato)	Term: April 1998 to 2/10/1999
Florêncio Siqueira de Carvalho (Mestre Florêncio)	Term: 2/10/1999 to 1/6/2000
José Luiz de Oliveira (Mestre Zé Luiz)	First Term: 1/6/2000 to 1/6/2003 Second Term: 1/6/2003 to 1/6/2006
Raimundo Monteiro de Souza (Mestre Monteiro)	Term: 1/6/2006 to 1/6/2009
Francisco Herculano de Oliveira (Mestre Herculano)	Term: 1/6/2009 to present day

* From February 8 to 12, 1982, Mestre Simão (Simão Pereira da Silva), who was in the place of Assistant Mestre, responded for the General Representation.
† From October 16 to 19, 1982, Mestre Zé Carlos (José Carlos Garcia) responded for the General Representation, and from October 19 to 30, 1982, Mestre Joanico (João Ferreira de Souza) responded for the General Representation.
‡ After the disincarnation of Mestre Manoel Nogueira, General Assistant Mestre Clóvis Cavalieri responded for the General Representation, from February 13 to April of 1998.

It is important to emphasize the mechanisms instituted, since the beginning, to prevent the concentration of decision-making authority or spiritual knowledge in the hands of one single person. As mentioned before, a directorate was created; both in the Beneficent Association in 1968, as well as in the Beneficent Spiritist Center União do Vegetal in 1971, with a president, vice-president, secretaries, treasurers and other positions. Since 1968, when the Association was created, directorate meetings have taken place monthly, open to all the members, and where everyone has the right to speak and to vote. Therefore, the presidents of núcleos, and the General Headquarters do not exercise their function on their own; they are assisted by other members of the directorate and the membership.

In the UDV, another important aspect of Mestre Gabriel's legacy is the interaction between material power and spiritual power, with the former serving the latter. Therefore, since the beginning of the structuring of this religious society there was a position equivalent to the General Representative Mestre (spiritual leader) interacting with the position of the president (material administrator). The president of the General Headquarters, until the end of the 1980's, responded legally and administratively for the entire UDV, whereas núcleo presidents were responsible for their respective locations.

The directorates of núcleos and the General Headquarters are elected every three years, and their work is supervised by a Fiscal Council. It is important to note that the members of the directorate do not receive any remuneration for their services, preserving the principles of the Center, which is the voluntary nature of its work. [18]

---

[17] The first mestre who occupied the post of Assistant Mestre was Mestre Paixão (Raimundo Pereira da Paixão), and in this position he assisted Mestre Gabriel between 1969 and July 22, 1971. After this date, at the decision of Mestre Gabriel, this post began to rotate every two months. At that time, in the rotation system, the following mestres occupied the position of Assistant Mestre: Mestre Ramos (07/22/1971 to 09/22/1971); Mestre Roberto Souto (09/22/1971 to 11/22/1971); Mestre Pernambuco (11/22/1971 to 01/22/1972); Mestre Joanico (01/22/1972 to 03/22/1972). In April of 1972, when Mestre Monteiro held the post of the General Representation, the Assistant Mestre was Mestre Sidon, who had taken the post on 03/22/1972 and held it until 05/22/1972. The rotation system for Assistant Mestre continued through the Representation of Mestre Monteiro, as it continues to this day.

[18] The material operation of the UDV is made possible through the monthly dues paid by each member, to pay for the expenses of the núcleos and the authorized distributions. The only individuals that have earnings within the UDV are the office employees of the General Directorate, located in Brasilia, and the property caretakers, who generally reside at the rural property of the núcleos and the authorized distributions. In addition to the monthly dues, the Participation Fund (CEBUDV 1989b) was created on March 31, 1988. This is an amount that every member of the UDV pays to support institution-wide expenses, such as overhead for the offices in Brasilia, housing for the General Representative Mestre in Brasilia, health insurance for the Mestres of the Origin (those trained by Mestre Gabriel) and their widows - who are considered the founding members of the Center, and other administrative initiatives that may become necessary.

Many events took place on a national level, especially during the eighties (some of which are described in this book) that began to impact the lives of UDV disciples. Subsequently, some support initiatives were established to assist in the medical and scientific field, in the legal realm and in the area of charitable works, attending to necessities and to face the challenges that were constantly arising. Therefore, out of necessity, the General Directorate of the UDV was created on August 26, 1989 (CEBUDV 1989b).[19]

After a long period of administrative improvements, which is still going on, the General Directorate of the Center is organized in the following manner:

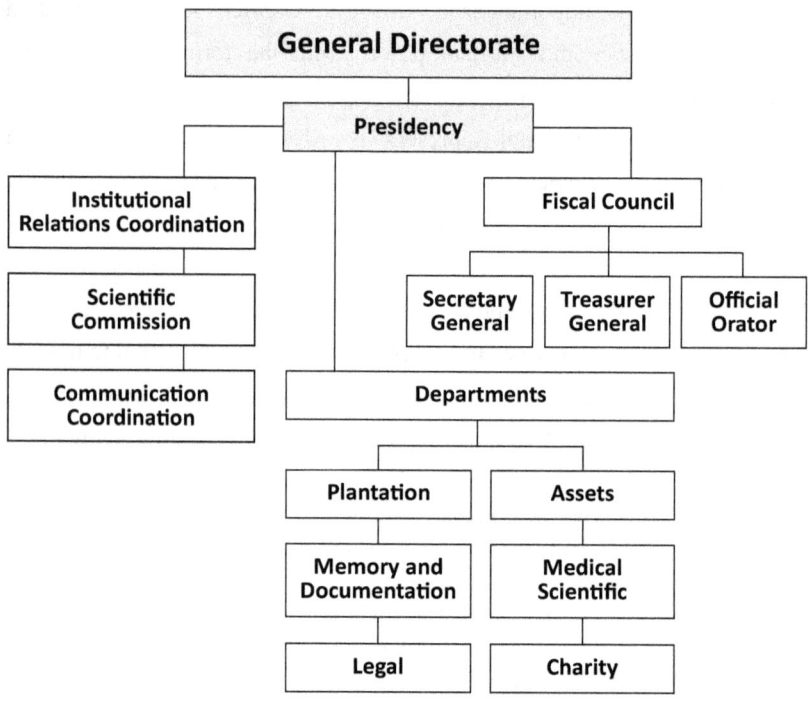

---

[19] The Presidents of the General Directorate and their respective administrative terms were the following: Edson Lodi Campos Soares (08/26/1989 to 01/06/1994), Edison Saraiva Neves (01/06/1994 to 01/06/2000), Edson Lodi Campos Soares (01/06/2000 to 01/06/2003), James Allen Segurado Paranayba (01/06/2003 to August 2008), Edson Lodi Campos Soares (August 2008 to 01/06/2009), Flavio Mesquita da Silva (01/06/2009 to 01/06/2012). It is important to observe that before the creation of the General Directorate, the post of President of the Center was exercised by the President of the General Headquarters. Thus, Mestre Hilton (Hilton Pereira Pinho), who was the president in the sixties, is considered the first president of the União do Vegetal.

The members of the General Directorate are elected every three years. The powers of the General Directorate are restricted to the material, social, cultural, charitable and educational aspects of the Center. Therefore, it is composed of a president, two vice-presidents, a general secretary, an adjunct secretary, a general treasurer, an adjunct treasurer, and an official orator. The actions of the General Directorate are supervised by a Fiscal Council, elected for the same period.

In order to better conduct its activities, the General Directorate is assisted by the Institutional Relations Coordination, the Communications Coordination and the Scientific Commission, and by six other Departments: Medical and Scientific, Plantation, Patrimony (Asset Management), Memory and Documentation, Legal, and Beneficence (Charitable Works).

The primary function of the Institutional Relations Coordination is contact with the government and with other religious societies who use ayahuasca.[20] The Communications Coordination has the responsibility to assist the presidency with press relations. The Scientific Commission maintains contact with researchers in disciplines other than the medical and pharmacological realm.[21][22] The Plantation Department is focused on the cultivation of the two plants used in the preparation of the Vegetal, the Mariri and the Chacrona, and also on the "companion" plants of these two species.[23] The Patrimony Department has the objective of administering the assets of the Center according to the laws of the country. The Department of Memory and Documentation is responsible for historical research within this religious society and for the preservation of the document archives.[24] The Legal Department works towards achieving legality and the institutionalization of the use of the Vegetal in Brazil.[25]

The Department of Charitable Works, also known as the Beneficence Department, promotes social assistance and educational initiatives to benefit both its internal membership and the public at large.[26]

As the President of the General Directorate is responsible for the material and administrative aspects of the Center, sharing his responsibility with a group of

---

[20] The texts in this book in the sections *The UDV Overseas* and *Historical Hoasca Institutions* describe some of the work carried out by the Coordination of Institutional Relations.

[21] See text by Milanez, in this book.

[22] See the texts by Gentil and Neves, Callaway and the section *Study with Adolescents*, in this book.

[23] See part III of this book, *Hoasca and the Environment*.

[24] See text by Motta and Gentil, in this book.

[25] See texts by Santos and Machado in the section *The UDV Overseas*, in this book.

[26] See text by Lima, in this book.

assistants, likewise, the General Representative Mestre is responsible for spiritual aspects, sharing his responsibilities with others who assist him. This administrative structure follows the path laid out by Mestre Gabriel, when he pointed to the co-existence of a President and a General Representative Mestre and to a participatory approach in the administration of the UDV.

When the General Headquarters moved from Porto Velho to Brasilia on November 1, 1982, a period of intense administrative organization took place due to the growth of the UDV. Since the beginning, the UDV has been cautious to maintain uniformity, both in the transmission of the teachings and in the material administration. Therefore, there has always been the recommendation that the members of the Cadre of Mestres be in close contact with one another to ensure this consistency.

In the late seventies and early eighties, the UDV had crossed the borders from the north into other regions, and the distances became an obstacle for the mestres being able to gather frequently; and when they did meet, the meetings were less than satisfactory. These meetings, initially called conclaves and later called conventions, had an overloaded agenda that ranged from the remembrance of the teachings of Mestre Gabriel to law reform; including participation in specific events at the hosting núcleos. Thus, it was clear that the conclaves and the conventions had lost the effectiveness of their decision-making power due to the growth of the UDV.

In the last 30 years, since the move of the General Headquarters to Brasilia, successive administrative reforms have been implemented with the purpose of developing an efficient and functional structure which guarantees, or at least creates the conditions for, a quality decision-making process, one which preserves administrative, disciplinary and doctrinal unity.

The General Administration is composed of the Cadre of Mestres of the Center, directed by the General Representative Mestre and relying upon the following collegiate bodies: Council of General Administration (Conselho da Administração Geral-CONAGE), General Representation (Representação Geral-RG), Council of Recordation of the Teachings of Mestre Gabriel (Conselho da Recordação dos Ensinos do Mestre Gabriel-CREMG)[27], Electoral College (Colégio Eleitoral- CE), Central Administrations (Administações Centrais-AC), Council of Central Administration (Conselho de Administração Central-CONACE) and the Administrations of the Núcleo.

---

[27] The Council of General Administration, the General Representation, and the Council of Recordation of the Teachings of Mestre Gabriel are based at the General Headquarters.

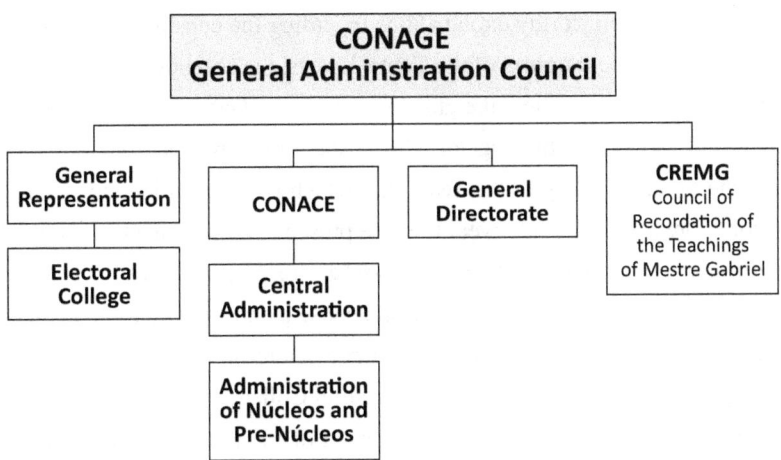

The Council of General Administration (CONAGE) is constituted by the members of the General Representation, the Council of Recordation of the Teachings of Mestre Gabriel, the Central Mestres of each region, the Mestres who have occupied the post of General Representative Mestre, the President of the General Directorate, and five other Mestres appointed by this Council. The CONAGE is a legislative, executive and supervisory body for the laws of the Center.

The General Representation (RG) is composed of the General Representative Mestre and the General Assistant Mestres. The Central Mestres are also part of the General Representation (within the attributes of the respective regions that are under their responsibility). The General Representation is agile, as it is composed of few members, one of which who is the highest authority of the Center. The General Representation presides over the General Administration and its departments. Its function is executive and supervisory.

The Council of Recordation of the Teachings of Mestre Gabriel (CREMG) is formed by the founding members of the Center, meaning the mestres who received the title of Mestre from the hands of Mestre Gabriel himself and had the opportunity to live alongside him. As the name of this Council suggests, its function is to serve as a consulting resource to preserve and to verify the Teachings of Mestre Gabriel.

The Electoral College is constituted by members of the General Representation, the Council of Recordation of the Teachings of Mestre Gabriel, all the mestres who served a full term as General Representative Mestre, four mestres from each region, one mestre from the General Headquarters and the President of the General Directorate. Its function is to elect the General Representative Mestre.

There are two noteworthy explanations regarding the constitution of the Electoral College. First, in a recent reform of the Center's laws, the decision to follow this system was approved in order to follow the guidance of Mestre Gabriel that the elections must happen during a session of the Vegetal. The reason for this is because within the light of the burracheira, the mystery of the Tea – that which is not examined by academic science – could present itself and reveal to those present, who, among the candidates, has the condition to be the General Representative Mestre.[28] Second, this became necessary due to the continuous growth of the UDV and consequently, the increase in members of the Cadre of Mestres. Thus, in order to preserve quality in the process of choosing its key leader, it was necessary to create the Electoral College.[29]

The Central Administrations are composed of the mestres based in each of the regions of the UDV. Among its responsibilities, the Central Administration elects the Central Mestre of the respective region, from a list of three candidates indicated by the General Representative Mestre. The Central Administration is also responsible for electing, by triplicate voting, the four mestres to be part of the Electoral College that elects the General Representative Mestre.

The Council of Central Administration (CONACE) is made up of the Central Mestre, the Representative Mestres of núcleos within the region, and by the mestres who have previously held the post of Central Mestre. Its purpose is to assure that the núcleos within the region follow the directives and principles of the UDV, and to be a link between the Council of General Administration and the region.

The Administration of each núcleo is composed of the Cadre of Mestres and the Body of Counsel based in the respective núcleos. Its responsibility is the local administration and to elect, at the appropriate time, the Representative Mestre.

The decision making structure of the UDV, as seen in the previous diagram, currently operates on various levels, facilitates a greater capacity for reflection by the entire leadership of the Center and functions as a regulatory system for relationships and the exercise of power. Concurrently, there is a system for the circulation of information (inputs and outputs) which moves in both directions vertically: what takes place in the local administration of the núcleos may be taken to the Central Administration, and is able to arrive, depending on its relevance, at the General Administration.

---

[28] *Burracheira* is the name given to the state experienced by those who ingest the Tea.

[29] It is important to mention that in the UDV there is no electoral campaigning. Those who are interested in nominating themselves simply announce a few months before that they want to be a candidate. Electoral campaigning is forbidden by the words of Mestre Gabriel: "those who campaign are showing that they do not have the conditions to occupy the place they want to occupy."

This movement exists in the other direction as well, from the General Administration to the núcleos. This flow of communication makes possible, in the first place, the preservation of the participatory character of the UDV.[30] Secondly, it facilitates an organizational standard resulting in the healthy growth of this religious society already numbering almost 14,000 members.

In the year of the UDV's Fiftieth Anniversary, we retrace our steps back to the rubber-tapping forests in the border between Brazil and Bolivia when Mestre Gabriel began the distribution of the Vegetal with his wife and children. Later, other rubber tappers and their families began to arrive. In the mid-sixties, in Porto Velho, there were around 50 disciples; in 1971, during the last days of the physical presence of Mestre Gabriel, his disciples amounted to 100 members (Makiuchi, no date), and some of them are still here with us, transmitting Mestre Gabriel's teachings.

At the time of publication of this book the UDV had 13,839 members who attend sessions and contribute to the cause of Mestre Gabriel.[31] These members are spread throughout the General Headquarters in Brasilia, 143 núcleos and 12 authorized distributions of the Vegetal in Brazil and overseas (see the map and tables below).

The religion created by José Gabriel da Costa continues to be based on the objective of bringing equilibrium to people's lives, shining the light found in the forest to increasingly broader horizons. This is the building of the world of Hoasca. The institutional format is simply its material infrastructure, and yet it is adaptable. This allows us to act in the world, through an organized unity of human efforts, for the achievement of an objective that at the present time is still beyond our capacity: Peace.

---

[30] The system of information is strengthened through letters that flow in both directions, as mentioned, and the laws of the Center are periodically updated and widely distributed in a publication called *Consolidação das Leis* (The Consolidation of the Laws). Also there is the newsletter called *Alto Falante* (Loud Speaker) that is published periodically.

[31] Data from May 2010. Only those over 18 years of age, who decide to associate of their free and spontaneous will, are considered members.

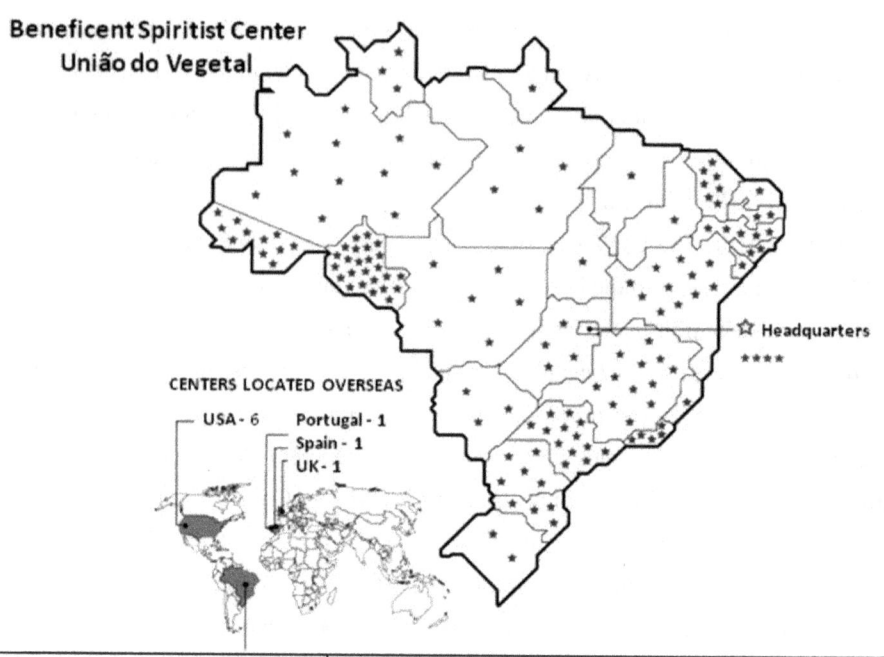

Beneficent Spiritist Center União do Vegetal

CENTERS LOCATED OVERSEAS
USA - 6
Portugal - 1
Spain - 1
UK - 1

☆ Headquarters

UDV CENTERS LOCATED IN BRAZIL		
Acre - 11	Goiás - 4	Rio de Janeiro - 5
Alagoas - 2	Maranhão - 1	Rio Grande do Norte - 1
Amapá - 1	Mato Grosso - 6	Rio Grande do Sul - 2
Amazonas - 11	Mato Grosso do Sul - 3	Rondônia - 25
Bahia - 11	Minas Gerais – 12	Roraima - 3
Ceará - 7	Pará - 4	Santa Catarina - 4
Distrito Federal - 4	Paraíba - 2	São Paulo - 13
Distrito Federal (Headquarters) - 1	Paraná - 5	Sergipe - 1
Espírito Santo - 1	Pernambuco - 5	Tocantins - 1
	Piauí - 1	TOTAL - 147

CENTRO ESPÍRITA BENEFICENTE UNIÃO DO VEGETAL

Centers in Brazil

STATE	CITY	NAME OF ADMINISTRATIVE UNIT
Acre	Cruzeiro do Sul	DAV de Santa Luzia
Acre	Cruzeiro do Sul	Núcleo Cruzeiro do Sul
Acre	Cruzeiro do Sul	Núcleo Mestre Francisco
Acre	Epitaciolândia	DAV Porto Rico
Acre	Feijó	Núcleo João Brandinho
Acre	Jordão	DAV Jordão
Acre	Marechal Taumaturgo	Núcleo Marechal
Acre	Rio Branco	Núcleo João Lango Moura

Acre	Rio Branco	Núcleo Jardim Real
Acre	Rio Branco	Núcleo Belo Jardim
Acre	Plácido de Castro	Núcleo Estrela Divina
Acre	Tarauacá	Núcleo Senhora das Águas
Acre	Tarauacá	Núcleo Água da Vida
Alagoas	Maceió	Núcleo Flor de Maria
Alagoas	Maceió	Núcleo Princesa Mariana
Amapá	Macapá	Núcleo Jardim Florido
Amazonas	Envira	Núcleo Mulateiro
Amazonas	Manaus	Núcleo Amor Vivíssimo
Amazonas	Manaus	Núcleo Caupuri
Amazonas	Manaus	Núcleo Flor do Norte
Amazonas	Manaus	Núcleo Tiuaco
Amazonas	Manaus	Núcleo Princesa Sama
Amazonas	Manaus	Núcleo Jardim do Norte
Amazonas	Manaus	Núcleo Mestre Vicente Marques
Amazonas	Manaus	Núcleo Águas Claras
Amazonas	Manaus	Núcleo Luz do Norte
Amazonas	Manaus	Núcleo Mestre Angilio
Amazonas	Manaus	Núcleo Menino Deus
Amazonas	Tefé	Núcleo Jardim do Chacronal
Bahia	Eunápolis	Núcleo Porto Seguro
Bahia	Feira de Santana	Núcleo Coração de Maria
Bahia	Ilhéus	Núcleo Reis Magos
Bahia	Ilhéus	Núcleo Encanto das Águas
Bahia	Ipiaú	Núcleo Amor Divino
Bahia	Lauro de Freitas	Núcleo Apuí
Bahia	Lauro de Freitas	Núcleo Vento Divino
Bahia	Salvador	Núcleo Estrela da Manhã
Bahia	Salvador	Núcleo Salvador
Bahia	Salvador	Núcleo Serenita
Bahia	Vitória da Conquista	Núcleo Vitória
Ceará	Crato	Núcleo Santa Fé do Cariri

Ceará	Fortaleza	Núcleo Tucunacá
Ceará	Fortaleza	Núcleo Fortaleza
Ceará	Fortaleza	Núcleo Flor Divina
Ceará	Fortaleza	Núcleo Cajueiro Pequenino
Ceará	Fortaleza	Núcleo Estrela Brilhante
Ceará	Sobral	Núcleo Mestre Sidom
Distrito Federal	Brasília	Sede Geral
Distrito Federal	Brasília	Núcleo Estrela Matutina
Distrito Federal	Brasília	Núcleo Canário Verde
Distrito Federal	Brazlândia	Núcleo Gaspar
Distrito Federal	Brazlândia	Núcleo Luz do Oriente
Espírito Santo	Vitória	Núcleo Príncipe Ancarilho
Goiás	Aparecida de Goiânia	Núcleo Rainha da Luz
Goiás	Chapadão do Céu	Núcleo Mestre Luziário
Goiás	Goiânia	Núcleo Rei Inca
Goiás	Terezópolis de Goiás	Núcleo Mestre Manoel Nogueira
Maranhão	São Luis	Núcleo Sereno do Mar
Mato Grosso	Alta Floresta	Núcleo Florestal
Mato Grosso	Barra do Garça	Núcleo Solinha
Mato Grosso	Cuiabá	Núcleo Arvoredo
Mato Grosso	Cuiabá	Núcleo Breuzim
Mato Grosso	Várzea Grande	Núcleo Santa Luzia
Mato Grosso	Várzea Grande	Núcleo Sagrada Família
Mato Grosso do Sul	Campo Grande	Núcleo Senhora Santana
Mato Grosso do Sul	Campo Grande	Núcleo São Joaquim
Mato Grosso do Sul	Campo Grande	Núcleo Luz de Maria
Minas Gerais	Belo Horizonte	Núcleo Rei Salomão
Minas Gerais	Belo Horizonte	Núcleo Flor Encantadora
Minas Gerais	Caldas	Núcleo Rainha das Águas
Minas Gerais	Divinópolis	Núcleo Divinópolis
Minas Gerais	Esmeraldas	Núcleo Menino Rei
Minas Gerais	Governador Valadares	Núcleo Luz Divina
Minas Gerais	Ipatinga	Núcleo Santana do Paraíso

Minas Gerais	Juiz de Fora	Núcleo Luz Dourada
Minas Gerais	Lagoa de Prata	Núcleo Lagoa da Prata
Minas Gerais	Nova Serrana	Núcleo Rei Rabino
Minas Gerais	Patrocínio	DAV de Patrocínio
Minas Gerais	Ubá	Núcleo Recanto das Flores
Minas Gerais	Uberlândia	Núcleo Sabiá
Pará	Belém	Núcleo Rei Canaã
Pará	Belém	Núcleo Príncipe Ram
Pará	Belém	Núcleo Augusto Cangulê
Pará	Santarém	Núcleo Castelo de Marfim
Paraíba	Campina Grande	Núcleo Campina Grande
Paraíba	João Pessoa	Núcleo Conselheiro Salomão Gabriel
Paraná	Curitiba	Núcleo São Cosme e São Damião
Paraná	Curitiba	Núcleo Monte Alegre
Paraná	Curitiba	Núcleo Coroa Divina
Paraná	Maringá	Núcleo Água boa
Paraná	Pato Branco	Núcleo Cores Divinas
Pernambuco	Abreu e Lima	Núcleo Mãe Gloriosa
Pernambuco	Caruaru	Núcleo Pau D'Arco
Pernambuco	Caruaru	Núcleo Mouraiá
Pernambuco	Olinda	Núcleo Imburana de Cheiro
Pernambuco	Recife	Núcleo Cajueiro
Piauí	Terezina	Núcleo Mestre Adamir
Rio de Janeiro	Nova Friburgo	Núcleo Lumiar
Rio de Janeiro	Petrópolis	Núcleo Camalango
Rio de Janeiro	Rio de Janeiro	Núcleo Pupuramanta
Rio de Janeiro	Rio de Janeiro	Núcleo Janaína
Rio de Janeiro	São João do Meriti	Núcleo Agulha de Marear
Rio Grande do Norte	Parnamirim	Núcleo Natal
Rio Grande do Sul	Itaara	DAV Itaara
Rio Grande do Sul	Porto Alegre	Núcleo Jardim das Flores
Rio Grande do Sul	Porto Alegre	Núcleo Porto Alegre
Rondônia	Alta Floresta D'Oeste	Núcleo Alta Floresta

Rondônia	Alto Paraíso	DAV de Alto Paraíso
Rondônia	Ariquemes	Núcleo Mestre Ramos
Rondônia	Buritis	Núcleo Mestre Nesclar
Rondônia	Cacoal	Núcleo Estrela Oriental
Rondônia	Campo Novo	Núcleo Campo Novo
Rondônia	Candeias do Jamari	Núcleo Erunaiá
Rondônia	Extrema	Núcleo Mestre Pojó
Rondônia	Guajará Mirim	Núcleo Palmeiral
Rondônia	Jarú	Núcleo Mestre Rubens
Rondônia	Ji-Paraná	Núcleo Estrela Guia
Rondônia	Machadinho D'Oeste	Núcleo Mestre Hilton
Rondônia	Ouro Preto D'Oeste	Núcleo Mestre Joanico
Rondônia	Porto Velho	Núcleo Mestre Gabriel
Rondônia	Porto Velho	Núcleo Estrela do Norte
Rondônia	Porto Velho	Núcleo Mestre Iagora
Rondônia	Porto Velho	Núcleo Mestre Bartolomeu
Rondônia	Porto Velho	Núcleo Mestre Pernambuco
Rondônia	Porto Velho	Núcleo São Miguel
Rondônia	Porto Velho	Núcleo Templo de Salomão
Rondônia	Porto Velho	Núcleo Caminho do Mestre
Rondônia	Presidente Médici	Núcleo Mestre Cícero
Rondônia	Rolim de Moura	DAV de Rolim de Moura
Rondônia	Seringueiras	Núcleo Mestre José Rodrigues Sobrinho
Rondônia	Vilhena	Núcleo Sereno de Luz
Roraima	Boa Vista	Núcleo Boa Vista
Roraima	Boa Vista	Núcleo Estrela do Oriente
Roraima	Boa Vista	Núcleo Santa Rosa
Roraima	Rorainópolis	Núcleo Mestre Constantino
Santa Catarina	Criciúma	Núcleo Aliança
Santa Catarina	Joaçaba	Núcleo Arco Íris
Santa Catarina	Florianópolis	Núcleo Estrela Dalva
Santa Catarina	Florianópolis	Núcleo Luz Abençoada

São Paulo	Arujá	Núcleo Castanheira
São Paulo	Campinas	Núcleo Lupunamanta
São Paulo	Campinas	Núcleo Alto das Cordilheiras
São Paulo	Campinas	Núcleo Princesa Encantada
São Paulo	Jundiaí	Núcleo Grande Ventura
São Paulo	Mogi das Cruzes	Núcleo Rei Davi
São Paulo	Piracicaba	Núcleo Estrela Encantadora
São Paulo	São Paulo	Núcleo Samaúma
São Paulo	São Paulo	Núcleo São João Batista
São Paulo	São Paulo	Núcleo Rei Divino
São Paulo	São Paulo	Núcleo Divino Manto
São Paulo	São Paulo	Núcleo Menino Galante
São Paulo	São Paulo	Núcleo Estrela Bonita
Sergipe	Nossa Senhora do Socorro	Núcleo Pedra Mar
Tocantins	Palmas	Núcleo Caminho Firme

Centers Overseas

COUNTRY	CITY/STATE	NAME OF THE ADMINISTRATIVE UNIT
USA	Edmonds / Washington	Núcleo Claridade Divina
USA	Palm City / Florida	Núcleo Jardim Florescendo
USA	Norwood / Colorado	Núcleo San Miguel
USA	San Rafael / California	Núcleo San Francisco
USA	Santa Fe / New Mexico	Núcleo Santa Fé
USA	Dallas / Texas	Núcleo Sagrada União
Spain	Caceres	Núcleo Imaculada Concepción
Spain	Valencia	DAV Valência
Portugal	Lisbon	DAV Lisboa
United Kingdom	London	DAV United Kingdom
Switzerland	Geneva	DAV Geneva

Bibliography

Araripe, Flaminio. "União do Vegetal: a Hoasca e a Religião do Sentir". Editora Três: *Revista Planeta,* n°. 105, edição de junho de 1981.

CEBUDV- Centro Espírita Beneficente União Do Vegetal. *Jornal Alto Falante.* Brasilia, Sede Geral: Edição de Julho de 1989.

CEBUDV - Centro Espírita Beneficente União Do Vegetal. *Jornal Alto Falante.* Brasilia, Sede Geral: Edição de Setembro/Outubro de 1989.

CEBUDV- Centro Espírita Beneficente União Do Vegetal. *Jornal Alto Falante.* Brasilia, Sede Geral: Edição de Março/Abril de 1989.

CEBUDV- Centro Espírita Beneficente União Do Vegetal. *Jornal Alto Falante.* Brasilia, Sede Geral: Edição de Janeiro/Fevereiro de 1992.

CEBUDV- Centro Espírita Beneficente União Do Vegetal. *Jornal Alto Falante.* Brasilia, Sede Geral: Edição de Abril/Junho de 1995.

CEBUDV-Centro Espírita Beneficente União Do Vegetal. Ata da Reunião do Conselho de Administração realizada no dia 11 de outubro de 2008. Brasilia, Sede Geral.

Convicção Do Mestre. *Jornal Alto Madeira,* 06/10/1967.

Dumont, Louis. "Homo hierarchicus: o sistema de castas e suas implicações." São Paulo: EDUSP, 1992.

Henman, Anthony Richard. "Uso del ayahuasca en un contexto autoritario. El caso de la União do Vegetal en Brasil." *America Indígena,* n° 46, vol 1, p. 219-234, 1986. Available at http://www.neip.info/index.php/content/view/90.html#et

Labate, Beatriz Caiuby e Araujo, Wladimyr Sena (orgs.) "O uso ritual da ayahuasca". Mercado de Letras, FAPESP: Campinas, São Paulo, 2002.

Labate, Beatriz Caiuby; Rose, Isabel Santana de e Santos, Rafael Guimarães dos (orgs.). "Religiões ayahuasqueiras: um balanço bibliográfico." Campinas: Mercado de Letras; São Paulo: FAPESP, 2008.

Macrae, Edward. "The ritual use of ayahuasca by three Brazilian religions", in: Coomber, R. e South, N. (orgs.) *"Drug use and cultural contexts "Beyond the West".* London: Free Association Books, p. 27-45, 2004. Available at http://www.neip.info/index.php/content/view/90.html#et

Makiuchi, Yuugi. "Biografia da Vida e Obra do Mestre Gabriel." (Biography of Mestre Gabriel) Mimeo, 27 pages, no date.

The Strength of Example: UDV, Memory and Mission

Raimundo Monteiro de Souza[1]

Ladies and gentleman, first I want to greet all of you on behalf of myself and my wife, Zildinha (Zilda Felícia da Costa Monteiro de Souza). This Second International Hoasca Congress, sponsored by the Beneficent Spiritist Center União do Vegetal (UDV) is destined to be part of our institution's history for its social and spiritual significance.

This is the first time that our religion, which was born in the heart of the Amazon on July 22, 1961, has had the opportunity to address the greater public, here in the capital of Brazil, to share its history, principles and objectives.

The União do Vegetal is a Christian Reincarnationist religion. Its origin is Brazilian, though its purpose is universal: to work for the evolution of the human being in the sense of perfecting moral, intellectual and spiritual virtues. It professes the belief in reincarnation with the objective of evolution. With every incarnation on earth the spirit has the opportunity to progress until one day arriving at perfection. The UDV believes and sustains the ethical and moral code expressed in the Ten Commandments of Moses, and sees Jesus Christ, the Son of God, as the savior of humanity. Above all, the União do Vegetal believes in the power of the example. This is a path that, through constancy in the duties and right conduct, shows human beings how to one day arrive in the presence of the Celestial Father, God. This is a path of salvation, with Jesus as its highest reference. Mestre Gabriel, José Gabriel da Costa, the founder of the União do Vegetal, is our trustworthy guide; a friendly light guiding our steps.

During our religious rituals held in our Spiritist temple, we make use of a sacred tea called Hoasca, or Vegetal, for the purpose of mental concentration. This tea, which is harmless to the health, is produced from the union of two plants that are native to the Amazon forest, the Mariri vine and the Chacrona leaf.

---

[1] Mestre of the Council of the Recordation of the Teachings of Mestre Gabriel, has held the post of General Representative Mestre several times, having occupied this place from 2006-2009, the period during which the 2nd International Hoasca Congress took place.

Academic researchers have been studying the phytochemical properties of this tea for many years. Though no conclusive scientific pronouncement has yet been achieved, the results of the meticulous studies, conducted by prominent national and international academic institutions, indicate its harmless nature, as stated in our Statutes.[2]

More than two decades ago the UDV created the Medical and Scientific Department (DEMEC), to assist the authorities and to orient our members. This department is composed of health professionals who are members of the UDV and promotes studies and research on multiple aspects of the Vegetal.[3] The main evidence of the tea's harmless nature, which no study can ignore, is the result of the observation of the behavior and health of our members. Since the UDV was created in 1961, there are now cases of families with three generations, all of whom utilize the Hoasca tea. This allows for the observation of not only their physical well-being, but also their moral and intellectual development.

Because our religion obtains its sacrament, the Hoasca tea, from nature, we have in our doctrine an inherent commitment to nature. We revere the divinity of nature and seek to express this reverence in our actions. For this reason, we have an ecological initiative called the Novo Encanto Association for Ecological Development.[4] This Association cares for a vast rubber-tapping forest preserve in the Amazon, where forestry management techniques that facilitate environmental preservation are developed.

It is with honor and joy that I participate in this Congress. This occasion takes me back to the modest beginnings of Mestre Gabriel's work, alongside a few hard-working men, the majority of them rubber–tappers in the Amazon, when we came together to build our first temple. We were in what was then the Territory of Rondonia, almost half a century ago, without material resources, every one of us giving all we had to

---

[2] Two significant international studies have been conducted. The first was the Human Pharmacology of Hoasca Project, which brought together nine research institutions in Brazil and overseas, the results of which were published and presented in 1995 at the First International Congress on Hoasca Studies. Among these nine institutions, the UDV is not included, as its participation through the Department of Medical and Scientific Studies was restricted to the logistical organization of the study. For more information see Brito (2004); Grob et al. (2004) and Andrade et al. (2004). The second research project is the study with adolescents from the UDV originally published in the *Journal of Psychoactive Drugs, no.37, v.2*, and is presented for the first time in the Portuguese language in this book (Portuguese version); see the articles in The Adolescents Study chapter.

[3] See also in this book the article by Gentil and Neves.

[4] To become familiar with the work developed by the Novo Encanto (New Enchantment) Association for Ecological Development, see in this book the articles in the chapter *Preservation and Improvement of the Landscape and the Environment*. More information can be found at: http://www.novoencanto.org.br/

further this work which reconnects us to the sacred and offers humanity a new opportunity for salvation.

Our institution does not disparage other religious traditions. It offers, through the communion with the Hoasca tea and through the wisdom of the sacred science of Solomon, attunement with spirituality and its highest ethical values.

I want in this opportunity to honor those who were present at the beginnings of this work, whose efforts have made it possible for us to be here today. I honor all of them through Raimunda Ferreira da Costa, Mestre Pequenina, the wife of Mestre Gabriel, and the Mestres of the Council of Recordation of the Teachings of Mestre Gabriel, who received from our great Mestre the mission of bringing the wisdom of this sacred work to humanity.

Today the União do Vegetal exists throughout Brazil, in the United States and in Europe. There are 155 núcleos and authorized distributions, nine of which are overseas. In addition to these, we have our general headquarters, located in Brasilia, Brazil. There are also several countries in Europe where people are organizing themselves to obtain the right to establish núcleos of the UDV. In the countries where the UDV has already arrived, we have taken the necessary steps before the authorities, as we have done in Brazil, in order to duly comply with that country's laws. In the United States, the North American brothers and sisters who are members of the UDV have definitively attained their religious rights through the recognition and approval of the Supreme Court of that country.[5] Therefore, it is with great sentiment that I contemplate this path we have traveled and witness the confirmation of Mestre Gabriel's words with respect to the Universal destiny of this sacred União do Vegetal.

Within our symbol of light, peace and love, and under the guardianship of Mestre Gabriel, it is my wish that this Second International Hoasca Congress may fully achieve its objectives.

Thank you and much happiness to all.

---

[5] See in this book the articles by Bronfman and Boyd. For a complete description of the of the UDV's legal process before the United States Supreme Court, go to http://udvusa.org

Bibliography

Andrade, E. N.; Brito, G. S.; Andrade, E. O.; Neves, E. S.; Mckenna, D.; Cavalcante, J. W.; Okimura, L.; Grob, C. And Callaway, J.C. "Human pharmacology of hoasca: clinical studies (Comparative Clinical Evaluation Among Long Term Users of Hoasca Tea And Control Groups – Physiological Evaluation of Acute Effects After Ingestion of The Hoasca Tea)." Labate, B. C. and Araujo, W.S. (orgs.), "O Uso Ritual da Ayahuasca" (Ritual use of Ayahuasca). Campinas: Mercado de Letras; São Paulo: FAPESP, p. 671-709, 2004.

Brito, G. S. De S. "Human Pharmacology of Hoasca: Tea Prepared From Hallucinogenic Plants Used In Ritual Context In Brazil." Labate, B. C. and Araujo, W.S. (Orgs.), O Uso Ritual da Ayahuasca (Ritual Use of Ayahuasca). Campinas: Mercado de Letras; São Paulo: FAPESP, p. 623-651, 2004.

Grob, C. S.; Mckenna, D. J.; Callaway, J. C.; Brito, G. S.; Andrade, E. O.; Oberlender, G.; Saide, O. L.; Labigalini Jr., E.; Tacla, C.; Miranda, C. T.; Strassman, R. J.; Boone, K. S. And Neves, E. S. "Human Pharmacology of Hoasca: Psychological Effects." Labate, B. C. and Araujo, W. S. (Orgs.), "O Uso Ritual da Ayahuasca" (Ritual Use of Ayahuasca). Campinas: Mercado de Letras; São Paulo: FAPESP, p. 653-669, 2004.

The Expansion of the UDV and its Achievements

James Allen Paranayba

Ladies and Gentlemen, members of this panel, authorities present, Mestres of the Council of Recordation of the Teachings of Mestre Gabriel, youth, scientists, Caianinhos and Caianinhas.[6]

When I came to the União do Vegetal, I was little more than a boy. I was twenty-years-old when I began to notice my parents' interest in a very strange tea. My father, who passed away some years ago, was an established architect in Brasilia. My mother was a social worker and is present here today. Both were people who would never be involved in the use of any illicit drugs. At that time we smoked cigarettes and drank alcohol.

Suddenly, both of them were interested in a strange tea used in a "session." We were very open in our family and so I made a comment about their experience: "Now that you are old, you are going to start messing with drugs?" My parents both laughed. It took some time before they convinced me to check out the Beneficent Spiritist Center União do Vegetal.

It was near Christmas in 1980 and my family had a strong tradition of always being together at this time of celebration. We decided, all three siblings, to go with our parents to experience the session for Christmas. It was then that we came to know this strange tea and to understand that it has nothing to do with drugs. As we continued to drink the tea we stopped smoking cigarettes, drinking alcohol and using illicit drugs.

This experience –my own impression of the Vegetal being strange – makes it easier for me to understand what we, *Caianinhos,* have gone through, having to explain and demonstrate to the authorities, over and over, that our society is essentially a religion. It is helpful for people to understand that this strange tea, that we call Vegetal, is harmless to the health of those who drink it, and that when we drink it we are taking communion of a sacrament, which we consider sacred. We understand why the authorities find it strange, and therefore we double our efforts to help them recognize that we are harmless to society at large and that the tea is harmless to our health.

---

[6] "Caianinhos" is a term used within the UDV to refer to the members, who are considered the spiritual disciples of Mestre Caiano.

We have been in this endeavor for decades.

There is an important phenomenon that occurs when we approach the authorities to give an explanation about this Vegetal used in our sessions. When the authorities obtain an initial explanation, we notice that their perception changes in regard to the Hoasca tea and to the *Hoasqueiros*.[7] There is a realization, way beyond stereotypes and simplistic definitions, that we are an organized, pluralistic society, mainly focused on the objective of living peacefully, practicing what our spiritual guide Mestre Gabriel teaches, reaffirming the words of Jesus: to love the other as you love yourself and love God above all things.

We have been to the offices of senators and too many meetings with state and federal representatives. We have met with judges and with the leaders of federal agencies, from the Esplanade of Ministries (equivalent to Capitol Hill) to police stations. We have participated in meetings with the civil and federal police, and public prosecutors. We have been to universities and have opened our doors to scientists.

Government and academic authorities have sought, and have always found, readily available information about our organization and the use of the Vegetal. We have noticed that once concrete information is acquired, personal statements are presented, and questions are addressed within the contextualized explanation of the use of this psychoactive beverage, the authorities acquiesce. They realize that they are not facing a threat to Brazilian society.

This is how we have conducted ourselves. We are not here to make propaganda or attract followers, as our Mestre Gabriel orients us not to do that. We do want, however, to explain the steps we have taken to demonstrate to the authorities the benefits that our society brings to all who arrive at our doors.

We were scrutinized by the Brazilian Federal Narcotics Council (CONFEN - within the Brazilian Justice Department) for six years. When the CONFEN was replaced by the Brazilian National Drug Policy Council (CONAD), we were scrutinized again, this time from within the Brazilian President's Office.[8] International researchers dedicated their equipment and methodological criteria to our activities to discover the effects of the Hoasca tea on our members and our children.[9]

---

[7] "Hoasqueiros" means those who drink Hoasca tea, and is a term used to refer to the members of the UDV.

[8] For more information on the steps taken by the UDV before the Federal Government see the chapter titled *The UDV in Brazil,* in this book.

[9] The author is referring to the Human Pharmacology of Hoasca Study and Hoasca in *Adolescence Study.* See the chapter *The Adolescents Study,* in this book

Throughout this process of examination of the use of Hoasca tea, we have focused our work on our main objective, which is to provide assistance to our membership and to the neediest sectors of Brazilian society, and this is the work we continue doing. Due to this charitable outreach work, the Brazilian President's Office has granted us the title of "Utilidade Publica" (institution of public benefit), awarded to the UDV on July 22, 1999.[10] Many of you may not be aware that the 22nd of July is the anniversary of the founding of the União do Vegetal.

All of our work then resulted in a good harvest in February of 1986, when CONFEN gave us a favorable decision and passed the resolution to remove the Banisteriopsis Caapi vine, one of the plants used to prepare the Hoasca tea, from the DIMED[11] schedule of proscribed substances (CONFEN Resolution no. 6).[12]

In November of 2004 CONAD updated its resolution no. 5, acknowledging our work over decades by guaranteeing our right to give Vegetal to our children and the right of pregnant women to drink the Vegetal.[13]

CONAD's Multi-disciplinary Working Group (GMT), composed of scientists and members of the UDV, recently created the regulation for this resolution and defined guidelines for the use of the tea, including that it not be sold and that it be used strictly within the rituals. These guidelines are congruent with the UDV's principles. This is our most recent advancement in Brazil.[14]

In the United States, our brothers there faced nothing less than the most powerful government on Earth. Those Caianinhos fought for years on end for their right to

---

[10] See article by Lima, in this book.

[11] DIMED was the Brazilian Health Ministry's National Division of Health and Drugs Surveillance, an agency that is now extinct. Eliseo Araujo Carlini, medical doctor and retired professor of psychopharmacology of the Escola Paulista de Medicina – UNIFESP (Sao Paulo Medical School), member of the Brazilian Academy of Sciences. See <http://www.abc.org.br/~ecarlini>.

[12] See the article by Santos, in this book.

[13] See the article by Machado, in this book.

[14] The Multi-disciplinary Working Group (GMT), established by the CONAD's (Brazilian National Drug Policy Council) Resolution no. 5, of November 4, 2004, was composed in the following manner, according to article 2: "the Multi-disciplinary Working Group will be composed of six members, indicated by the CONAD, from the following disciplines: anthropology, pharmacology/biochemistry, sociology, psychology, psychiatry and law. Furthermore, the group will include six additional members, invited by the CONAD, representing the religious groups that use the Hoasca tea. The designation of the people who would compose the Multi-disciplinary Working Group took place after the seminar in March 2006, in Rio Branco, Acre. Several original members were substituted at different points, and on November 23, 2006, the final report was presented to General Jorge Armando Felix, Chief Minister of the Institutional Safety Office and President of the CONAD. The said report was only published several years later in the *Diário Oficial da União* (Official Registry of Brazil) on January 26, 2010.

study the Divine Science with a tea that opens the doors of consciousness. Our tea was seized on May 21, 1999, in a dramatic government operation, from a small office in New Mexico's state capital, Santa Fe.[15] The final decision is yet to be issued. After the favorable decision by the US Supreme Court permitting the use of the tea by the UDV, the powerful American government is still insisting that the UDV be submitted to a bureaucratic process and restrictions for the use of controlled substances. This is perhaps a last attempt to give public agents the means to interfere with our unrestricted activities in that country.[16]

We opened our doors to academic research for the Human Pharmacology of Hoasca study that was conducted in 1993, through a partnership among nine scientific institutions in three countries.[17] Our members were examined by scientists while the effect of the tea was active in their bodies.

In 2001 the adolescent sons and daughters of our members made themselves available to researchers for the Hoasca in Adolescence Study. Psychiatrists, anthropologists, psychologists and sociologists studied this new and strange phenomenon that is the resurgence of the use of Hoasca tea.[18]

These are the events discussed in this Congress. With the goal of detailing the entire structure of the Center so that it can be presented to Brazilian Society and the world, we organized teams of volunteers in the fields of law, medicine, anthropology and communications. Through our presentations it will become clear that the decision

---

[15] See article by Bronfman and Boyd in this book.

[16] On July 19, 2010, two years after this speech was given at the Second International Hoasca Congress, a final agreement was reached and signed between representatives of the Government of the United States and the disciples of the UDV in that country, bringing conclusion to the legal action that began 11 years before. The agreement allows for the full expression of the UDV's religious activities within a system of mutually accepted protocols reached through negotiation and mediated by the Federal Judiciary in the United States. See www.udvusa.com for details.

[17] The following institutions were involved in this study: University of California – Los Angeles (UCLA), Minneapolis University, Kuopio University (Finland), Escola Paulista de Medicina-UNIFESP (Paulista School of Medicine), Universidade do Estado do Rio de Janeiro-UERJ (State University of Rio de Janeiro), Universidade Federal da Amazonia-UFAM (Federal University of Amazonia), Universidade Estadual de Campinas-UNICAMP (State University of Campinas), Instituto Nacional de Pesquisa da Amazonia-INPA (National Institute of Amazonian Research), and Sociedade Brasileira de Psiquiatria-SBP (Brazilian Psychiatric Society). In addition to these nine scientific institutions, researchers from the University of New Mexico (USA) and Pardue University (Finland) assisted as consultants. The UDV, through its Department of Medical and Scientific Studies, supported the study by handling the logistics coordination. For more information on this study, as well as the list of institutions that participated in the Human Pharmacology of Hoasca Project, see Brito (2004); Grob et al. (2004) and Andrade et al. (2004).

[18] See article by Bronfman and Boyd in this book.

of the US Supreme Court was a signal to the world of the necessity to re-evaluate the position of the authorities on the religious use of the Vegetal.

Unfortunately, deviations do occur, and there are cases in which Hoasca tea is used outside of the religious context. However, those who become aware of the UDV's work and take a closer look at the work of other organizations such as the Barquinha or Alto Santo, will clearly see what our principles are: We are against the commercial and recreational use of the tea. We produce it only according to our needs for strict use in our sessions. The use of Hoasca tea is not mixed up with the use of drugs that cause disorientation, personality distortions and the breaking down of families.

The American government was not able to prove that the Hoasca tea belonging to the UDV had been diverted in any way or that the health of any member of the UDV had been harmed. The use of the tea by 13 thousand UDV members, thousands of families, continues to confirm that the tea is harmless to human health.[19]

After the decision in Washington D.C., issued on February 21, 2006, the discussion began in Europe on how to treat the issue of the religious use of Hoasca tea.[20] Soon after this Congress we will be presenting our institution's work in Heidelberg, Germany, at an international conference on this subject.[21]

Governments will need to revisit and discuss this theme, not only in regards to the chemical properties of dimethyltriptamine, DMT, which is the active principle in the Chacrona (Psychotria Viridis). The Court of Justice in Holland, repeating what was done in Brazil, analyzed the subject from a sociological perspective.[22] The results of these processes in Europe, the United States and here in Brazil is that we will conclude a long cycle of formal clarifications on the use of Hoasca tea in the West. These

---

[19] As of May 2010 the exact number of UDV members ages 18 years and older was 13,839.

[20] The US Supreme Court held a hearing on November 1, 2005, to deliberate over the right to the ritualistic use of Hoasca tea by the Beneficent Spiritist Center União do Vegetal. The unanimous decision was issued on February 21, 2006. See http://www.udvusa.com/pdf/SupremeCourtDecision.pdf.

[21] The conference is "Globalization of the uses of Ayahuasca: an Amazonian psychoactive and its users," organized by Henrik Jungaberle, Rolf Verres and Bia Labate, held at the University of Heildelberg on May 16-18, 2008. See http://www.ritualdynamik.de/ritualdynamik/archiv/2Archiv-2008_pdfs/AyahuascaConference SchuekleMay2008.pdf

[22] This refers to case no. 13/067455-99, tried on May 21, 2001, involving Geerdina Johana Cornelia Fijneman, a disciple of the Centro Ecletico da Fluente Luz Universal Raimundo Irineu Serra – CEFLURIS (Raimundo Irineu Serra Ecletic Center of Fluid Universal Light), who was arrested in a Daime Church in Amsterdam for possession of 17.5 liters of Ayahuasca. Holland's Supreme Court upheld the defendant's Right to Religious Exercise. For the Abridged Judgment of this case, see http://mestreirineu.org/law_texts/2001%20Dutch%20Daime%20Case%20 Abridged%20Judgement.pdf.

victories that have been gained to date, namely the recognition by Brazilian and international authorities, are encouraging to those who have been fighting for decades for the most fundamental right of choosing their own religion and the religion they want to teach their children.

Despite these victories, we *Hoasqueiros*, along with our families, still face other challenges that go beyond the government agencies and official decisions. Ladies and gentlemen, in this third millennium, a time in which we had imagined in our childhoods that all the great problems of humanity would be solved, we still suffer the prejudice caused by lack of understanding about the Vegetal and from the attitudes of public agents who are unaware of the decisions made by the CONAD. The official decisions have already been made and the resolutions approved. And yet in the chambers and at the desks of managers and public agents, through personal decisions, without legal foundation, attempts are made to bar our activities.

In São Paulo we had 22 liters confiscated. No official allegation was provided. The Vegetal was investigated and nothing that justified the confiscation was announced.[23]

In Brasilia, Federal District, due to a complaint from a judge from the state of São Paulo, the Brazilian Department of Child Protection began a preliminary investigation. Our children were evaluated by civil agents and now have on their records that they were questioned by the police for their religious practices.[24]

One case here, another there, shows us that we still face the challenge of being legally accepted. The use of the tea was never illegal. Today, in addition to that, we have the decision of governments here in Brazil and overseas, making official their approval of the use of the tea. Nonetheless, it is necessary to make a greater effort to be able to exist as a society.

What we want, ladies and gentlemen, is to be a part of the global community.

---

[23] On September 13, 2007, federal agents (São Paulo) confiscated 22 liters of the tea. Criminal agents from the Federal Police carried out their investigation and determined that the substances are not on the schedule of prohibited psychotropic and narcotic plants. Thus, in the archive of the Federal Justice's Fourth Criminal Court, record no. 2007.61.81.015775-1, is an exemption from filing that was issued since the required findings for criminal action were absent. The case was dismissed and closed by the Federal Police.

[24] Stemming from a complaint sent via email, a judge from São Paulo opened a preliminary investigation through the First Youth Court of the TJDFT -Tribunal de Justiça do Distrito Federal e dos Territórios (Court of the Federal District and of the Territories). The CEBUDV provided all the explanations and documents that were requested. Three children, daughters of members, corroborated with the investigation, and were interviewed by civil officers; however, since there was no formal complaint made at the end of the investigation, case no. 3120-3/2005 was archived on August 28, 2006.

Today, guided by Mestre Gabriel, we are able to say, "We are not a problem. We are here to stay, and we are here to be part of the solution."

During this Congress we will demonstrate our commitment to environmental sustainability through the work we do with the plants used to make our tea. We conduct ourselves with the objective of a seeking knowledge and a better life for everyone. We are looking for solutions for environmental sustainability through our ecological association, our plantation department, and also in the harvesting of the native plants from the forest.[25]

We have contributed to the work of social integration in Brazil through our youth and adult literacy outreach program. We are developing the prototype of an open-source software program that is a tool for literacy lessons. In this approach, both the student and the teacher use the computer for literacy instruction, and learn to use the Internet as well. Since 2007 this endeavor has been conducted in partnership with *"Casa Brasil"* (Brazil House), part of the Federal Presidency and the Ceará State Education Department. This program's pedagogical framework is based on the work of world-renowned Brazilian educator Paulo Freire. The program was designed to be constantly updated, an interactive open-source software.[26]

Through this program we are offering solutions for youth and adult literacy to the greater society. The people served by this program are supported in becoming integrated into the Third Millennium, leaving illiteracy behind them and entering the world of communications via the Internet and computers. This allows them access to a more competitive labor market, giving them the opportunity to achieve autonomy and independence.

Essentially, we are addressing these issues in order to be able to exercise our constitutional right to religious freedom and participate in building a better world. We believe that the world begins to improve through the transformation of each one of us. It is necessary to respect our neighbor's rights, so that one day, we may arrive at being able to love our neighbor. *Scientification,* for us Caianinhos, disciples of Mestre Gabriel, is a path of eternal learning.[27]

We seek peace and we structure our society in a transparent way, cooperating with the executive, legislative, judicial and academic authorities. This is what you will see during this Congress.

---

[25] These topics are addressed in Part III – Hoasca and the Environment, in this book.

[26] For more information see http://www.udv.org.br/A+luz+das+letras/O+bem+que+faz/93/.

[27] "Scientification" is a term used in the UDV that means a "constant search for spiritual consciousness."

To conclude my words for this opening ceremony, I wish to speak of the gratitude I have for my parents. When I was a child I heard it said that men ought to walk on a straight path and that the parents' role is to teach their children to find this path.

I see that my father, who has already passed away, and especially my mother, fulfilled their mission in a noble way. They offered this path of light to me and to my siblings, where we have learned to walk in rectitude. My wife and I, together for 25 years, consider ourselves to be apprentices on this path of the União do Vegetal. Yet we exercise our right, as parents, to point our children toward this path of rectitude, following in the footsteps of my parents who brought me here.

What we want is simply to follow the path offered by the União do Vegetal, in peace, guided by the doctrine of a simple and exemplary man: Mestre Gabriel, and to learn how to live within the symbol of the União: Light, Peace and Love.

Bibliography

Andrade, E. N.; Brito, G. S.; Andrade, E. O.; Neves, E. S.; Mckenna, D.; Cavalcante, J. W.; Okimura, L.; Grob, C.; And Callaway, J. C. "Human Pharmacology of Hoasca: Clinical Studies (Comparative Clinical Evaluation Between Long Term Hoasca Tea Users and Controls – Physiological Evaluation of Acute Effects After Ingestion Of Hoasca Tea)." Labate, B. C. and Araujo, W. S. (Orgs.) "The Ritual Use of Ayahuasca." Campinas: Mercado De Letras; São Paulo: FAPESP, p. 671-709, 2004.

Brito, G. De S. "Human Pharmacology of Hoasca. Tea Prepared From Hallucinogenic Plants Used In Ritual Context In Brazil." Labate, B. C. and Araujo, W. S. (Orgs.) "The Ritual Use of Ayahuasca." Campinas: Mercado de Letras; São Paulo: Fapesp, p. 623-651, 2004.

CONAD. Conselho Nacional Antidrogas. Resolution No. 5, November 4, 2004. Brasilia: Diario Oficial da União, Executive Power, November 8, Section I, p. 8, 2004.

CONAD. Conselho Nacional de Politicas Sobre Drogas. Resolution No. 1, January 25, 2010. Brasilia: Diario Oficial da União, Executive Power, January 26, Section I, p. 57-60, 2010.

CONFEN. Conselho Federal De Entorpecentes. Resolution No. 6, February 4, 1986. Diario Oficial da União, Executive Power, Brasilia, DF, February 5, 1986. Section I, p. 2054, 1986.

DIMED. Divisão Nacional de Vigilancia Sanitaria de Medicamentos (1995). Portaria No. 02, March 8, 1995. Diario Oficial da União, Executive Power, Brasilia, DF, March 13, 1995. Section I, p. 4421-4434.

Grob, C. S.; Mckenna, D. J.; Callaway, J. C.; Brito, G. S.; Andrade, E. O., Oberlender, G.; Saide, O.L.; Labigalini Jr., E.; Tacla, C.; Miranda, C. T.; Strassman, R. J.; Boone, K. S. And Neves, E. S. "Human Pharmacology of Hoasca: Psychological Effects." Labate, B. C. and Araujo, W. S. (Orgs.) "The Ritual Use of Ayahuasca." Campinas: Mercado de Letras; São Paulo: FAPESP, p. 653-669, 2004.

6: Opening Speeches at the Second International HOASCA Congress

Citizenship of the Forest: The Heritage of a Sacred Right

Perpétua Almeida[28]

Greetings to all of you present, to my fellow panelists, to the President of the União, to the President of this Congress, and to the Representative of the Attorney General's Office. I want to salute this entire panel by honoring Mr. Raimundo Monteiro de Souza, the General Representative Mestre of the União do Vegetal.[29] Through this symbolic gesture, I salute all the elders, which is a value that the União, the Barquinha, and the Alto Santo all hold: respect for elders. I also want to salute all the women in this Congress by honoring Mestre Pequenina, who holds an important place representing the União do Vegetal, as the widow of Mestre Gabriel.

I also want to honor my friend Madrinha Peregrina of the CICLU-Alto Santo, the widow of Mestre Irineu, from Rio Branco, Acre, whose absence is justified, though nonetheless felt.[30]

I also salute all the men here present, by honoring a friend from the state of Acre, Mr. Francisco Araújo, leader of the Barquinha, who has the same fortitude and energy of our friend Mestre Daniel.[31]

In addition I want to salute two other colleagues from parliament who are present: my friend Wolney Queiróz (PDT/Pernambuco) and my friend Ilderlei Cordeiro (PPS/Acre), both federal congressmen.

This Congress, where so many members of the União do Vegetal are present, along with so many guests and participants from other organizations that use the Hoasca tea

---

[28] Perpétua Almeida - Congresswoman (PCB – Acre), supporter (2008) of the project Ayahuasca as Immaterial Heritage of Brazilian Culture, with IPHAN (National Institute of Historical and Artistic Heritage).

[29] Raimundo Monteiro de Souza, Mestre Monteiro, occupied the position of General Representative Mestre from 01/06/2006 to 01/06/2009.

[30] Peregrina Gomes Serra, Madrinha Peregrina, director of the Center originally created by Mestre Irineu, *Centro de Iluminação Cristã Luz Universal (CICLU) – Alto Santo* (Universal Light Center for Christian Illumination – CICLU – High Saint).

[31] See article by Araújo Neto, in this book.

in their rituals, is a historical landmark in the Brazilian social movement. And this is how it needs to be recognized. I know there have been other congresses; however, this one is taking place in a special context. Precisely because the União do Vegetal is concerned with this historical moment that the world is passing through, struggling for survival. Precisely because at the beginning of this new century, in which the world and our country, face apprehension regarding the future, the importance of this Congress needs to go on the record. It is considerable that people like you are presenting your organization, your research and your perspective to society in order to guarantee this sacred right. These people, who use the Hoasca tea in a religious context and seek to be closer to nature, are requesting to be acknowledged.

Present here today, and throughout my life, are dear friends who are members of Centers such as the UDV, Barquinha or Alto Santo, with whom I interact frequently in Acre. This gives me the responsibility to contribute, so that this religion of the forest, born in the heart of the Amazon, the only genuinely Brazilian and Amazonian religion, may be respected and recognized by the national public power. Presently, in all states of Brazil, in the US and in Europe, the groups that utilize the Hoasca tea for religious purposes are being recognized.

The Chacrona and the Mariri originate in the heart of the Amazon forest. This fact increases our responsibility to care well for our home, for this cause and for our planet. With this in mind, we proposed to the Brazilian government, through the Brazilian Ministry of Culture and the Institute of Historical and Artistic Heritage, that the use of the Hoasca tea in religious ritual be recognized as a Brazilian Intangible Cultural Heritage.[32]

This event took place recently at the CICLU-Alto Santo in Acre, with the presence of many representatives of the different Hoasca tea Centers, in which Madrinha Peregrina received the visit of the Minister of Culture. I hope that our enthusiasm and firmness influences the Ministry of Culture and the IPHAN (National Institute of Historical and Artistic Heritage) to grant our request, which is justified.

When we delivered the document to Minister Gilberto Gil, Toninho Alves, a member of the CICLU-Alto Santo, said that the request to recognize the use of the Hoasca tea in religious ritual as a Brazilian cultural heritage is to request that the Brazilian people be the stewards of a great treasure, found within the forest by these three great

---

[32] Congresswoman Perpétua Almeida was one of the main organizers of the appeal that was made by the Hoasca tea religions to then Minister of Culture Gilberto Gil, on April 30, 2008, to recognize the use of the Hoasca tea in religious ritual as a Brazilian Intangible Cultural Heritage.

Mestres.[33] It would be an opportunity to place this treasure in the hands of the Brazilian society. This is the recognition that we are seeking.

The Brazilian Government must recognize that this page of its history is well-written by people like you, each one of you here today – and those who are absent but are with us in spirit – who have worked and continue to work so that love, light and union may be present in Brazilian society.

In the Acre state anthem it says: "we have in our soul the enchantments of heaven;" as far as I know, and I don't know much, I perceive that all of you, thousands of Hoasca tea drinkers, all over the world, are seeking to get closer to these enchantments.

The caring for nature, for children, for elders, and the contribution to a society that hopes for better days, makes you special citizens, and this increases the responsibility of each one of you here today.

In the state of Acre we have a concept also created by our friend Antônio Alves. He coined the term: *"florestania"* (forestship). It means something like citizenship of the forest. It seems to me that all of you who use the Hoasca tea in your religious rituals are exactly that: *"florestanos"* (foresteans, or citizens of the forest) in your essence, due to your respect for diversity, respect for culture, and your respect for our great Brazilian Amazon forest.

To Mestre Monteiro, who lived in my hometown, Cruzeiro do Sul, in the state of Acre, and is today the General Representative Mestre of the União do Vegetal, I wish for you success in the leadership of this Center.

To Mestre Pequenina, this exemplary woman who was a rubber tapper, and who, with her husband, founded the Beneficent Spiritist Center União do Vegetal, may you achieve your objectives. May humanity be able to assimilate more and more the words that you, and all the members of the UDV, have as a symbol of faith: Light, Peace, and Love.

To conclude, I want to reaffirm our commitment, along with other colleagues here present, to engage the National Congress in this cause so that Brazil can become the guardian of this treasure that is the religious use of the Hoasca tea. We will devote our efforts so that the Ministry of Culture, as it learns more about Brazilian history, as it learns more about the rituals of Amazonia, will be able to recognize the use of the Hoasca tea in religious ritual as an Intangible Cultural Heritage of Brazil.

In closing, I salute all of you, in the presence of the spirits of Mestre Irineu, Mestre Gabriel, and Mestre Daniel. I am wishing to all of you a valuable, grand, and victorious Congress. Thank you very much!

---

[33] See article by Alves, in this book

PART I
Hoasca and Science

The Formation of the Medical and Scientific Department and the Scientific Commission

Lucia R.B. Gentil [1]
Edison Saraiva Neves [2]

The UDV and the Government

In 1967, in what is now the state of Rondônia in north Brazil, the União do Vegetal became public for the first time as a result of the arrest of Mestre José Gabriel da Costa by the chief of police.

After his arrest, the disciples of the UDV published an article in the Alto Madeira newspaper in Porto Velho, titled "The Conviction of the Mestre," making public the story of Mestre Gabriel and the objectives of the UDV.[3] The following year the UDV was registered in the public records office.

In 1985, the Divisão Nacional de Vigilancia Sanitaria de Medicamentos - DIMED (Brazilian National Health and Drug Administration), through Ordinance no. 2/85, included the *Banisteriospsis caapi* in the list of proscribed substances. Consequently, health professionals who were members of the UDV organized themselves in order to obtain scientific information about the Hoasca tea and engage in scientific dialogue with academia. The following year, the Center for Medical Studies was created, presently the Medical and Scientific Department (DEMEC), which through its Scientific Commission accompanies the bio-medical studies that are conducted within the UDV. In 1985 the Conselho Federal de Entorpecentes – CONFEN (Brazilian Federal

---

[1] Lúcia R. B. Gentil – geographer and social scientist from the University of Campinas, specialist in education.

[2] Edison Saraiva Neves – medical doctor, general clinical nutrologist, has previously occupied the following offices: president of the General Directorate, president of the Center of Medical Studies of the CEBUDV, director of the Department of Beneficence, and member of the Deliberative Council of the Novo Encanto Association for Ecological Development.

[3] Article published in the Alto Madeira newspaper, issue of October 6, 1967 (CEBUDV, 1967). This article is read in every "escala" (scheduled) session of the UDV. The "escala" sessions take place on the first and third Saturday of every month.

Narcotics Council), via Resolution no. 04/85, designated a Working Group constituted of anthropologists, sociologists, psychologists, lawyers and medical doctors, to study the various Hoasca tea religions, including the UDV. The result of this study was CONFEN's Resolution no. 06, of February 4, 1986, which mandated the temporary suspension of the *Banisteriopsis caapi* from DIMED's list of proscribed substances.

The minutes of CONFEN's 5th Ordinary Meeting on Ayahuasca, held on August 24, 1992, restated that *Banisteriopsis caapi* must remain excluded from DIMED's proscribed substances list and that the re-evaluation of the subject would only take place based on new evidence.

On November 4, 2004, the Conselho Nacional Antidrogas – CONAD (Brazilian National Drug Policy Council) guaranteed the legalization of the ritualistic use of Hoasca tea by minors, stating that the use of the tea by minors shall be within the parents' criteria, in the appropriate exercise of their parental rights.[4]

Studies and Congresses: The Constitution of DEMEC

The proposal to carry out research and studies on Hoasca tea dates back to the seventies when a doctor used the *Alto Madeira* newspaper to attack the UDV. He alleged that a narcotic tea was being used in the rituals of the União do Vegetal. Consequently, the Directorate of the UDV published an explanation in the same newspaper on September 18, 1977, stating that the doors of the Center were open for any research.

The idea to develop research and studies, as well as the proposal to establish a qualified dialogue with academic researchers, only became concrete in the mid-eighties when the Center for Medical Studies of the UDV (CEM-UDV) was created. This was the embryo of the existing DEMEC, with medical doctor Edison Saraiva Neves as its first coordinator. When an arbitrary decision was made by the DIMED, without scientific back up, to list the Mariri as a proscribed substance in Brazil, the members of the UDV who were health professionals began to develop the Center for Medical Studies of the UDV (CEM-UDV). One of the first measures of the CEM-UDV, knowing that the DIMED decision was not based on scientific backing, was to request that a study be conducted that would include the fields of sociology, chemistry, pharmacology, anthropology, culture and constitutional law. At that time this comprehensive proposal for a broad study did not become concrete, however, the health professionals

---

[4] For more information regarding the dialogue between the UDV and CONFEN and CONAD, see the articles of Santos and Machado, in this book.

were well aware of the necessity to develop such a study.

The idea to carry out a comprehensive study on Hoasca tea, as well as the means to make it feasible, began to materialize in 1991, when the Beneficent Spiritist Center União do Vegetal (CEBUDV) realized its 1st Health Congress in the city of São Paulo.[5]

Several scientists were invited as presenters, such as the anthropologist Clodomir Monteiro from the Federal University of Acre, Luis Eduardo Luna from the Swedish School of Economics and Business Administration in Helsinki, Finland, and ethnopharmacologist Dennis McKenna, from the University of Minnesota, USA.

The UDV launched its proposal to conduct a bio-medical study, which coincided with the objectives of Eduardo Luna and Dennis McKenna (an idea dating back to 1985 in Ecuador, when logistical challenges caused the study not to be conducted). At that time the CEM-UDV had within its structure a Scientific Commission coordinated by medical doctor Glacus De Souza Brito.

Members of the UDV became motivated to promote research and, at that time, the Brazilian Medical Homeopathy Association published the study titled *"Patogenesia homeopática do chá Hoasca"* (Homeopathic pathogenesis of the Hoasca tea), in addition to the master's thesis of Labigalini Jr. (1998).

Another important result of the 1st Health Congress of the UDV was the health professionals' Letter of Principles:

The health professionals of the Beneficent Spiritist Center União do Vegetal,

- considering the agreements set forth in the Code of Medical Ethics (CEM Resolution no. 1246/88), the Psychologists' Code of Professional Ethics (CPF Resolution no. 002/87), the International Code of Medical Ethics, the Nuremberg Code, Declarations of Geneva and Helsinki and the Universal Declaration of Human Rights;
- considering that, in its statutes, the Beneficent Spiritist Center União do Vegetal has the objectives of using the Hoasca tea, and also developing the human being in the sense of perfecting his moral, intellectual and spiritual virtues;
- considering that the use of the Hoasca tea is not authorized for any type of therapy, and considering this opportunity to provide a public clarification regarding the guiding principles of the Center for Medical Studies of the UDV and its health professionals, DECLARE THAT:

---

[5] This Congress took place May 30 to June 2, 1991, called "The religious use of the Hoasca tea and its multiple repercussions on individuals: Social, religious and psychosomatic." Approximately 120 people attended this Congress (CEBUDV, July/91).

1. They will not use the Hoasca tea in a professional manner without scientific substantiation that it has therapeutic properties, either within the UDV or outside.
2. They will limit their professional activities within the UDV to medical emergencies and observation of scientific studies on the Hoasca tea, when authorized by the Center for Medical Studies of the UDV.
3. They will not make use of their profession or of their membership in the UDV to refer clients to the UDV with the objective of using the tea in a therapeutic manner.
4. They recognize the Center for Medical Studies of the UDV as the supervisory department for study and scientific research related to the Hoasca tea, conducted by the members of the UDV.
5. All studies and research supervised by the Center for Medical Studies will comply with existing internal and external norms, especially the norms of the Medical Code of Ethics and the Professional Psychologists' Code of Ethics.
6. The research and scientific studies supervised by the Center for Medical Studies will be guided by impartiality, integrity and decency, and that the individuals will abstain from divulging results of such studies, which will only be done properly by the Center for Medical Studies of the UDV.
7. The present Letter of Principles may be re-evaluated, in the case that scientific evidence of the therapeutic capacity of the Hoasca tea is substantiated.

São Paulo, June 2, 1991
The health professionals of the UDV present
at the 1st Health Congress of the União do Vegetal

In 1992, Dennis McKenna configured a protocol for the bio-medical study, and in the following year he began the field-work phase at Núcleo Caupuri, a núcleo of the UDV in Manaus, for the Human Pharmacology of Hoasca Project, or Hoasca Project. This project was coordinated by Dr. Charles Grob, head of the Children and Adolescent Division at the University of California Medical School at Los Angeles, with the logistical support of the Center for Medical Studies of the UDV.

There were two objectives in this study: to track any possible general and mental health hazards in long term users within a religious context and to investigate the pharmacological effect in the central nervous system.

In September of 1993, the 2nd National Health Congress of the CEM-UDV took place with the objective of presenting the preliminary results of the ongoing Human

Pharmacology of Hoasca study.⁶ In 1995, we had the 3rd National Congress of Medical Studies and the 1st International Hoasca Studies Conference where we presented the final results of the Human Pharmacology of Hoasca study.⁷ The studies continued in 1997 with the "Hoasca in Adolescence Project: A Study on the Behavior of Adolescents in the UDV," also coordinated by Dr. Charles Grob (UCLA).⁸

An important decision was made in 1997, when the General Representative Mestre was Mestre Manoel Nogueira, to transform the Center for Medical Studies into The Medical and Scientific Department (DEMEC). This is an important distinction because the word *"center"* seemed to indicate that CEM was separate from the Beneficent Spiritist *Center* União do Vegetal, and the word "department" more appropriately indicates that the DEMEC is a department within the UDV.

Research in the Area of Human Sciences: The Constitution of the Scientific Commission

The UDV is a religion that originated in a rubber-tapping region of the Amazon forest, near the border with Bolivia, in 1961. Its history is linked to the history of Brazil, interrelated with the economic history of the rubber cycle, with the expansion of the agricultural boundaries towards the north and with the urban growth experienced by the country after this period. Nonetheless, despite its development within urban centers, the UDV has and maintains its roots firmly planted in the Amazon forest and in the *"caboclo"* culture.⁹

Though the UDV is not the only religion that uses the Hoasca tea, its distinctive characteristics are:

a) its unified doctrine based in Christianity, which also includes elements of African and Indigenous cultures;

b) its organizational structure composed of the General Headquarters, núcleos, administrative departments, and deliberative councils;¹⁰

---

⁶ The 2nd National Health Congress took place September 4-7, 1993, at a rural hotel in Campinas, São Paulo, its theme being "The União do Vegetal and the Integral Development of the Human Being." More than 400 participants attended this Congress (CEBUDV, August 93/February 94).

⁷ The 3rd National Congress of Medical Studies and the 1st International Hoasca Studies Conference were combined into one event which took place November 2-4, 1995, at the Hotel Gloria in Rio de Janeiro (CEBUDV, August/September/October/93).

⁸ See section *The Adolescent Study*, in this book.

⁹ "Caboclo" is the term used to refer to Brazilian people of mixed European and indigenous descent, who make up a majority of the population in the forest region where the UDV originated.

¹⁰ For more information on the organizational structure of the UDV, see Gentil and Gentil (2002) and the Introduction of this book.

c) its use of the Hoasca tea only in religious rituals.

The UDV's origins, its distinctive elements, its level of organizational development and its structured growth have drawn the attention of social scientists, especially in the area of anthropology. As in the area of biological sciences, this dialogue with anthropologists has always been welcomed by the UDV. As previously mentioned, anthropologists Eduardo Luna (Finland) and Clodomiro Monteiro (Federal University of Acre-UFAC) were invited to attend the 1st National Health Congress in 1991. In addition to Luna and Monteiro, Dr. Jean Langdon, a professor from the Federal University of Santa Catarina (UFSC), was also invited to the 2nd Congress in 1993 in Campinas, São Paulo. At the 3rd Congress in 1995 in Rio de Janeiro we had the presence of Dr. Edward MacRae from the Federal University of Bahia (UFBA).

In this way, through the initiative of the UDV, a scientific dialogue has been a part of the process of structuring our institution. Among the UDV's membership are disciples who work or are students within departments of human science and philosophy of various universities, who are interested in studying, understanding and systematizing this individual and collective phenomenon: the use of the Hoasca tea.

Thus the General Directorate began to receive many requests to approve studies by social scientists, both from UDV members and non-members. These studies required field research, access to documentation, interviews with members, attendance of sessions and participant observation. For this reason it became necessary to develop a means of accompanying these projects.

In 1996 an initial structure was created for a scientific commission that would focus on human sciences studies. Since then several works have been written on the UDV. As has been said, the UDV has always initiated and been receptive to dialogue with the scientific realm, however, the institution has a structure that must be respected by scientists, especially regarding its spiritual teachings.

Being a religion of initiation, the UDV has different levels of teachings, the transmission of which is done orally, within high criteria, and within the ritual of the sessions. The fundamental criteria for the transmission of these teachings is the conditions that the disciple has to be able to adequately understand them, which, according to the doctrine of the UDV, only happens when the disciple has the necessary "degree of memory" or consciousness (Gentil & Gentil, 2002). Therefore, the disciples need to be attending the UDV sessions for a period of time in order to mature their understanding of its organizational structure and its doctrine, to be able to receive the teachings and to learn how to maintain the necessary discretion regarding the transmission of teachings to those who are not yet in the same hierarchical degree.

The same way that the UDV respects the work of scientists, the UDV expects a comparable attitude from the academics who are interested in studying it. There are ways that are not condoned by the UDV to gain access to the teachings (for example, through dissident groups or "pirated" recordings of the stories and *"chamadas"*). Gaining access to the teachings in those ways is damaging to the respect that is necessary for researchers to have toward the subject of their study, is contradictory to good ethics and, most importantly, disrespectful of the religious structure that has brought innumerable benefits to thousands of followers.

For this reason, the original proposal of 1996 evolved into the formation, in April of 2004, of the Scientific Commission, currently directed by Luiz Fernando Milanez, which is responsible for facilitating the dialogue between the UDV and academia.[11]

Bibliography

CEBUDV – Centro Espirita Beneficente União Do Vegetal. "Convicção do Mestre." *Jornal Alto Madeira,* October 6 edition, Porto Velho, Rondônia, 1967.

CEBUDV – Centro Espirita Beneficente União do Vegetal. *Jornal Alto Falante.* Sede Geral, July, Brasilia, DF, 1991.

CEBUDV – Centro Espirita Beneficente União do Vegetal. *Jornal Alto Falante.* Sede Geral, August/February, Brasilia, DF, 1993/1994.

CEBUDV – Centro Espirita Beneficente União do Vegetal. *Jornal Alto Falante.* Sede Geral, August/September/October, Brasilia, DF, 1995.

CONFEN – Conselho Federal de Entorpecentes. *Resolution no. 04, July 30, 1985.* Brasilia: Diário Oficial da União, Poder Executivo, Aug. 8., Section I, p. 11397, 1985.

_____. Conselho Federal de Entorpecentes. *Resolution no. 06, February 4, 1986.* Brasilia: Diário Oficial da União, Poder Executivo, Feb. 5., Section I, p. 2054, 1986.

_____. Conselho Federal se Entorpecentes. Ata da 5ª Reunião do Conselho Federal de Entorpecentes – CONFEN. Diário Oficial da União, Poder Executivo, Brasilia, DF, August 24, 1992. Section 1, p. 11467, 1992.

CONAD – Conselho Nacional Antidrogas. Resolução no. 5, November 4, 2004. Brasilia: Diário Oficial da União, Poder Executivo, November 8, Section I, p. 8, 2004.

---

[11] For more information on the Scientific Commission see the chapter by Milanez, in this book.

DIMED – Divisão Nacional de Vigilancia Sanitaria de Medicamentos. *Portaria no, 02, March 8, 1985.* Brasilia: Diário Oficial da União, Poder Executivo, March 13, 1985, Section I, p. 4421-4434, 1985.

Gentil, Lúcia R. B and Gentil, Henrique S. "O Uso Psicoativo Em Um Contexto Religioso: A União do Vegetal." Labate, Beatriz C. and Araujo, Wladimir, S. (Orgs.). "O Uso Ritual da Ayahuasca." Campinas: Mercado De Letras, 2002.

Labigalini Jr., E. "O Uso da Ayahuasca Em Um Contexto Religioso Por Ex Dependentes de Álcool: Um Estudo Qualitativo." Tese de Mestrado Em Saúde Mental. São Paulo: Unifesp/EPM 1998.

8: The Constitution of the DEMEC and the Scientific Commission

Objectives and Procedures of the Scientific Commission of the UDV

Luiz Fernando Milanez

A Brief History

In the process of the institutional organization of the União do Vegetal many things were developed because of a necessity that arose, and the same is true of the Scientific Commission. In 1985 an ordinance of the DIMED (National Health and Drug Administration of the Brazilian Health Department) included the Banisteriopsis caapi (Mariri) on its list of prohibited substances. At that time, the UDV temporarily suspended sessions with the Vegetal for two months in all its núcleos and requested a review of this measure by the Brazilian Federal Narcotics Council. In the following year, 1986, after the issue was duly studied, the Vegetal and the plants were provisionally removed from DIMED's list, and in 1992 they were removed permanently. Thus, the legal use of the Vegetal in religious rituals was secured.

Those of us who have been drinking the Vegetal for some years know, through our own experience, the wellness it brings to us. For us, the Vegetal is proven harmless to the health. It is proven harmless by the individuals who have been participating in the UDV since its beginnings. They have been drinking this tea for nearly 50 years and they continue to enjoy good health physically, mentally and spiritually, despite the fact that they are well advanced in years. Nevertheless, we needed to have scientific proof to demonstrate the harmlessness of the tea to the authorities. In 1986, the UDV created the Center for Medical Studies – the present Medical and Scientific Department, DEMEC – due to the urgent need for an institutional technical dialogue, with the purpose of facilitating research within the UDV done by Universities, providing internal support and consulting with governmental authorities and the scientific community. Parallel to this, the UDV created a Legal Department for the purpose of bringing the process of institutionalization to completion and securing the definitive legalization of the religious use of the Vegetal.

The first step towards the organization of a scientific effort was taken in 1991 at the 1st UDV Health Congress, in São Paulo. At this Congress, despite the small number of participants, approximately 120 members and guests, an exchange began between the UDV and scientists from many disciplines.

At that time, when the UDV only had approximately 1,500 active members, it opened its doors to research, and the Hoasca Project then took place in Manaus in 1993. This was the first bio-medical study in the history of the use of the tea, which brought together a pool of researchers from nine academic institutions from three countries to carry out a study on the human pharmacology of the Hoasca tea. In 1995 the 3rd UDV Congress, and the 1st International Hoasca Congress, was held in Rio de Janeiro, where the official final results of the Human Pharmacology of Hoasca study were presented.

The Center for Medical Studies (CEM), subsequently DEMEC, maintained a Scientific Commission from the beginning, coordinated by Dr. Glacus de Souza Brito, which worked in the same manner as the present Scientific Commission, though it only attended to bio-medical projects. This characterizes the pioneering role of the UDV in the realm of research of the Hoasca tea and the dialogue with the scientific community. The first studies that took place within the UDV were of a bio-medical character, with the purpose of proving that the tea is harmless. The DEMEC now also has a Clinical Commission and a Mental Health Commission.

The rapid expansion of the UDV and segments of Santo Daime in large urban centers in the nineties became the subject of study in anthropology departments of some universities. In addition to this, through UDV members that are affiliated with these fields through universities, requests for the approval of dissertation studies began to arrive at the General Directorate. In 1995 and 1996, two master degree dissertations by UDV members were developed, the first in science of religion, and the second in social anthropology. At that moment there was the necessity to closely accompany these studies to be certain of the fidelity of the information regarding our institution, and to be careful so that the teachings, reserved stories, and chamadas would not be published or analyzed in congresses or round tables.

Immediately there was a significant increase in the number of researchers, inside and outside the UDV, interested in developing studies in the area of human sciences, with the UDV as the subject of these studies. Therefore it became necessary for the UDV to have a Scientific Commission that could work with research in other fields in addition to the medical field.

Núcleo Lupunamanta, in Campinas, through the initiative of Lúcia Gentil, sent a formal request on July 12, 2002, for the creation of a technical commission that would evaluate proposals, as well as accompany and review the scientific works done by researchers from educational institutions regarding the União do Vegetal.

Justifications for the Creation of a Scientific Commission

1. To assist the General Directorate in managing the number of research proposals received;
2. To address the need of establishing more permanent procedures and criteria in order to deal with the growing interest from the scientific community, both internal and external;
3. To facilitate the General Directorate's ability to concentrate its attention on this subject, through the focusing capacity that this commission could provide;
4. To promote works that consider, primarily, the interests of the Center;
5. To guarantee the accuracy of the information, and to assure that the scientific studies are compatible with the objectives of our Institution.

The UDV's Scientific Commission

The Council of the General Representation of the UDV met on April 9-10, 2004, and approved the constitution of the Scientific Commission, with the purpose of analyzing, approving and overseeing projects whose focus is the Vegetal, the UDV, and its membership. At that time, Luiz Fernando Milanez was appointed as the coordinator of the Commission. Thus the Scientific Commission of the UDV was created with more attributes than those originally granted to it through the DEMEC, centralizing the information from all fields of knowledge, and reporting directly to the Institutional Relations Coordination of the UDV.

Objectives

1. To provide consulting support to the General Directorate;
2. To define timelines, criteria and procedures for the development of this Commissions' activities;
3. To examine research proposals and data surveys for the Center, evaluating them from the perspective of our Institutions' interests and contributing to the decision-making process of the General Directorate;

4. To accompany the development of the research, studies, and surveys approved by the General Directorate through to their completion.
5. To define, in accordance with the General Directorate, criteria for providing information about the Center, such as:
   – Information related to the religious rituals;
   – Information from the Department of Memory and Documentation;
   – Information from the Department of Charitable Works;
   – Data from the socio-economic census of the members of the UDV;
   – Data from the survey of the Department of Plantation of Mariri and Chacrona;
   – Location maps of núcleos and areas of plantation, etc.

Procedures

All affiliates of the CEBUDV who wish to conduct research within the Center that will be published as an academic paper, book or chapter in a book, article, dissertation or thesis, must submit a proposal to the coordinator of the Scientific Commission before starting the project.[1] Each proposal will be analyzed by two researchers from our team of advisors, who will issue a recommendation of approval, reformulation, or refusal.

We have in the UDV approximately 80 members with accredited academic backgrounds, with doctorate degrees or who are doctoral candidates, in various academic fields of study (medicine, psychology, anthropology, education, agronomy, biology, architecture, science of religion, literature, ecology, etc.) who assist voluntarily in this work of proposal evaluation.[2] The objective of the Commission is to analyze, authorize, and supervise the development of these works in order to aid the process in whatever way possible, to guarantee the accuracy of the information that could in the future become a reference, and to guard the doctrinal content of the UDV.

For those who are not members of the UDV, the procedure is the same, so that they may count on our support, collaboration and supervisory assistance.

---

[1] For more information see commissaocientifica@udv.org.br

[2] Number of members as of May 2008.

Bibliography

Andrade, A. P. *"O Fenômeno do Chá e a Religiosidade Cabocla – Um Estudo Centrado na União do Vegetal."* Dissertação de Mestrado. São Bernardo do Campo: Programa de Pós-Graduação Em Ciências da Religião, Universidade de Metodista de Ensino Superior (UMESP), 1995.

Andrade, E, N.; Brito, G. S.; Andrade, E. O.; Neves, E. S.; Mckenna, D.; Cavalcante, J.W.; Okimura, L.; Grob, C. And Callaway, J. C. *"Human Pharmacology Of Hoasca: Clinical Studies (Comparative Clinical Evaluation Among Users Of Hoasca Tea Over Prolonged Periods And Controls- Physiological Evaluation Of Acute Effects After Ingestion Of Hoasca Tea),"* Labate, B. C. and Araujo, W. S. (Orgs.) *O Uso Ritual Da Ayahuasca.* Campinas: Mercado De Letras, São Paulo: FAPESP, p. 671-709, 2004.

Brissac, S, G, T. *"A Estrela do Norte Iluminando Até o Sul: Uma Etnografia da União do Vegetal Em Um Context Urbano."* Dissertação de Mestrado do Programa de Pós-Graduação Em Antropologia Social. Rio de Janeiro: Museu Nacional/UFRJ, 1999.

Brito, G. De S. *"Human Pharmacology of Hoasca. Tea Prepared From Hallucinogenic Plants Used In Ritual Context In Brazil,"* Labate, B. C. And Araujo, Wladimir, S. (Orgs), *O Uso Ritual da Ayahuasca.* Campinas: Mercado de Letras; São Paulo: FAPESP, p. 623-651, 2004.

Gentil, Lúcia R. B And Gentil, Henrique S. *"O Uso de Psicoativo Em Um Context Religioso: A União do Vegetal,"* Labate, B. C. And Araujo, Wladimir, S. (Orgs), *O Uso Ritual da Ayahuasca.* Campinas: Mercado de Letras; São Paulo: FAPESP, 2002.

Grob, C. S.; Mckenna, D. J.; Callaway, J. C.; Brito, G. S.; Andrade, E. O.; Oberlender, G.; Saide, O. L.; Labigliani Jr., E.; Tacla, C.; Miranda, C. T.; Strassman, R. J.; Boonke, K. S. and Neves, E. S. *"Human Pharmacology Of Hoasca: Psychological Effects,"* Labate, B. C. and Araujo, W. S. (Orgs), *O Uso Ritual Da Ayahuasca.* Campinas: Mercado de Letras; São Paulo: FAPESP, p. 653-669, 2004.

Hoasca Project: Personal View of the Hoasca Project

J.C. Callaway[1]

When people ask me to describe Hoasca, I often begin by saying it is a unique plant-based technology that stimulates the mind in many ways; initially as a direct experience for the individual, and secondly how this individual subsequently interacts with society.

Many other things may be said, both productive and potentially unproductive, because other sacred beverages are also made from the same plants, and most people outside of the UDV are not able to notice that Hoasca is different. From a scientific point of view, Hoasca is at least chemically different from most other forms of "ayahuasca."[2] It is more similar in alkaloid content to the indigenous teas made by the Shuar.[3]

This is also important because the institutions of justice and science will continue to focus on certain alkaloids that are found in Hoasca, and their effects on the individual and society. Medical science, in particular, can be expected to eventually explore any useful findings and possibly apply them to specific problems in the modern world, such as treating alcoholism and other forms of drug abuse.

It is unlikely that either justice or science will fully accept or even understand the divine aspects of Hoasca, as this aspect of divinity is currently beyond the limits of these institutions. But these issues are really not so important to me because the main message is within the experience, and the experience speaks for itself.

I began to read about ayahuasca in the early 1980s, primarily through the published academic works of Harvard ethnobotanist Richard Schultes and other great

---

[1] Dr. J.C. Callaway, Ph.D., Doctor of Neuroscience, professor of the pharmacology and toxicology department at the University of Kuopio, Finland.

[2] The author is comparing the Hoasca tea utilized in the religious rituals of the UDV and the Ayahuasca tea used in other contexts, such as in other indigenous societies that have used the tea for hundreds of years. The difference in alkaloid levels is partly explained due to the subtypes of *Banisteriopsis* and *Psychotria viridis* utilized.

[3] The Shuar is an indigenous group in Ecuador that utilizes this tea.

researchers. The experiences that were described in the scientific literature seemed both incredible and inaccessible to me at that time. I was especially interested in the molecular similarities and possible correlations between neurotransmitters in the human brain, the biochemistry of normal dreaming and the alkaloids that are found in ayahuasca. There seemed to be some common link between these molecules and their actions in the brain, like a new set of keys that could unlock deeper mysteries of the mind. I was surprised at how little scientific information was available on these topics. Although more is known now, there is still much more that remains unknown in this regard.

Another mystery for me was to try and understand how people could have discovered such an amazing effect from the combination of two plants. I spent about 10 years searching and reading all of the information I could possibly find on ayahuasca and related topics. There were not very many people who were available discuss these issues during this time. Since 1995, there has been an explosion of interest in ayahuasca, and much has been learned from a scientific point of view, but science has not been able to say very much at all about the divine nature of this unique experience or its useful impact on the individual and society.

The deeper mystery of ayahuasca will continue to be a frontier of science for many more years, although this ancient technology of the mind cannot be easily accepted or understood by the science of today. This technology will continue to be a personal experience that can only be achieved by drinking the tea within an appropriate context. It is because of this unique experience that a relatively small number of people have continued to maintain this ancient technology over the years.

I had not heard of the UDV until 1992, when I met and had discussions with Dr. Dennis McKenna. He had recently attended a UDV conference in Brazil, and had some very interesting stories to tell.[4] Dennis was already an established scientist at that time, and someone who I admired. He was beginning to organize a research project and collect medical scientists for the Hoasca Project.[5] Dr. Charlie Grob, a medical doctor who I also knew and also admired, had already promised to be the principle investigator for this project. It was an honor for me to be asked and, of course, I was immediately interested and ready to go. I had no idea what to expect, and it was hard for me to imagine such an ambitious scientific project in an unfamiliar culture. There

---

[4] This was the UDV's I National Health Congress which took place in São Paulo in 1991. See article by Neves and Gentil in this book.

[5] See papers by Brito (2004), Grob et al. (2004) and Andrade *et al.* (2004). The scientists mentioned above, Charles Grob, Dennis Mckenna and Jace Callaway, are the main international researchers who participated in the Hoasca Project.

were only few details that were available to me at that time. Were these indigenous people, far from modern civilization? At that point, I had no idea that ayahuasca was even used as a sacrament by a "modern" organized religion. Soon after I arrived in São Paulo, in June of 1993, I met Mestre Glacus de Souza Brito, and my lack of information was quickly replaced with something much more interesting than the childhood jungle fantasies that had filled my mind for so many years.[6]

Part of my job was to fully experience the phenomenon we were about to study. The first time that I tasted Hoasca was soon after I arrived, in a small núcleo near Campinas, away from the busy noise of São Paulo. The Mestre began the first of several short songs, the *chamadas*.[7] My ordinary senses were quickly modified and the acute sensation of the altered state lasted about three hours. The environment was new to me, but somehow familiar and I never had any feeling of fear or danger. However, drinking even a small amount of Hoasca can be a humbling experience. For me, at least in some ways, it was like coming home to a place I had never been before. The first impressions were that of a sincere and intentional community, as if this small room of about 50 people were floating together on a journey along a tranquil river. Only a few of these people were actually known to me, yet I felt relaxed, welcomed and a universal connection to all during these few precious hours of ordinary time. The session eventually came to an end, with everything back to "normal", but with a memory of incredible clarity. The work we had come to do in Brazil now seemed simple and trivial, almost silly, compared to what I had just experienced. I understood and accepted that this work had to be done, while I also understood and reluctantly accepted that our work could only be superficial at best.

There was no sense to talk much about this experience with Dennis and Charlie. It was still too fresh and complex. Besides "Wow" or "Oh Man", we really did not

---

[6] Glacus de Souza Brito, a doctor at the immunology department of the University of São Paulo Medical School, was of great importance in the development of the medical-scientific research conducted in the UDV. He made a significant contribution in the elaboration of the Hoasca Project research protocols. Following is his description of how the idea came about at UDV's I National Health Congress in 1991: "Dennis McKenna (Minneapolis University) and Luis Eduardo Luna (Swedish School of Economics and Business Administration in Helsinki, Finland) presented only references of studies conducted with indigenous tribes in Colombia and Peru. These indigenous groups mixed other plants in their teas. At that moment I offered a challenge to Dennis McKenna that the information they were presenting about the tea did not correspond to the actual reality of the UDV and the other plants being used also did not reflect the practice of the UDV. I proposed we conduct a study with a tea prepared by a mestre of the UDV, in the ritual manner of the UDV. This proposal was immediately accepted. At the moment the seed of the Hoasca Project was planted and it came to fruition two years later."

[7] *Chamadas* are hymns sang by only one person at a time in the rituals of the UDV.

have much of a common vocabulary to even begin a serious discussion of what we had just experienced. We all seemed to be experiencing much of the same things, more or less, and each in our own way. None of us had ever been in such a unique research environment, and we soon agreed that we would not be able to measure or analyze very much of the actual experience that an individual has with Hoasca. We were certainly allowed, and even encouraged to take all the samples and ask all the questions that we wanted, so access was not a problem. We were thoroughly impressed by the scale and enormity of the effects of the Hoasca tea, but a bit disappointed by the inability of our science to measure or to even recognize the magnitude of the experience; the proverbial elephant in the room. There was not a sample that could be taken or question that could be asked that would give us any more information than we already had about this experience.

As part of our investigation, Charlie was prepared to conduct a psychological inventory of our volunteers, which he did, but this simple examination of the mind could only give the most rudimentary data on the effects of Hoasca. This was like trying to understand the contents of a book by looking at its shadow. From the perspective of modern psychiatry the information from Hoasca, these messages to the mind, could only be compared to psychosis. However, Dennis, Charlie and I intuitively knew this effect was quite the opposite of psychosis. We were in full agreement on that. But there was no time to make big changes in our protocol, and we didn't have anything else that could be used in substitution of our planned work. So we all quickly agreed to continue our primary mission; to collect and measure certain fundamental aspects of this complex phenomenon, and try not to allow ourselves to become overly concerned by these mysterious details. In short, we had to ignore the elephant in the room and stay focused on the things that we knew; the plants, the pharmacology and, to a lesser extent, the people and their personal relationship to Hoasca.

There were only a few clearly defined goals in the Hoasca Project. This was a prospective study; a general survey of the plants, the tea and the people. Such a thing had never been done before, and certainly not for a religious practice. We were given unprecedented access to everything, and there was never anything that was too sacred to see, touch or taste.

As scientists, we were completely amazed that we were invited into the central mysteries of a religious group that had no fear or outsiders or anything to hide. It was unusual to imagine how any religion could be so secure as to allow a group of scientist to come in and do as they pleased, and then leave without any preconditions. This situation was both novel and surreal. Where was the problem here? What horrible things were not being told or shown? From the beginning, we looked for possible "problems". That was part of our job, as independent investigators. In this regard we failed to find any significant problems that can be related to the use of Hoasca. I believe that if there were serious problems, we would have at least seen signs of them by now. I now accept that looking for such possible problems was a necessary waste of time.

After 15 years, I have obtained some fundamental answers from our research on Hoasca, but I still have more questions about the nature of the experience, and I especially wonder why humans even have the capacity for such an experience. I have also become older, so I am unable to say exactly where the changes in my life have come from during this particular span of time. However, this project has had a profound and positive impact on my life, which is something unexpected from a scientific project. In essence, our results can only provide some basic information on this phenomenon; such as the identification of specific alkaloids in the plants, in the tea and for only a few hours in the people who drink this tea. We know that Hoasca offers a reliable technology to connect and reconnect with the divine and a deeper sense of self, and this connection carries with it a strong sense of personal life purpose and of one's purpose in the larger community. Such things are written about in all religious traditions. There is a profound and comfortable feeling, a timeless eternity, that comes with this experience; a state of no beginning or end. Could this be near heaven? Such places exist in all religions. Perhaps the fundamental difference is that Hoasca provides a reliable and active sacrament for this communion, while most other religions apparently do not. This may have been the case in the distant past, in the beginning of all great religions, but somehow was diluted or even forgotten over time. The UDV also provides a context for this experience, which insures a reasonable certainty that one will feel the "force" and see the "light" after consuming even a small amount of Hoasca tea within this religious context. In summary, Hoasca is a sacrament that does not require much faith, and the UDV provides a context for the efficient use of this experience.

Now that the work has been done and the articles have been published, it is not a matter of "if" the world will take a stronger interest in Hoasca but "when", and how quickly. There is now no way to ignore this fact or make it go away. A critical description of Hoasca has now entered the published scientific literature, and now cyberspace, which has stimulated a free flowing discussion of this and related phenomena.

About 15 scientific articles have been published directly from the results of the

Hoasca Project since 1994.[8] Before that time, there were only 21 published articles in the scientific literature that could be identified with the key work "ayahuasca", according to PubMed, from 1953 to 1994.[9] As of this writing, there are now 84 published scientific articles for "ayahuasca" from 1953- 2008. As of late November of 2008, a total of seven articles have been published on "ayahuasca", compared to the period between 1953-1994, when only one scientific article was published every second year. Clearly, the published results from the Hoasca Project have stimulated a global interest within the scientific and lay communities. This is unusual by most any standard. In this regard, it can be said that the Hoasca Project has been an impressive success, and it has been a great honor for me to be a part of this project. My experience with the UDV continues to deepen over time, and I always feel warmly welcomed in this very large family.

The UDV International Conferences have also been extremely successful in presenting the medical and scientific information, in addition to respective information on the environment and society. The most recent conference, in Brasilia during May of 2008, was exceptional in every way, and especially in the high level of quality and in the number of interested people who attended. These events are always very well planned and organized, and always with the highest available level of communications technologies, which includes simultaneous translations. I am always impressed by the fact that UDV members have such a keen interest and exceptionally high level of scientific knowledge about the chemical and physical aspects of Hoasca. In other words, this information that is presented at these conferences is not just to impress external authorities, but it is actively absorbed, discussed and understood by the people who use Hoasca. To me, it has been especially rewarding to observe the growing interest and participation in these conferences over the years, and especially to reconnect with familiar faces. These conferences also serve as practical examples of the UDV's ability to effectively organize and facilitate such complex functions. Any institution would be completely satisfied with such accomplishments. Moreover, the efficient documentation, follow up and distribution of information from these events is taken very seriously, which is especially important for the future of any organization. With a patient optimism, which is

---

[8] Callaway is mostly referring to articles related to the bio-medical field. Considering, however, multi-disciplinary subjects, the scientific-academic production has been more extensive. Refer to Labate, Rose and Santos, 2008, for a bibliographic survey of the Ayahuasca field of knowledge.

[9] PubMed is a site of the United States National Library of Medicine with access to medical articles published in specialized journals. See http://www.ncbi.nlm.nih.gov/pubmed/

something new for me, I look forward to see how this phenomenon continues to develop in my remaining years.

Bibliography

Andrade, E, N.; Brito, G. S.; Andrade, E. O.; Neves, E. S.; Mckenna, D.; Cavalcante, J.W.; Okimura, L.; Grob, C. And Callaway, J. C. "Human Pharmacology of Hoasca: Clinical Studies (Comparative Clinical Evaluation Among Users of Hoasca Tea Over Prolonged Periods and Controls- Physiological Evaluation of Acute Effects After Ingestion of Hoasca Tea)." In Labate, B. C. and Araujo, W. S. (Orgs.) "O Uso Ritual da Ayahuasca." Campinas: Mercado de Letras, São Paulo: FAPESP, p. 671-709, 2004.

Brito, G. de S. "Human Pharmacology of Hoasca. Tea Prepared From Hallucinogenic Plants Used In Ritual Context In Brazil." In Labate, B. C. and Araujo, Wladimir, S. (Orgs), "O Uso Ritual da Ayahuasca." Campinas: Mercado de Letras; São Paulo: FAPESP, p. 623-651, 2004.

Grob, C. S.; Mckenna, D. J.; Callaway, J. C.; Brito, G. S.; Andrade, E. O.; Oberlender, G.; Saide, O. L.; Labigalini Jr., E.; Tacla, C.; Miranda, C. T.; Strassman, R. J.; Boonke, K. S. and Neves, E. S. "Human Pharmacology of Hoasca: Psychological Effects," In Labate, B. C. and Araujo,W. S. (Orgs), "O Uso Ritual da Ayahuasca." Campinas: Mercado de Letras; São Paulo: FAPESP, p. 653-669, 2004.

Labate, Beatriz C.; Rose, I.S. and Santos, R.G. (orgs.) "Religiões ayahuasqueiras: um balanço bibliográfico: O Uso Ritual da Ayahuasca." Campinas: Mercado De Letras, 2008.

Hoasca in Adolescence: A Study on the Health and Behavior of Adolescent Users of Hoasca in a Ritual Context[1]

Otávio Castello de Campos Pereira

The objective of this chapter is to present a historical perspective of the conception and development of the "Hoasca in Adolescence" project and its relationship to the process of institutionalization of the Beneficent Spiritist Center União do Vegetal (UDV). Financed in its majority by the not-for-profit Heffter Institute, the project was developed by a multinational team from the University of California, Los Angeles (UCLA) and the Universidade Federal de São Paulo- UNIFESP (Federal University of São Paulo).[2] Its objective is to evaluate the physical and mental health of adolescents who regularly attended the rituals of the UDV, and to specify if the long-term ritual consumption of the tea might have harmed their development.

The results, published in the *Journal of Psychoactive Drugs* in 2005, and republished here in the following chapters, provide evidence that the adolescents of the UDV presented a physical and mental development similar to the comparison group, and suggested that the ritual use of the Hoasca tea could prevent drug abuse in adolescence. The findings revealed that the UDV adolescents showed a tendency toward valuing ethical principles in general and had better relationships with their fathers, in relation to the comparison group.

At the conclusion of one of the publications the authors affirm that *"no evidence was found of any harmful effect of the Ayahuasca in the adolescents who participated with their families in the ritual ceremonies."* (Grob and Silveira 2005 a,b,c,; Grob and De Rios 2005)

---

[1] I thank Dr. Glacus Brito, who at that time was the Director of the Medical and Scientific Department of the UDV, for the invitation to collaborate on this research project, and for his availability and dedication in orienting a young doctor. I also thank Dr. Prof. Dartiu Xavier da Silveira, Dr. Evelyn D. Xavier da Silveira, Dr. Luiza B. Alonso and Dr. Charles Grob for the learning I acquired and for the trust in my logistical coordination. I also thank Prof. Joaze Bernardino, for persevering in convincing this author to write this article.

[2] For more information about the Heffter Institute, see the site http://www.heffter.org

History

The ritual use of the Hoasca tea, also known academically as Ayahuasca, has drawn an increasing interest from the scientific community. Until the late eighties the existing research was mostly related to anthropological aspects or botanical aspects and the biochemistry of its components – the vine Banisteriopsis caapi and the shrub Psychotria Viridis. It was only in 1993 that the first bio-medical study took place, to determine the effects of the tea on the human organism – the *Hoasca Project*. In this study, scientists from nine institutions in three countries (United States, Finland and Brazil) conducted an investigation of the clinical and psychiatric aspects of the health of UDV members in the city of Manaus, Brazil.[3] The results were presented at the 1st International Conference on Hoasca Studies in Rio de Janeiro, which clearly indicated that the individuals evaluated enjoyed good health, both physical and mental, without any suggested pattern of drug abuse or addiction. Moreover, the religious affiliation was temporally associated with the remission of psychiatric disorders (such as anxiety and those related to alcoholism), suggesting that the experience with the Hoasca tea had a profound impact on the course of life of those individuals.[4]

One of the pillars of the Hoasca Project was Charles S. Grob, M.D., head of the UCLA Child and Adolescent Psychiatry Department. During the presentation of the results of the Project at the Conference in 1995, Dr. Grob expressed an interest in assessing the mental and psychological health of adolescents that drink the Hoasca tea.

Concurrently, despite the results of the Hoasca Project having indicated an existing safety in the ritual use of the tea by adults, segments of the government and the public persisted in questioning any possible harm to the development of the children and adolescents who participated in the UDV's religious rituals. Therefore the UDV, consistent with its historical practice, initiated the invitation for independent researchers to carry out a scientific investigation on this subject.

Subsequently, in 1997, Luiza Alonzo, Ph.D., presented the first proposal for a qualitative study with adolescents of the UDV, to be carried out jointly with UCLA. During the planning stage the researchers opted for a study that could also evaluate quantitative aspects and invited the Psychiatry Department from UNIFESP, whose scientists also took part in the *Hoasca Study*.

---

[3] The UDV is not included among the institutions that carried out this study because the UDV only participated by providing logistical support, having no influence in the methodology or the results.

[4] For more information, see: Brito (2004); Grob *et.al.* (2004) and Andrade *et. al.* (2004).

In 2000, while observing the Census of the UDV and the norm-setting of the neuropsychological tests, the Brazilian scientists decided on the strategy to study adolescents from large urban centers. Given the population contingency and the logistical viability, the cities of Brasilia, São Paulo and Campinas were chosen. Some months later the American and Brazilian teams met in California to finalize their plans and adjust their methodology.

With the approval of UNIFESP and the financial backing of the Heffter Institute, the study began in 2001 with the initial field work of data collection, which will be discussed next. In 2004 the researchers met again in California to discuss the results, which after its publication in 2005, was also presented in the 2nd International Hoasca Congress in May of 2008.

Justification

The uses of psychoactive substances to expand consciousness have been recorded since the beginning of humanity. It is an under-studied phenomenon which is receiving attention from the scientific community, including for its therapeutic potential. If on one hand there exists the recreational use of substances, usually associated with risk factors for the individual and the society, on the other hand there are traditional practices related to the search for transcendence and spirituality, a phenomenon that has been scientifically recognized as something very different from what is referred to as "drug use" by society at large.

In this scenario, in which social groups have questioned if Hoasca in its ritualistic use could be a powerful, potentially harmful "drug," the existence of a legally sanctioned context in which a psychoactive beverage is utilized as a sacrament is something new, and deserves the attention of the scientific community.

Although the Hoasca Project has indicated the absence of any harm to the physical and mental health of adults, segments of society and the Brazilian Government questioned if the use of the tea by adolescents posed any risk, not yet studied, to the individual or to society.[5] Such suspicion is based on widely observed drug consumption by adolescents (such as cocaine, marijuana and others) that frequently causes injurious consequences and negatively interferes in the development of adolescents specifically in the dimensions of sociability, honesty, study habits and cognitive

---

[5] For more information on the questions regarding the use of Hoasca by minors, see the chapter by Machado, in this book.

function. Consequently, questions regarding what impact the continuous use of a psychoactive sacrament would have in the development of an adolescent.

Objectives

The main objective of this research project was to evaluate the long term effects of the sacramental use of the Hoasca tea on the physical and mental health of adolescents who participate regularly in the sessions of the UDV, two sessions per month, and the impact this practice might have had on their development.

More specifically, the study endeavored to (1) evaluate the mental state of the adolescents studied, tracking possible psychiatric disorders, including drug use patterns; (2) understand the subjects' cognitive function in its multiple aspects; (3) understand the psycho-social universe of the adolescents: their values, beliefs, myths and vision of the future.

Methodology

The results of the Hoasca Project showed that the sacramental use of the Hoasca tea is inseparable from its ritual context. Therefore the researchers understood that a qualitative and quantitative approach would be the most suitable for better investigating aspects of physical and mental health as well as the psychosocial factors that make up the reality of these adolescents and the long-term effects possibly associated with the use of the tea.

Furthermore, to increase the credibility of the results, a comparative study model was chosen, and a *control* group was recruited, composed of adolescents who had never used the beverage. In this way it would be possible to contrast the results of both groups, and also compare them with the normal patterns of the general population. Additionally, specifically for the neuropsychological comparison, a control group would facilitate the use of a blind study, in which the researcher does not know to which group each subject belongs. The researcher only obtains the information regarding the individual's group affiliation after the statistics of the results are calculated. Therefore, this is a methodological refinement that grants greater credibility to the results.

Working with the objective of developing a blind comparative study (blind study) for the neuropsychological evaluations, the researchers initially planned to evaluate the subjects in offices set up specifically for the study. Nonetheless, this set up was not favorable for controlling specific conditions that could alter the results, such as: motivation of the individual while being evaluated, hours of sleep on the evening before the evaluation; alcohol, drug and caffeine consumption, as well as others.

The solution found was to confine the participants from both groups in a rural hotel setting for the data collection phase. This way the environment of the study could be better controlled and the model employed with greater reliability. Also, most importantly, the attraction for a group of adolescents of the same age to interact, in a leisure environment, without cost to the participant, could contribute to motivating the chosen adolescents to be engaged in the study.

In 2001 the UDV and control group adolescents from Brasilia were lodged for four days at a rural hotel outside Brasilia, and the São Paulo adolescents were lodged at a quiet seaside inn outside São Paulo in September of the same year. A team from *Projeto Pegadas Brasil* (Tracking Project Brazil), a group that specializes in youth environmental education and campouts, coordinated outdoor activities and entertainment during the evaluation periods, in such a way that the collection of data from each adolescent, totaling approximately four hours, was distributed throughout the entire stay.[6] These activities also assisted the researchers in maintaining a controlled environment with respect to tobacco and drug use, and other necessary conditions to avoid predictable biases, which could negatively interfere with the reliability of the results.

Sample

The recruiting of UDV adolescents started through a census that took place in all the núcleos and authorized distributions of the UDV near the cities of Brasilia, Campinas and São Paulo. Variables of interest to the study were collected for all the adolescents in those communities and compiled in a database, assigning an identification number to each individual. Next, the adolescents who fit the criteria by age and a minimum attendance at the rituals were listed and chosen randomly to be invited to participate in the study. The next step was to organize meetings with the adolescents and their parents to present the proposal for the study and formalize the invitation, emphasizing the voluntary nature of their participation. All participants and their parents/legal guardians signed a written consent. Finally, two lists were created, one with the adolescents chosen for the sample and another of alternates, also chosen randomly, in case of any eventual necessary substitution.

---

[6] The Tracking Project http://www.thetrackingproject.org/international/brasil.htm

Ranking by sex, age and academic grade of UDV participants provided the elements necessary for the pairing with the comparison group, or control. These were recruited among students of the Marista School in Brasilia and the Arquidiocesano School in São Paulo (both private Catholic schools). Three groups were randomly chosen from each high school grade. Spreadsheets were created listing each individual's name, age and sex. Next, subsets were selected for pairing with the sample group from the UDV, matching with the variables mentioned. For example, for a UDV 16 year-old male high school sophomore, a list was assembled with adolescents from the control group with the same characteristics who would be invited to participate in the study. In this manner an exact match of the characteristics was organized for the invitation criteria of the controls. The next step was to randomly choose candidates from each subset and formally invite them to participate in the study. Meetings with the students and their parents/legal guardians took place for the presentation of the study, emphasizing the voluntary aspect. Written consents were signed in the same manner as with the UDV group. After the control group was defined, a list of alternates was composed, respecting the same criteria, in case of necessary substitutions. In addition, a teacher from each institution was assigned to accompany the entire study, at the request of the researchers.

Procedures

The multiple evaluations used were developed in previously prepared environments within the hotel facilities. To guarantee that the effects of the Hoasca tea that were detected were resulting from long-term use, all the UDV adolescents abstained from the use of the Hoasca tea for a minimum of 20 days before the start of the study.

The neuropsychological assessment consisted of the application of a battery of tests by two neuropsychologists and one computer test, both of which were previously measured. As mentioned earlier, neither professional knew to which group the adolescents belonged (the UDV or the control). All subjects had the following functions evaluated: memory, attention, language, concentration, executive functioning, processing speed, visuomotor and visuoconstructional abilities. Special care was taken with factors that could interfere in the results (for example: insufficient sleep hours, tobacco, alcohol, illicit drugs and caffeine consumption).

The psychiatric assessment consisted of the application of instruments to track psychiatric disorders in each participant, evaluating the psychiatric state as a whole: depression, anxiety, drug use, drug misuse, attention deficit disorders and self-image disorders. Individual interviews were carried out by a psychiatrist on a subset of the sample adolescents from the UDV and the control group, chosen equally at random.

The clinical evaluation was done by a medical doctor specializing in adolescents, with interviews and a physical exam for all the participants, aiming to evaluate the general state of health, pubescent development and to track clinical history that may justify any findings in the psychiatric and neuropsychological assessments.

Focus groups and individual interviews were used for the qualitative assessment with a randomly selected subset from the sample groups. In these meetings topics related to daily life were discussed, without judgment of what is considered right or wrong, encompassing nine main topics: family life, friends and acquaintances, questions about the future, social integration and alienation, sexual experiences, religious affiliation, and previous experiences with illicit drugs. In the focus groups – experiential meetings with six to eight participants with pre-defined duration and topics – hypothetical daily life situations were presented to assess drug use, social alienation, sex life, and moral and ethical values.

It is important to highlight that during the recruiting, and especially throughout the collection of data, specific instructions were given for the adolescents to be completely sincere responding to the test, and in exchange the researchers guaranteed that all the information collected would be protected by secrecy and never would be evaluated from a moral perspective.

Results and Conclusions

The analysis of the characteristics of the participant sample showed that both groups – UDV adolescents and *controls* – were very similar in relation to age, gender, academic grade level, and socio-economic status, and therefore comparable.

The rate of refusal at the time of enrollment, a fact not yet published, is important to note. Overall, only four UDV adolescents declined to participate after they were randomly selected and invited, and six of the control group also presented the same behavior. The refusals were motivated by schedule conflicts with previous engagements, specifically, academic and sport competitions. Hence, only two UDV adolescents and three from the controls declined to participate for lack of interest in the study. The entire sample participated willingly and was engaged in the process of the study.

A total of 84 adolescents were assessed, male and female, between 15 and 19 years old. Approximately half of the sample was recruited from Brasilia and the other half from Sao Paulo and Campinas. None of the participants from the control group had previously experienced the Hoasca tea and the adolescents from the UDV had abstained from drinking the tea for a minimum of 20 days before the evaluations; they had been drinking the Hoasca tea regularly on an average of more than four years and, in 60% of the cases, since birth. Therefore, it was considered that the sample of UDV adolescents were regular participants in the rituals with repeated exposure to the effects of the Hoasca tea throughout their lives.

As to the actual results, the researchers state in their publications that in general terms all the assessments showed no significant differences between the groups, and place them within normalcy. Some interesting differences were observed, sometimes in favor of one group, other times in favor of the other:

1. The interpretation of the data from the neurological assessment that took place after the conclusion of the statistical analysis and the revealing of the blind strategy, demonstrated a similar performance in both groups on the majority of the tests, with results that place them within normalcy for the age and grade level of the participants. The researchers concluded that: "Ayahuasca had no toxic or pernicious effect in the neuro-cognitive function of the adolescents" (Grob and Silveira 2005c);
2. The psychiatric investigation showed a similar psychopathological profile between the two groups, indicating that both are within the population normalcy, except that the control group presented a slightly higher incidence of attention deficit disorders, body dysmorphic disorder and anxiety. These findings suggest a tendency that would require further study to determine conclusive confirmation and possible causes (Grob and Silveira 2005a);
3. Regarding substance use, in general the groups were found to be comparable, except for the significantly lower proportion of alcohol use by UDV adolescents. This finding might be explained by the strong doctrinal recommendation of abstinence from alcoholic beverages. Furthermore, the authors consider that this finding can be related to the possible pharmacological effect of the tea, whose therapeutic potential on alcohol and drug disorders has already been indicated in previous studies (Grob and Silveira 2005b);
4. The clinical assessment, the objective of which is to subsidize the interpretation of the neuropsychological and psychiatric results,[7] established that the

---

[7] The results of the clinical evaluation are not yet published

pubertal development of all the adolescents is in the range of normalcy, having found no evidence of present or previous diagnostics of clinical concern for this study;

5. The interviews and focus groups held during the qualitative assessment revealed few differences between the groups. Neither makes significant use of drugs or alcohol, and both understand the economic and social importance of the family as a place of protection and care. Generally, they are adolescents who do not like confrontational situations and who live in environments where spiritual values are taught. Discrete differences were observed between the two groups. While the UDV adolescents contribute more often to the domestic routine and have a closer proximity to their fathers (even those with divorced parents); the control group was observed to have a greater perception of the violence and corruption in society; females in the control group were observed as having less association with patterns historically defined as feminine. The researchers observed that in the UDV the use of the Hoasca tea is within the context of a ritual, not viewed as something banal, and that "[the tea] is not used for a personal interest or need, as among drug users." They affirmed in their publication: "for the adolescents, the UDV functions as a social network, providing support and safety in a tranquil and nurturing environment." The researchers concluded, "the use of the tea cannot be separated from the context in which it is used, nor from the groups that use it. What this study allows to be concluded is that, for the adolescents of the UDV, the use of the Hoasca tea takes place within a religious and group context, with a strong orientation towards family values, participation in domestic life, tension-free family relations, closeness with fathers, future expectations avowed by the UDV, explicit gender hierarchy and closer friendships with those who share the same religious belief."[8]

Meaning of the Results

During the development of this study the researchers opted to focus the assessment on factors that would be most sensitive to detecting any harm that might be caused by the use of the Hoasca tea: cognitive function and occurrences of psychiatric disorders among the adolescents most exposed to the substance. This proposal is

---

[8] See Alonso in this publication.

based on the substantially documented scientific premise that the habitual consumption of drugs (such as marijuana, cocaine, crack and others) may cause cognitive and psychiatric harm. In other words, the researchers' starting point for assessing mental health issues was to consider the ritual use of the Hoasca tea as a potential abuse drug, and to investigate it through the same methods used to study other drug misuse. This way they could guarantee that the risk of the tea causing harm to the mental health of the adolescents would be adequately assessed.

The results found among the adolescents whose absolute majority had frequent contact with the tea since birth, were revealing: they showed a pattern not only similar to adolescents of the same socioeconomic status who had never used the psychoactive substance, but also may indicate that the ritual experience with the Hoasca tea may have had a protective effect against drug and alcohol abuse. Therefore, the findings of this study corroborated the understanding already found in the scientific literature: "the use of Hoasca... is clearly a very different phenomenon from the conventional notion of 'drug abuse.'" (Grob 1996).

Concurrently, the qualitative evaluation, which in summary sought to understand the universe of those adolescents – exploring how they live, what they think, how they interact with society, among other aspects – also confirmed that they are similar to the control group. The researchers placed the individual and community behavior of UDV adolescents amid values considered healthy and morally acceptable in society by affirming that the use of the Hoasca sacrament is inseparable from its context. Simplistically, we can say that these adolescents are "common adolescents." Neither better nor worse, just "common."

Therefore, the results as a whole describe a reality very different from the one expected from adolescents who use drugs, whose lives are frequently harmed by damage to individual and social development, often leading to a significant state of personal, familial, academic or professional disorientation. Nonetheless, it is necessary to keep in mind that, if on the one hand, the results of this study show that the UDV adolescents are not harmed by the effects of the tea, on the other, it is important to emphasize that these young hoasqueiros are not exempt from using drugs and alcohol, or from having psychiatric disorders. This study demonstrated that the UDV adolescents have a similar profile to the adolescents in the control group, within a population standard expected for the same age group and with tendencies indicating that the ritual use of the tea could be beneficial to health. In order to benefit from these findings, it is necessary to bring this awareness to those responsible for working with and educating the youth in the UDV.

Future Research

In relation to this present study, we consider that further studies can be conducted to confirm some of the tendencies found, in those aspects for which the results were not statistically significant. We also understand that it could be interesting to reevaluate these same UDV adolescents 10 years later, to observe their neuropsychological and psychiatric profiles at the start of adulthood.

Furthermore, the psychosocial aspects of the religious use of the Hoasca tea need to be further studied, as its characteristic of being psycho-integrative seems to be a rare phenomenon and a unique opportunity for understanding human behavior. More specifically, the indications of the tea's therapeutic potential need to be studied further in order to be confirmed and so that margins of safety may be well established.

Regarding the Logistical Support and the Role of the DEMEC-UDV

Having scientific studies conducted within the UDV is a phenomenon intimately related to its process of institutionalization (Castello, 2010). While understanding that it is not common for a religious institution to actively assist with research within its midst, a few considerations will be presented regarding the historical work developed by the Medical and Scientific Department of the UDV, the DEMEC.

The DEMEC was established through the initiative of health professionals of the UDV. Motivated by the necessities of the Center's process of institutionalization, they proposed the creation of a department that could act as a liaison with the medical and scientific community as a whole. Ten years later, in 1986, the creation of the *Center for Medical Studies* (CEM) was finally approved. Its initial activities focused on the cataloging of all the scientific information related to the Hoasca tea and the plants used in its preparation. In 1991, the CEM organized the 1st Health Congress of the UDV with the objective of bringing together members of the Center and researchers interested in the scientific aspects of the Hoasca tea. At that time there was a convergence of interests and the UDV opened its doors to researcher Dennis McKenna, Ph.D., for the first biomedical studies on the Hoasca tea, which came to be the *Hoasca Project*. The CEM provided intra-institutional facilitation and logistical support for the development of the study.

Later, in 1997, the CEM was restructured and renamed the Medical and Scientific Studies Department – DEMEC. Its activities remained related to all the medical and scientific aspects of the tea. In addition to developing activities to attend to the internal demands of the UDV related to its institutionalization process, DEMEC maintained its traditional role as collaborator in the implementation of research. Because of this, its participation in the Hoasca in Adolescence study naturally was to provide institutional facilitation and logistical coordination for the field work phase.[9]

After this brief contextual explanation, we note a few observations with respect to the logistical support work done by the DEMEC. It is a challenge to seek to assist the scientists in what is demanded of them and at the same time maintain the guiding principle of non-interference. Due to this, we seek to create the conditions established by the researchers so that they can apply the scientific methods that they have determined to be the most appropriate, and to allow them to arrive at conclusions in a competent and unbiased manner, based on scientific rigor.

We compare the work carried out by the DEMEC in the field work phase of a study to that of organizing a symphony orchestra performance: the logistics pertain to physical organization, transportation, lodging, meals, and the stage infrastructure so the performance can take place. The research-scientist is responsible for choosing the instruments, the repertoire, taking command of the baton, and for the performance itself.

This historical perspective on the DEMEC is a tribute by this author to the doctors who were the directors of the DEMEC-UDV since the time of its inception: Dr. Edison Saraiva Neves, Dr. Glacus de Souza Brito, Dr. Helio Gonçalves and Dr. José Roberto Campos de Souza.[10] These pioneers, along with many other valuable scientists, have contributed significantly to the development of the biomedical studies of the Hoasca tea.

---

[9] For more information on the constitution of the Center for Medical and Scientific Studies (CEM) and the Medical and Scientific Department of the UDV (DEMEC), see Gentil and Neves in this publication.

[10] Dr. Edison Saraiva Neves was the first director of the CEM, from its creation in 1986 until 1994. From 1994 to January 5, 2003, Dr. Glacus de Souza Brito was responsible (noting that in 1997 the CEM became the Medical and Scientific Studies Department of the UDV (DEMEC) and Dr. Brito became its first director. From January 6, 2003 to January 5, 2006, Dr. Helio Gonçalves was the director of the DEMEC. Following, Dr. José Roberto Campos de Souza directed the department from January 6, 2006 to May 01, 2010. Dr. Ariovaldo Ribeiro Filho was the director from May 2, 2010 to January 5, 2012, and Dr. Tadeu Feijão will be responsible from January 6, 2012 until January 5, 2015.

Bibliography

Andrade, E, N.; Brito, G. S.; Andrade, E. O.; Neves, E. S.; Mckenna, D.; Cavalcante, J.W.; Okimura, L.; Grob, C. and Callaway, J. C., "Human pharmacology of hoasca: clinical studies (comparative clinical evaluation among users of Hoasca tea over prolonged periods and controls- physiological evaluation of acute effects after ingestion of Hoasca tea)." In Labate, B. C. and Araujo, W. S. (Editors) *O uso ritual da Ayahuasca.* p. 671-709. Campinas: Mercado de Letras, São Paulo, FAPESP, 2004.

Brito, G. de S. "Human pharmacology of Hoasca. Tea prepared from hallucinogenic plants used in ritual context in Brazil." In Labate, B. C. And Araujo, Wladimir, S. (editors), "O Uso Ritual da Ayahuasca," p. 623-651. Campinas: Mercado de Letras; São Paulo: Fapesp, 2004.

Callaway, J. C.; Airaksine, M. M.; Mckenna, D. J.; Brito, G. S. And Grob, C. S. "Platelet serotonin uptake sites increased in drinkers of Ayahuasca." *Psychopharmacology* 116, p. 385-387, 1994.

Callaway, J. C.; Raymon, L. P.; Hearn, W. L.; Mckenna, D. J.; Grob, C. S.; Brito, G. S. and Mash, D. C. "Quantitation of N,N-dimethyltryptamine and harmala alkaloids in human plasma after oral dosing with Ayahuasca." *Journal of Analytical Toxicology* 20, p. 492-497, 1996.

Castello, O. And Brito, G. S. "Ayahuasca (Hoasca): Histórico, botânica, fitoquímica, farmacologia, efeitos clinicos e neuropsicológicos." Document not published. Copyright Registered at the Fundação Biblioteca Nacional, number 214.259 (livro: 373 folha: 419), 1999.

Castello, O. "Considerações medico-cientificas a respeito do chá Hoasca e sua inofensividade a saúde" – julho, 2009. Available at: http://www.udv.org.br/alto-falante/2010/abril/LinhaDoTempo_InofensividadeDoCha_2008.pdf.

Castello, O. "Evidências científicas da inofensividade do Vegetal." *Jornal Alto Falante,* April, 2010. Brasília: Centro Espírita Beneficente UDV.

Grob *et. al.* "Human pharmacology of Hoasca, a plant hallucinogen used in ritual context in Brazil." *Journal of Nervous and Mental Disease* 184, pp. 86-94, 1996.

Grob, C. S. "A psicologia da Ayahuasca". In Metzner, Ralph. Editor. "Ayahuasca - alucinógenos, consciência e o espírito da natureza," p. 195-225. Rio de Janeiro: Editora Gryphus, 2002.

Grob, C. S.; Mckenna, D. J.; Callaway, J. C.; Brito, G. S.; Andrade, E. O.; Oberlender, G.; Saide, O. L.; Labigalini Jr., E.; Tacla, C.; Miranda, C. T.; Strassman, R. J.; Boonke, K. S. and Neves, E. S. "Human pharmacology of Hoasca: psychological effects." In Labate, B. C. and Araujo, W. S. (Editors). *"O Uso Ritual Da Ayahuasca"*. p. 653-669. Campinas, Mercado De Letras; São Paulo, FAPESP, 2004.

Grob, C. S. and Silveira, D. X. *et al.* "Ayahuasca in adolescence: a preliminary psychiatric assessment." *Journal of Psychoactive Drugs,* 37 (2), p. 129, 2005a. Presented in full in this book.

Grob, C. S. and Silveira, D. X. *et al.* "Reports on psychoactive drug use among adolescents using Ayahuasca within a religious context." *Journal of Psychoactive Drugs,* 37 (2), p. 141, 2005b. Presented in full in this book.

Grob, C. S. and Silveira, E. D. *et al.* "Ayahuasca in adolescence: a neuropsychological assessment." *Journal of Psychoactive Drugs,* 37 (2), p. 123, 2005c. Presented in full in this book.

Grob, C. S. and Rios, M. D. *et al.* "Ayahuasca in adolescence: qualitative results." *Journal of Psychoactive Drugs,* 37 (2), p. 135, 2005. Presented in full in this book.

Labigalini Jr. *"O uso de Ayahuasca em um context religioso por ex-dependentes de álcool – um estudo qualitative."* Tese de Mestrado em Saúde Mental. São Paulo, Universidade Federal de São Paulo, 2008.

Mckenna, D. (2002). "Ayahuasca: uma história etnofarmacológica," In Metzner, Ralph. Editor. *"Ayahuasca - alucinógenos, consciência e o espírito da natureza,"* p. 172-194. Rio de Janeiro: Editora Gryphus, 2002.

Miranda. "Alternative religion and outcome of alcohol dependence in Brazil." *Letter. Addiction (90),* p. 847-848. 1995.

Ayahuasca in Adolescence: A Neuropsychological Assessment[1]

Evelyn Doering-Silveira, M.Sc
Enrique Lopez, Psy.D
Charles S. Grob, M.D.
Marlene Dobkin de Rios, Ph.D.
Luisa B. Nunes Alonso, Ph.D.
Cristiane Tacla, Psy.
Itiro Shirakawa, M.D., Ph.D.
Paulo H. Bertolucci, M.D., Ph.D.
Dartiu Xavier Da Silveira, M.D.

Ayahuasca is a hallucinogenic beverage made essentially of two Amazonian plants. It is prepared by boiling the stems of a vine named *Banisteriopsis caapi* and the leaves of *Psychotria viridis,* although other plants are of- ten mixed in as well. This psychedelic tea has been used for centuries by native Indian and mestizo shamans in Peru, Colombia, and Ecuador for healing and divination. In the eighteenth century ayahuasca was taken up by the colonists as a result of their proximity to tribal peoples during the Colonial period. The mixing of native contexts with nonnative settings resulted in the incorporation of ayahuasca as a psychoactive ritual sacrament in ceremonies by several different religious movements. In Brazil, ayahuasca is used as sacrament within the context of religious practice by the syncretic churches União do Vegetal (UDV) and Santo Daime, among others; this practice was legally approved in 1987. Churches using ayahuasca in Brazil differ somewhat from one another as to their principles, rituals, and composition of the tea.

---

[1] This article was originally published in the *Journal of Psychoactive Drugs;* Jun 2005; 37, 2; p. 123-128. Reproduced with permission of the copyright owner, the Haight Ashbury Publications, San Francisco, California, Copyright 2005. This research was funded in part with a grant from the Heffter Research Institute, Santa Fe, New Mexico and from the Fundação de Amparo a Pesquisa do Estado de Sao Paulo (FAPESP), Brazil. Special thanks are due to Dr. Glacus Da Souza Brito and Dr. Otávio Castillo Campos Pereira, who served as liaison between the União do Vegetal Church and the Research Team.

According to the laws of the UDV, the use of ayahuasca is restricted to religious ceremonies where multigenerational families meet twice a month for approximately four hours. In sound accordance with the principles of this church (UDV), adolescents are encouraged to voluntarily join their parents and drink the ayahuasca tea during the ritual ceremonies. Adherents commonly believe that ayahuasca is harmless and potentially beneficial for adolescents (e.g., prophylaxis against drug abuse) as long as it is imbibed in a religious context. To date, however, this assumption has never been confirmed by means of controlled studies on the effects of periodic ritual use of ayahuasca by adolescents.

In 1993, a multinational research team composed of American and Brazilian physicians, psychologists and social scientists conducted a comprehensive study with UDV adult members in Manaus, the large capital city of the state of Amazon located in the heart of the Brazilian tropical rainforest. This was the first investigation of what is called the Hoasca Project. Phase I evaluations of pharmacokinetics, neuroendocrine assays, and serotonin function were carried out as well as psychiatric, medical health, and baseline neuropsychological screenings (Callaway et al. 1999, 1996, 1994; Mc Kenna et al. 1998; Grob et al. 1996). Contrasting the findings from 15 men who had been UDV members for at least 10 years (subjects) with demographically-matched controls who did not belong to the UDV and had never consumed ayahuasca, this pilot investigation concluded that there was no evidence of any injurious effect which could have been induced or caused by or be related to the ritualistic use of ayahuasca. On the contrary, these long-term UDV members reported a marked decline in severe psychiatric disorders, including discontinuation of cigarette, alcohol, and recreational drug use following their entry into this sect. Dramatic improvements in their personal values, behavioral compliance, and sense of purpose were described as well. Neuropsychological testing of long term adult UDV members and matched controls found the UDV members to have statistically significant superior concentration and short-term memory on some measures, though overall both groups scored well.

Currently, in Brazil, adolescent membership of the UDV is estimated at over 1,200.[2] A thorough investigation of UDV adolescents' cognitive profile is definitely warranted when one considers the slow but ever-growing population that consumes

---

[2] These numbers correspond to the time when the research was conducted in 2001. Presently, the UDV has an estimated 17,000 members. It is important to note that adolescents are not members of the UDV until they become 18 years of age. At this age they can voluntarily become a member and begin to have rights and responsibilities within this religious institution. At the time of membership all members start to wear the UDV uniform.

ayahuasca worldwide on a regular basis, and the significant proportion of younger people who are among them.

Objective

The primary objective of this study is to assess the effects of long-term use of ayahuasca on adolescent cognitive functioning.

Subjects and Method

Sample – Eighty-four adolescents from three cities in Brazil (São Paulo, Campinas, and Brasilia) voluntarily participated in this study. Ayahuasca-consuming adolescents were randomly selected among participants of three distinct UDV churches, whereas the comparison group included randomly selected adolescents according to pairing criteria. Interviews were conducted by a trained psychiatrist in 2001 in two different Brazilian cities. Four of the adolescents (one subject and three controls) were not paired and as such were automatically excluded from the statistical analysis. As a result two groups of 40 adolescents (N = 80) between the ages of 15 and 19, from both sexes, were considered in this study. The first group, hereafter designated as the *subjects,* was composed of 40 adolescents from the Brazilian syncretic church UDV (União do Vegetal) who had drunk ayahuasca within a ritual context at least 24 times during the last two years prior to the neuropsychological assessment. They were 22 males and 18 females, with a mean age of 16.52 years and a standard deviation of 1.34. Most of them were White (78.9%) and their educational level ranged from first year in high school to first year in college. The second group, hereafter designated as the control group, was a comparison group composed of 40 adolescents who had never drunk ayahuasca (22 males and 18 females) matched on sex, age, race, and educational level to the subject group, with a mean age of 16.62 years and a standard deviation of 1.00. They were mostly White (82.1 %) and their educational level ranged from first year in high school to third year in high school. Both groups had similar social and economic profiles, belonged to the same community, and shared the same environmental influences (although they did not attend the same schools). Subjects were recruited from various public and private schools whereas the comparison group of adolescents was selected from two private schools only.

Procedure - Data collection was accomplished in setting purpose fully aimed at enhancing both subjects' and control's maximal motivation and collaborative attitudes as well as safeguarding the neuropsychological assessment against undesirable interferences. Thus, 20 subjects and 20 controls from Brasilia were taken on a four-day stay to a hotel located in a farm near Brasilia. Subjects and controls from São Paulo and Campinas were taken on a two-day stay to a hotel located on a quiet beach near São Paulo during two consecutive weekends (10 subjects and 10 controls at a time). Having both subjects and controls exposed to the same environmental and psychological conditions allowed for a closer monitoring of possible confounding variables such as cigarette smoking, alcohol and drug use, poor sleeping hours, caffeine ingestion, and use of medicine, among others. Both subject and control tobacco smokers had refrained from cigarette smoking at least one hour before the assessment. Caffeine ingestion was available exclusively during breakfast time. No alcoholic beverages and other drugs were consumed 24 hours before the neuropsychological assessment. Sleeping times ranged from six to eight hours during the nights spent either at the farm hotel or at the beach hotel. Subjects had kept a minimal 20-day interval since last ingestion of ayahuasca on occasion of the neuropsychological assessment. Comfortable, quiet and well lit assessment rooms were provided. Researchers involved in data collection remained "blind" to the identity of participants throughout the study.

All adolescents and their respective parents and/or legal guardians were asked to sign an informed consent before enrollment in the study.

Neuropsychological Assessment - A comprehensive battery of neuropsychological tests was devised to assess the overall level of cognitive functioning of the adolescents. All 40 experimental adolescent subjects and 40 controls were administered a neuropsychological battery. Neuropsychological tests that assessed attention, concentration, intelligence, language, memory, executive functioning, processing speed, visuomotor skills and visuoconstructional abilities were administered. The following measures were administered: Trailmaking Test, Stroop-Victoria version, Rey-Osterrieth Complex Figure Test (ROCFT), the Conners' Continuous Performance Test II (CPT-II), and the World Health Organization/University of California at Los Angeles Auditory Verbal Learning Test (WHO/UCLA Auditory Verbal Learning Test). Additionally, subtests of the Wechsler Adult Scale of Intelligence-III (WAIS-III) were used. The following subtests were administered from the WAIS-III: Digit Span, Digit Symbol, Symbol Search, and Object Assembly. It is important to note that Portuguese versions were administered for verbal measures. For nonverbal measures, instructions were given in Portuguese.

The Trailmaking Test, which measures sequencing, visual attention and scanning, psychomotor speed, and mental flexibility, requires that a connection be made between 25 encircled numbers randomly arranged on a page in proper order using a pencil for Part A and the connection of 25 encircled numbers and letters in alternating order for Part B (Lezak 2004).

The Digit Span subtest is used as one of the measures to calculate Verbal Intelligence and the Working Memory Index of the WAIS-III. It is used to assess verbal attention.

The Digit Span subtest consists of two parts. In the first part, individuals are required to repeat sequences of three to nine digits long (Digit Forward); in the second part, examinees are asked to repeat backwards sequences of two to eight digits long (Digit Backwards). The Digit Symbol and Symbol Search are subtests from the WAIS-III that are used to assess psychomotor speed. They both are used to calculate the Processing Speed Index. The Digit Symbol subtest consists of a series of numbers, each of which is paired with its own corresponding symbol. Using a key, the individual writes the symbol corresponding to its number (Wechsler 1997). In the Symbol Search subtest, individuals scan two groups of symbols and indicate whether the target symbol appears in the search group. In the Object Assembly subtest, examinees are required to assemble puzzles as quickly as possible. It measures visual-spatial constructional abilities.

The Stroop-Victoria version is a test that measures selective attention and cognitive flexibility; it has three separate conditions (Spreen & Strauss 1998). In the first part, individuals are asked to read randomized color blocks (red, green, yellow, and blue). In the second part, the examinees are required to read words printed in different ink colors. In the last condition, individuals are given a card where color names are printed in different colored ink (the printed word never corresponds to the color name); this requires the subjects to name the color of the ink while disregarding the printed word. The Rey-Osterrieth Complex Figure Test is used to measure visuomotor skills, visual-spatial constructional ability, and visual memory (Mitrushina et al. 2005). On this measure, individuals are asked to copy a complex figure and then reproduce the design from memory 30 minutes later.

The Conners' Continuous Performance Test Second Edition (CPT-II) is a computerized task used to assess abilities such as sustained attention, vigilance, reaction time, and impulsivity (Conners 2005). In this task, individuals are asked to press the space bar for all letters that are displayed on the computer screen except the letter X. There are six blocks, each displaying 60 letters at different interstimulus intervals. The test lasts approximately 14 minutes. A computerized report is generated at the end that includes the total number of omitted letters (omission), number of Xs pressed (commissions), and a variety of other measures related to visual attention (Hit Rate, Hit Rate SE, Variability of SE, D-prime, Beta, Perseverations, Hit RT Block Change, Hit RT SE Block Change, Hit RT ISI Change, and Hit RT SE ISI Change).

The WHO/UCLA Auditory Verbal Learning Test is a verbal memory-list test that assesses verbal learning and memory (Mitrushina et al. 2005). In this measure, examinees are read out loud a list of 15 items (list A) for five consecutive trials, each followed by a free recall test. After the fifth trial, individuals are presented with an interference trial (list B) of 15 items (Trial VI). Immediately following the interference trial, individuals are asked to recall the first list without further presentation (Short Delay Recall, Trial VII). After about a 30-minute delay, individuals are again asked to recall the words from list A (Long Delay Recall, Trial VIII). Finally, a recognition trial (Trial IX) is administered where individuals are to identify words recognized from list A.

Data Analysis

Descriptive statistics were followed by the comparison between ayahuasca-using subjects and control groups. Strength of associations was tested with chi-square for categorical variables, whereas t-test was used for comparing continuous variables.

Results – Overall, no significant differences in performance were found between adolescent ayahuasca users and matched controls on most of the neuropsychological measures. Results of the neuropsychological l measures between both ayahuasca users and controls are available in Table 1.

On a neuropsychological measure of visual search, sequencing, visual attention, psychomotor speed, and mental flexibility, there was no difference between the two groups (Trail Making Test A and B, $p < 0.31$ and $p < 0.26$, respectively . On a measure of verbal attention, both subjects and controls did not score significantly different in their total Digit Span scores ($p < 0.61$). Additionally, no difference was found on Digit Span Forward and Digit Span Backward ($p < 0.53$ and $p < 0.46$, respectively). Ayahuasca users and match controls did not score significantly different on both subtests that measure processing speed (Digit Symbol, $p < 0.27$; Symbol Search, $p < 0.67$). Again, there was no difference between both groups on the Object Assembly subtest ($p < 0.30$). On all conditions of the Stroop test, both groups did not score significantly differently (Stroop I, II, and III; $p < 0.40$, $p < 0.08$, and $p < 0.95$, respectively). Ayahuasca users and matched controls did not differ in performance on the ROCFf in both the copy and memory conditions ($p < 0.23$, $p < 0.88$, respectively). On all measures of the Continuous Performance Test, the subjects and controls did not differ significantly (p values on all CPT measures ranged from $p < 0.24$ *top* < 1.00).

Subjects and matched controls scored similarly on most trials of the WHO/UCLA Auditory Verbal Learning Test. However, they seemed to differ on two of the initial trials (Trial II, $p < 0.00$, and Trial IV, $p < 0.01$). Trials I, Trial III, Trial V were not significantly different ($p < 0.34$, $p < 0.12$, and $p < 0.36$, respectively). The total score of all initial trials (Total I-V) was also statistically significant ($p < 0.01$). As expected, performances on Trial VI (interference list) were comparable among groups. Short-delay memory recall (Trial VII), long-delay memory recall (Trial VIII), and recognition recall (Trial IX) were not significantly different ($p < 0.09$, $p < 0.18$, and $p < 0.17$, respectively). Table 1 displays scores on neuropsychological measures for the adolescent ayahuasca users and matched controls.

TABLE 1

Neuropsychological Performance of Adolescents Who Drink Ayahuasca within a Religious Context (N = 40) Compared to a Matched Control Group (N = 40)

	AYAHUASCA		COMPARISON GROUP		STATISTICS	
	Mean	SD	Mean	SD	t	p
TRAILMAKING TEST						
Trail A	29.20	8.86	27.25	8.26	1.02	0.31
Trail B	61.38	25.10	56.00	15.82	1.15	0.26
WAIS-III						
Digit Span Forward	9.38	2.32	9.03	2.69	0.62	0.53

Digit Span Backward	6.83	2.26	6.48	1.97	0.74	0.46
Digit Span Total	16.45	4.27	16.00	3.46	0.52	0.61
Digit Symbol (Coding)	77.80	10.07	81.58	18.73	-1.12	0.27
Symbol Search	37.20	6.24	37.83	6.83	-0.43	0.67
Object Assembly	32.35	9.26	34.17	6.18	-1.04	0.30
STROOP-VICTORIA VERSION						
Stroop I	13.03	2.27	12.60	2.22	0.85	0.40
Stroop II	16.20	3.89	14.75	3.34	1.79	0.08
Stroop III	24.95	7.14	25.05	8.00	-0.06	0.95
REY-OSTERRIETH TEST						
Rey Figure Copy	34.64	1.46	34.08	2.58	1.20	0.23
Rey Figure Recall	21.89	5.00	21.69	6.79	0.15	0.88
CONTINUOUS PERFORMANCE TEST						
CPT Omissions	2.64	4.99	1.65	1.90	1.17	0.24
CPT Commissions	10.37	6.80	10.80	5.97	-2.97	0.77
Hit Rate	406.93	77.43	400.25	73.70	0.40	0.69
Hit Rate SE	6.06	2.72	5.78	2.09	0.50	0.62
Variability of SE	7.49	5.22	7.40	5.05	0.08	0.94
D-prime	0.86	0.40	0.86	0.48	0.00	1.00
Beta	0.84	0.98	0.80	1.03	0.17	0.86
Perseverations	0.62	1.27	0.52	0.93	0.40	0.69
WHO/UCLAAVLT Trial I	6.73	2.34	7.20	2.05	-9.64	0.34
Trial II	10.05	2.17	11.55	1.66	-3.47	0.00*
Trial III	11.70	2.09	12.40	1.93	-1.56	0.12
Trial IV	12.48	1.82	13.38	1.23	-2.58	0.01*
Trial V	12.90	1.45	13.23	1.72	-0.92	0.36
Total I-V	53.85	7.50	57.75	5.51	-2.65	0.01*
Interference List (Trial VI)	6.58	1.83	6.83	1.81	-6.13	0.54
Short-delay (Trial VII)	12.15	1.90	12.83	1.58	-1.73	0.09
Long-delay (Trial VIII)	12.40	1.93	12.93	1.55	-1.34	0.18
Recognition (Trial IX)	14.55	0.82	14.78	0.62	-1.39	0.17

*Statistically significant ($p < 0.05$).

On a neuropsychological measure of visual search, sequencing, visual attention, psychomotor speed, and mental flexibility, there was no difference between the two groups (Trail Making Test A and B, $p < 0.31$ and $p < 0.26$, respectively. On a measure of verbal attention, both subjects and controls did not score significantly different in their total Digit Span scores ($p < 0.61$). Additionally, no difference was found on Digit Span Forward and Digit Span Back ward ($p < 0.53$ and $p < 0.46$, respectively). Ayahuasca users and match controls did not score significantly different on both subtests that measure processing speed (Digit Symbol, $p < 0.27$; Symbol Search, $p < 0.67$). Again, there was no difference between both groups on the Object Assembly subtest ($p < 0.30$). On all conditions of the Stroop test, both groups did not score significantly differently (Stroop I, II, and III; $p < 0.40$, $p < 0.08$, and $p < 0.95$, respectively). Ayahuasca users and matched controls did not differ in performance on the ROCFf in both the copy and memory conditions ($p < 0.23$, $p < 0.88$, respectively). On all measures of the Continuous Performance Test, the subjects and controls did not differ significantly (p values on all CPT measures ranged from $p < 0.24$ to $p < 1.00$).

Subjects and matched controls scored similarly on most trials of the WHO/UCLA Auditory Verbal Learning Test. However, they seemed to differ on two of the initial trials (Trial II, $p < 0.00$, and Trial IV, $p < 0.01$). Trials I, Trial III, Trial V were not significantly different ($p < 0.34$, $p < 0.12$, and $p < 0.36$, respectively). The total score of all initial trials (Total 1-V) was also statistically significant ($p < 0.01$). As expected, performances on Trial VI (interference list) were comparable among groups. Short-delay memory recall (Trial VII), long-delay memory recall (Trial VIII), and recognition recall (Trial IX) were not significantly different ($p < 0.09$, $p < 0.18$, and $p < 0.17$, respectively). Table 1 displays scores on neuropsychological measures for the adolescent ayahuasca users and matched controls.

Discussion

This is the first study to focus on cognition of long term ayahuasca-using adolescents. To date there is no scientific information on the consequences of this activity, whether beneficial or deleterious, although the Hoasca Project (referred to in the Introduction to this issue of the *Journal of Psychoactive Drugs*) details some of the consequences for adult participants. The primary finding of the present study is that no overall differences in neuropsychological performance were found between the group of ayahuasca-consuming adolescents and the group of adolescents who had never used the substance. Current scientific knowledge places great emphasis on education acting as a protector against brain insults. Since good performance on neuropsychological tests is greatly influenced by educational level the authors considered good academic achievement a central aspect in this study. Both the experimental subjects and controls had maintained good academic levels, which may have contributed to their good performance.

However, it is important to note that both groups performed well and presented similar results in most neuropsychological measures except for two trials from a verbal learning memory list test, with lower scores for the ayahuasca-consuming adolescents. Although two of the initial five trials (Trial II and IV) did show a statistically significant difference between groups on the WHO/UCLA Auditory Verbal Learning Test, the groups differed only on initial trials, which are not truly indicative of memory differences between both groups. The initial trials are more likely to be assessing learning and encoding abilities and strategies (Mitrushina et al. 2005). On memory trials, later trials (Trial VI, Trial VII, and Trial IX), both adolescent groups did not statistically differ.

It is also important to note that the mean raw scores of the initial trials (Trial II and IV) of both subjects and controls were in the average range in regards to normative data among similar aged adolescents on a similar memory list task (Geffen et al. 1990). This indicates that the mean raw scores of both groups did not significantly differ when compared to adolescent normative data.

Even though this data overall supports the theory that there was not a difference between ayahuasca users and matched controls on neuropsychological measures, one can argue that the difference in scores may suggest that ayahuasca users might differ on subtle cognitive abilities (i.e., learning and encoding). Therefore, it is important that further studies elucidate these findings. Additionally, results are limited because of the small sample size and because long-term effects were not addressed. Results may also not generalize among other populations. Again, further studies are necessary.

While additional investigations are recommended, in this pilot research study, the authors found no evidence of injurious effects of ayahuasca on adolescents who participated with their families in ceremonial rituals using psychoactive substances. In Western society, it is indeed a unique phenomenon when young people are permitted to ingest a powerful hallucinogen. We have been allowed access to study the effects and have found, at least in this pilot preliminary investigation, that ayahuasca did not have a toxic or deleterious effect on adolescent neurocognitive functioning.

The question arises that since the UDV adolescents use much less alcohol, marijuana and other intoxicants according to data published in this same issue (Doering-Silveira et al. 2005) all of which are known to have negative effects on cognition when used excessively, whether ayahuasca may protect the UDV adolescents from further harm.

Bibliography

Callaway, J.C.; McKenna, D.J.; Grob, C.S.; Brito, G.S.; Raymon, L.P.; Poland, R.E.; Andrade, E.N. & Mash, D.C. "Pharmacokinetics of hoasca alkaloids in healthy humans." *Journal of Ethnopharmacology* 65: 243-56, 1999.

Callaway, J.C.; Raymon, L.P.; Hearn, W.L.; McKenna, D.J.; Grob, C.S. & Brito, G.S. "Quantitation of N,N-dimethyltryptamine and harmala alkaloids in human plasma after oral dosing with ayahuasca." *Journal of Analytical Toxicology* 20: 492-97, 1996.

Callaway, J.C.; Airaksinen, M.M.; McKenna, D.J.; Grob, C.S. & Brito, G.S. "Platelet serotonin uptake sites increased in drinkers of ayahuasca." *Psychopharmacology* 116: 385-87, 1994.

Conners, C.K. *Conners' Continuous Performance Test-II (CPT-11).* Toronto: Multi-Health Systems Inc., 2005.

Doering-Silveira, E.; Grob, C.S.; De Rios, M.D.; Lopez, E.; Alonso, L.K.; Tacla, C.; Brito, G.S. & Da Silveira, D.X. "Report on psychoactive drug use among adolescents using ayahuasca within a religious context." *Journal of Psychoactive Drugs* 37 (2), 2005.

Geffen, G.; Moar, K.J.; O'Hanlon, A.P.; Clark, C.R. & Geffen, L.B. "Performance measures of 16- to 86-year-old males and females on the Auditory Verbal Learning Test." *Clinical Neuropsychologist* 4 (I): 45-63, 1990.

Grob, C.S.; McKenna, D.J.; Callaway, J.C.; Brito, G.S.; Neves, E.S.; Oberlander, G.; Saide, O.L.; Labigalini, E.; Tacla, C.; Miranda, C.T.; Strassman, R.J. & Boone, K.B. "Human psychopharmacology of Hoasca, a plant hallucinogen used in ritual context in Brazil." *Journal of Nervous and Mental Disorders* 184 (2): 86-94, 1996.

Lezak, M.D. "*Neuropsychological Assessment*" Fourth Edition. New York: Oxford University Press, 2004.

McKenna, D.J.; Callaway, J.C. & Grob, C.S. "The scientific investigation of ayahuasca. A review of past and current research." *Heffter Review of Psychedelic Research* 1: 65-77.

Mitrushina, M.N.; Boone, K.B.; Razani, J. & D'Elia, L.F. 2005, 1998. *Handbook of Normative Data for Neuropsychological Assessment-Second Edition.* New York: Oxford University Press.

Spreen, O. & Strauss, E. A *Compendium of Neuropsychological Tests-Second Edition.* New York: Oxford University Press, 1998.

Wechsler, D. *Manual for the Wechsler Adult Scale of Intelligence Third Edition (WAIS-III).* San Antonio, Texas: The Psychological Corporation, 1997.

Ayahuasca in Adolescence:
A Preliminary Psychiatric Assessment[1]

Dartiu Xavier da Silveira, Ph.D.
Charles S. Grob, M.D.
Marlene Dobkin de Rios, Ph.D.
Enrique Lopez, Psy.D.
Luisa K. Alonso, Ph.D.
Cristiane Tacla, Psy.
Evelyn Doering-Silveira, M.Sc.

Ayahuasca is a hallucinogenic concoction of plants used as a psychoactive ritual sacrament in ceremonies of the syncretic churches União do Vegetal (UDV) and Santo Daime. In Brazil, law has sanctioned the use of ayahuasca within the context of religious practice since 1987. Ayahuasca is consumed only during religious ceremonies, which last approximately four hours, being regularly scheduled twice monthly and often attended by multigenerational families. Within the UDV, adolescents are offered the opportunity to voluntarily join their parents and participate in ritual ceremonies where ayahuasca is consumed, and it is a common belief among members of the UDV that ayahuasca presents no risk for adolescents as long as they take it within a religious context. Nevertheless, to date there have been no controlled studies on the effects of periodic ritual ayahuasca use on adolescents.

In 1993, a comprehensive research investigation of ayahuasca use in long-term adult members of the UDV called the Hoasca Project was conducted in the Brazilian Amazon city of Manaus (Callaway et al. 1999, 1996 1994; McKenna et al. 1998; Grob et al. 1996). Phase I evaluations of pharmacokinetics, neuroendocrine assays,

---

[1] This article was originally published in the Journal of Psychoactive Drugs; Jun 2005; 37, 2; p. 123-128. Reproduced with permission of the copyright owner, the Haight Ashbury Publications, San Francisco, California, Copyright 2005. This research was funded in part with a grant from the Heffter Research Institute, Santa Fe, New Mexico and from the Fundação de Amparo a Pesquisa do Estado de Sao Paulo (FAPESP), Brazil. Special thanks are due to Dr. Glacus Da Souza Brito and Dr. Otávio Castillo Campos Pereira, who served as liaison between the União do Vegetal Church and the Research Team.

serotonin function, and psychiatric and medical health were then conducted. Contrasting the findings on 15 subjects from the UDV for at least 10 years with matched controls who had never consumed ayahuasca; this pilot investigation concluded that there was no evidence of injurious effect induced by ritual use of ayahuasca. Indeed, UDV subjects appeared to have experienced a remission of severe psychiatric disorders, including drug and alcohol abuse, following their entry into this religion.

Currently, the membership of the UDV in Brazil is estimated at close to 9,000, including approximately 1,200 adolescents.[2] Considering the proportion of this age group within the population that uses these psychoactive substances on a regular basis, it is advisable to investigate the adolescents' psychiatric status and behavioral functioning.

The main objective of this study is to evaluate the mental condition of these adolescents through screening instruments for psychiatric disorders.

Method

Sample and Procedure

The study involved 40 adolescents, from both sexes, ages ranging from 15 to 19 years of age, who had drunk ayahuasca in a ritual context for at least 24 times in the last two years prior to the assessment. They were compared to a comparison group of 40 adolescents who had never drunk ayahuasca matched by sex, age, and educational level. Both groups live in the same communities and share the same environmental influences.

Ayahuasca-consuming adolescents were randomly selected among participants of three distinct UDV churches where as the comparison group included randomly selected adolescents according to pairing criteria. After a twenty-day washout period, ayahuasca adolescents were interviewed together with comparison group and asked to complete a series of scales aiming to screen for psychiatric conditions. Interviews were conducted by a trained psychiatrist in 2001 in two different Brazilian cities. Both adolescents and their parents were asked to sign an informed consent before enrollment in the study.

Instruments

Measurement of psychiatric morbidity in the community and clinical settings in

---

[2] These numbers corresponds to the time when the research was conducted in 2001. Presently, the UDV has an estimated 17,000 members.

the last decades has been achieved basically by the use of standardized methods of measurement (Cooper 1987; Eastwood 1971). Many tests used in case identification are usually referred to as "screening tests" (Goldberg 1989) and have been developed to be used in a first stage assessment in populational studies to identify probable cases that will later have their "caseness" status confirmed or not in a second stage. Such a test is devised to be easy and quick to administer, usually does not involve rich diagnostic detail, but enables proper measurement of the condition. Tests used here are acceptable scientific tools both in the sense they proved they consistently measure a given phenomenon (reliability) and in the sense that they are actually measuring what they are designed to measure (validity; see Bartko & Carpenter 1976).

Subjects were assessed in terms of mental status by means of the following psychiatric screening instruments: SRQ (Self Report Questionnaire) to assess overall psychic condition (Iacoponi & Mari 1988; Mari & Williams 1986); CES-D (Center for Epidemiological Studies Depression Scale) for depression (Da Silveira & Jorge 2002); Beck Anxiety Inventory and STAI (State-Trait Anxiety Inventory) as a screening for anxiety disorders (Gorenstein & Andrade 1996); DUSI (Drug Use Screening Inventory) to identify drug misuse (De Micheli & Formigoni 2002; Tarter et al. 1996, 1992); Conners' Adolescent Self-Rating sub scale to detect Attention Deficit Disorder (Doering-Silveira & Da Silveira In press); and BSQ (Body Shape Questionnaire) to investigate self image related disorders. (Di Pietro & Da Silveira In press).

Data Analysis

Descriptive statistics were followed by comparisons between ayahuasca and control Groups. Strength of associations was tested with chi-square for categorical variables, whereas t-test was used for comparing continuous variables.

TABLE 1		
Demographic Characteristics of Adolescent Study (N = 80)		
	Ayahuasca Group (N = 40)	Comparison Group (N = 40)
Age	16.52 years (SD= 1.34)	16.62 years (SD= 1.0)
Sex: Male	N = 22 (55.0 %)	N = 22 (55.0 %)
Female	N = 22 (55.0 %)	N = 18 (45.0 %)
Civil status: Single	N = 38 (95.0 %)	N = 37 (92.5 %)
Residence: Living with Parents	N = 37 (92.5 %)	N = 39 (97.5 %)
Ethnic group: White	N = 30 (75.0 %)	N = 33 (82.5 %)

Results

Demographic Data

In the ayahuasca group, 22 adolescents (55%) were male and 18 (45%) were female. Their mean age was 16.52± 1.34 years. Education level ranged from the first year in high school to first year in college. Ethnic breakdown showed 30 (75% of the sample) were White and 10 (25%) classified themselves as of mixed ethnic origin. Ninety five percent of the subjects were single and most of them (92.5%) lived with their parents. In the comparison group, 22 adolescents (55%) were male and 18 (45%) were female. Their mean age was 16.62 ± 1.0 years. They were mostly White (82.5%) and their educational level ranged from first year in high school to third year in high school (first year in high school= 7; second year = 15; third year = 18). Thirty-seven adolescents (92.5%) were single and most of them (97.5%) lived with their parents (see Table 1).

Pattern of Ayahuasca Consumption

Twenty-five adolescents (63%) started drinking ayahuasca systematically during childhood (before the age of 13) while 15 of them (37%) began to drink when adolescents (after they were 13 years old). The time span of systematic (at least once a month) ayahuasca use was 4.05 ± 2.28 years. At the time of assessment, the adolescents abstained from drinking ayahuasca for at least 20 days, with a mean abstinence period of 41.16 ± 15.55 days. Only one adolescent (2.5 %) reported having drunk ayahuasca outside of a religious context and 39 (97.5%) reported that the experience had a profoundly positive influence on their lives.

TABLE 2
Number and Percentages of Subjects Scoring Positively for Psychiatric Diagnoses in Ayahuasca and Comparison Adolescent Groups (N = 80)

Scales	Cut-offs	Ayahuasca		Comparison Group		Statistical Significance
	(N = 40)	(N = 40)				p
		n	%	n	%	
Self-Report questionnaire	7/ 8	3	7.5	4	10.0	n.s.
CAGE (SRQ subscale)	1/2	1	2.5	0	0	n.s.
DUSI	2/3	1	2.5	0	0	n.s.
Beck Anxiety	15/16	3	7.5	2.5	n.s.	
STAI-state	21/22	2	5.0	7	17.5	n.s.
STAI –trait	21/22	24	60.0	32	80.0	0.087
CES-D	15/16	12	30.0	11	27.5	n.s.
Body shape questionnaire	110/111	4	10.0	11	27.5	0.083
ADD	2/3	2.5	7	17.5	0.057	

Psychiatric Assessment

In the ayahuasca group three adolescents (7.5%) had high scores on psychiatric symptoms. In terms of substance use disorders, one adolescent (2.5%) scored positively for problem drinking and another one (2.5%) for substance misuses. Concerning anxiety symptoms, 24 (60.0%) were anxious at the time of assessment but only three adolescents (7.5%) presented high scores on Beck Anxiety Scale and two adolescents (5.0%) on STAI-State scale. Twelve teenagers (30%) presented with depressive symptoms. In the assessment for other psychiatric disorders, four adolescents (10.0%) screened positively for body dysmorphic disorder and one (2.5%) fulfilled DSM IV criteria (three or more items) for attention deficit disorder-inattentive type. Except for the high proportion of depressive subjects in this sample, overall percentages are comparable with general population rates.

In the comparison group, four adolescents (10.0%) presented high scores on psychiatric symptoms. None of the adolescents scored positively either for alcohol related problems or for substance abuse or dependence [see above comment]. Although 32 (80.0%) adolescents reported anxiety symptoms at the time of assessment, only one (2.5%) presented high scores on the Beck Anxiety Scale, but seven adolescents (17.5%) scored high on STAI-State scale. Eleven of them (27.5%) were probably depressive. In the assessment for other psychiatric disorders, 11 adolescents (27.5%) screened positively for body dysmorphic disorder and seven (17.5%) fulfilled DSM IV criteria for Attention Deficit Disorder-Inattentive type.

Comparing both groups (see Table 2), adolescents of the comparison group demonstrated a trend to have more problems than adolescents from the ayahuasca group with anxiety symptoms ($p = 0.087$), self image ($p = 0.083$), and inattentiveness ($p = 0.057$). After stratification by gender (see Table 3), differences among the ayahuasca and the comparison group were more expressive among women; the exception was for attention problems, where six boys from the control group and only one from ayahuasca group fulfilled diagnostic criteria for A.D.D. Eleven girls from the ayahuasca group presented high scores for anxiety (STAI-Trait) whereas 17 girls from the comparison group scored high for the condition. Concerning the body shape questionnaire, only one male adolescent from each group scored high on the instrument, whereas 13 female adolescents presented high scores, with three of them being from the ayahuasca group and 10 from the comparison group.

TABLE 3
Number and Percentages of Subjects Scoring Positively for Psychiatric Diagnoses in Ayahuasca and Comparison Adolescent Groups, Stratified by Sex (N = 80)

Scales	Ayahuasca Group		Comparison Group	
	N	%	N	%
Men (N = 22)				
STAI-Trait	13	59.1	15	68.2
Body shape questionnaire	1	4.1	1	4.5
DSM IV ADD	1	4.1	6	27.3
Women (N = 18)				
STAI-Trait	11	61.1	17	94.4
Body shape questionnaire	3	16.7	10	55.6
DSM IV ADD	0	0	1	5.6

Discussion

In the preliminary pilot investigation of adult long-term ayahuasca users held in Brazil named the Hoasca Project (Grob et al. 1996), diagnostic interviews identified considerable past psychiatric histories preceding their entry into the ayahuasca church. Interestingly, psychopathology remitted following their regular attendance at ayahuasca ceremonies. It is still unclear if the reported changes can be attributed to the effect of the substance itself or to the religious affiliating process. Besides ayahuasca ingestion, set and setting may have also played a considerable role in this favorable outcome. Members of the syncretic church stressed, as do many other religious groups, the importance of a protective and supportive community (Grob 1999).

In the present study adolescents drinking ayahuasca within a religious context were overall comparable to controls in terms of psychopathological profile. Nevertheless slight differences could be observed in favor of the ayahuasca group in terms of less anxiety symptoms, less body image dysmorphia, and fewer attention deficit disorders. Only trends could be observed between groups, but the small sample size may be responsible for differences not reaching statistical significance.

Church members often report that the more they engage in ayahuasca rituals, the more they "learn" how to focus their attention. This may be reflected in the lower frequency of probable attention deficit cases among them. It is not possible yet to determine if this is the due to a direct effect of ayahuasca in the brain or to the possibility of better training of attentional skills in this particular environment.

The Hoasca project also identified significant personality differences between ayahuasca using and nonusing groups (Grob et al. 1996). Ayahuasca using subjects were considered to be more confident, optimistic, outgoing, energetic, persistent, reflective, and scored higher than controls in measures of social desirability and emotional maturity (Grob 1999). This phenomenon, probably reflecting the strong sense of belonging to a well-structured religious community, can also eventually explain the smaller proportion of ayahuasca using adolescents reporting anxiety symptoms and concerns over body image.

This cross-sectional study made it possible to establish the lower frequencies of psychiatric symptoms in the ayahuasca-consuming adolescents in comparison with nonusing ones. However, it is not possible to know if psychopathological less affected adolescents are more prone to adhere to the religious group or if the affiliation to such a community exerts a "protective" effect on these adolescents, whatever mechanisms involved may be.

Bibliography

Bartko, J .L & Carpenter, W.T. "On the methods and theory of reliability." *Journal of Mental and Nervous Diseases* 163: 307- 17, 1976.

Callaway, J .C.; McKenna, D.J .; Grob, C.S.; Brito, G.S.; Raymon, L.P.; Poland, R.E.; Andrade, E.N. & Mash, D.C. "Pharmacokinetics of Hoasca alkaloids in healthy humans." *Journal of Ethnopharmacology,* 65: 243-56, 1999.

Callaway, J.C.; Raymon, L.P. ; Heam, W.L.; McKenna , D.J.; Grob, C.S. & Brito, G.S., "Quantitation of N,N-dimethyltryptamine and harmala alkaloids in human plasma after oral dosing with ayahuasca. *Journal of Analytical Toxicology* 20: 492-97, 1996.

Callaway, J.C.; Airaksinen, M.M.; McKenna, D.J.; Grob, C.S. & Brito, G.S. "Platelet serotonin uptake sites increased in drinkers of ayahuasca." *Psychopharmacology* 116: 385-87, 1994.

Cooper, B. "Psychiatric Epidemiology-Progress and Prospects". Kent, U.K.: Cross Helm, 1987.

Da Silveira, D.X. & Jorge, M.R. "Reliability and factor structure of the Brazilian version of the Center For Epidemiologic Studies Depression." *Psychological Reports* 91: 865-74, 2002.

De Micheli, D. & Formigoni, M.L. 2002. "Psychometric properties of the Brazilian version of the Drug Use Screening Inventory." Alcohol: Clinical and Experimental Research 26 (10): 1523-8, 2002.

Di Pietro, M. & Da Silveira, D.X. In review. "Reliability and dimensionality of the Brazilian version of the Body Shape Questionnaire.

Doering-Silveira, E. & Da Silveira, D.X. In review. "Using Conners' Adolescent Self-Rating Sub-scale to detect attention deficit disorder."

Eastwood, M.R. "Screening for psychiatric disorder." *Psychological Medicine* 1: 197-208, 1971.

Goldberg, D.P. Screening for psychiatric disorders. In: P. Williams; G. Wilkinson & K. Rawnsley (Eds.) *The Scope of Epidemiological Psychiatry.* London: Routledge, 1989.

Gorenstein, C. & Andrade, L. "Validation of a Portuguese Version of the Beck Depression Inventory and the State-Trait Anxiety Inventory in Brazilian subjects." *British Journal of Medical and Biological Research* 29: 453-57, 1996.

Grob, C.S. "The psychology of ayahuasca." In: R. Metzner (Ed.) *Ayahuasca: Hallucinogens, Consciousness, and the Spirit of Nature.* New York: Thunder's Mouth Press, 1999.

Grob, C.S.; McKenna, DJ.; Callaway, J.C.; Brito, G.S.; Neves, E.S.; Oberlander, G.; Saide, O.L.; Iacoponi, E. & Mari, J.J 1988. Reliability and factor structure of the Portuguese version of Self Reporting Questionnaire. *International Journal of Social Psychiatry* 35 (3): 213-222, 1988.

Labigalini, E.; Tacla, C.; Miranda, C.T.; Strassman, R.J. & Boone, K.B. "Human psychopharmacology of Hoasca, a plant hallucinogen used in ritual context in Brazil." *Journal of Nervous and Mental Disorders* 184 (2): 86-94, 1996.

McKenna, DJ.; Callaway, J.C. & Grob, C.S. "The scientific investigation of ayahuasca. A review of past and current research." *Hejfter Review of Psychedelic Research* 1: 65-77, 1998.

Mari, J.J. & Williams, P. "A validity study of Psychiatric Screening Questionnaire (SRQ-20) in primary care in the city of São Paulo. *British Journal of Psychiatry* 148: 23-6, 1986.

Tarter, R.E.; Kirisci, L. & Mezzich, A. "The DUSI: School adjustment correlates of substance abuse." *Measurement and Evaluation in Counseling and Development* 29: 25-34, 1996.

Tarter, R.E.; Laird, S.B.; Bukstein, O. & Kaminer, Y. "Validation of the Drug Use Screening Inventory: Preliminary findings." *Psychology of Addictive Behaviors* 6: 233-36, 1992.

13: The Adolescent Study

Report on Psychoactive Drug Use Among Adolescents Using Ayahuasca Within a Religious Context[1]

Evelyn Doering-Silveira, M.Sc.
Charles S. Grob, M.D.
Marlene Dobkin de Rios, Ph.D.
Enrique Lopez, Psy.D.
Luisa K. Alonso, Ph.D.
Cristiane Tacla, Psy.
Dartiu Xavier da Silveira, MD, Ph.D.

Ayahuasca is a hallucinogenic mixture of Amazonian plants used as a psychoactive ritual sacrament in ceremonies of the syncretic churches União do Vegetal (UDV) and Santo Daime. These Brazilian ayahuasca churches have expanded their base in the last decades from Brazil to North America and Europe, attracting thousands of people. Ayahuasca use is supposed to occur only during religious ceremonies, which last approximately four hours, being regularly scheduled twice a month and often attended by multigenerational families. Within the rituals, adolescents are offered the opportunity to voluntarily join with their parents and participate in ceremonies where ayahuasca is consumed. It is said that ayahuasca apparently offers no risk for adolescents as long as it is used within a ritual context. Nevertheless, to date there have been no accurate assessments of patterns of other psychoactive substance use among adolescents who drink ayahuasca within a religious setting.

In Brazil it is currently estimated that almost two thousand adolescents participate in ayahuasca ceremonies. Considering the proportion of this age group that uses ayahuasca on a regular basis, the aim of this study is to evaluate patterns of psychoactive substance use among these adolescents.

---

[1] This article was originally published in the *Journal of Psychoactive Drugs;* Jun 2005; 37, 2; p. 141-144. Reproduced with permission of the copyright owner, the Haight Ashbury Publications, San Francisco, California, Copyright 2005. This research was funded in part with a grant from the Heffter Research Institute, Santa Fe, New Mexico and from the Fundação de Amparo a Pesquisa do Estado de Sao Paulo (FAPESP), Brazil. Special thanks are due to Dr. Glacus Da Souza Brito and Dr. Otávio Castillo Campos Pereira, who served as liaison between the União do Vegetal Church and the Research Team.

Method

Sample and Procedure

The study involved 84 adolescents of both sexes, ranging from 15 to 19 years of age. Forty-one adolescents had drunk ayahuasca in a ritual context for at least twice month during the two-year period preceding evaluation. They were compared to a group of 43 adolescents of similar sex, age and educational level. Both groups lived in the same communities and shared the same environmental influences.

Adolescents were interviewed and asked about previous experiences regarding use of a variety of psychoactive substances. The comparison group had never used ayahuasca.

Both adolescents and their parents were asked to sign an informed consent before enrollment in the study. The ayahuasca-consuming adolescents were randomly selected among participants of three distinct UDV churches, whereas the comparison group included randomly selected adolescents according to pairing criteria. Interviews were conducted by a trained psychiatrist in 2001 in two different Brazilian cities.

Instruments

Participants were assessed in terms of patterns of psychoactive drug use according to the World Health Organization criteria: lifetime use (those who had ever experimented with a given substance); last year use (those who had used a substance at least once during the 12-month period preceding assessment); and recent use (those having used a given substance at least once during the 30-day period prior to evaluation).

Data Analysis

Descriptive statistics were followed by the comparison between ayahuasca and control groups. Strength of associations was tested with chi-square for categorical variables.

TABLE 1			
Proportion of Psychoactive Drug Users during the Last Year among Adolescents Using Ayahuasca Compared to Controls (N = 84)			
Psychoactive Drug	UDV	Control	Statistic
	%	%	%
Alcohol	46.3	74.4	X2 = 5.8; P = 0.016
Amphetamines		7.9	
Cannabis	32.5	34.9	
Cocaine/crack		2.6	
Hallucinogens		7.9	
Tranquilizers	2.8		
Opiates			
Anticho linergics			
Tobacco	28.3	22.0	
Solvents	8.1	19.5	
Steroids	2.8		
Barbiturates			

Results

Demographic Data

In the ayahuasca group, 23 adolescents (56.1%) were male and 18 (43.9%) were female. Their mean age was 16.49 ± 1.34 years. Educational level ranged from last year in high school to first year in college. Concerning ethnic distribution, 31 (75.6%) of them were White and all others classified themselves as of mixed ethnic origin. Thirty-nine adolescents (95.1%) were single and most of them (92.5%) lived with their parents.

In the comparison group, 23 adolescents (53.5%) were male and 20 (46.5%) were female. Their mean age was 16.65 ± 1.0 years. They were mostly White (81.4%) and their educational level ranged from first year in high school to third year in high school (first year = 7, second year = 14, third year = 17). Forty adolescents (93.0%) were single and most of them (97.5%) lived with their parents. Both groups displayed similar demographic characteristics.

Pattern of Ayahuasca Consumption

Twenty-five adolescents (60%) started drinking ayahuasca systematically during childhood (before they were 13 years old) while 15 of them (40%) began to drink when adolescents (after their 13th birthday). In one adolescent this information was missing.

The time span of systematic (at least once a month) ayahuasca use was 4.05 ± 2.28 years. By the time of assessment adolescents abstained from drinking ayahuasca for at least twenty days, with the mean time of abstinence 41.16 ± 15.55 days.

Pattern of Psychoactive Drug Use

Lifetime use. No statistically significant differences were observed in the comparison of ayahuasca users with the comparison group in terms of lifetime frequency of psychoactive drug use. Nevertheless, it was observed that a higher proportion of lifetime cocaine users among UDV adolescents (10.3%) existed compared to controls (2.4%). The frequency of use for those who had ever used tobacco among UDV members (52.5%) was also higher than that reported by adolescents from the comparison group (34.9%).

Drug use during the last year. In terms of psychoactive substance use during the 12-month period preceding assessment, a higher proportion of alcohol users was recorded among controls (74.4%) than among UDV members (46.3%). This difference reached statistical significance ($p < 0.05$). Compared to UDV adolescents, a higher proportion of controls reported last year use of amphetamines, cannabis, cocaine, hallucinogens, and solvents, although these differences were not statistically significant. Tobacco, steroids and tranquilizers were used slightly more often by UDV members than by controls (see Table 1), but not to a statistically significant degree.

Recent drug use. During the 30-day period, preceding the assessment (recent use), 65.1% of adolescents from the comparison group reported alcohol use while only 32.5% of UDV members did so. This difference was statistically significant ($p < 0.01$). In terms of amphetamine use, a trend of higher consumption was observed ($p = 0.87$) among controls, since none of the five adolescents (12.2% of the control group) reporting amphetamine use in the previous month were UDV members. Concerning all other substances, no significant differences could be detected among groups. Among UDV members, the proportion of recent users of any psychoactive drug was less than 10%, except for alcohol (32.5%), minor stimulants, e.g., Guaraná and coffee (26.3%), tobacco (21.1%), and cannabis (10.8 %; see Table 2).

Discussion

In many instances, psychoactive drugs are used to reduce anxiety, inhibitions, and low self-esteem, among other undesirable feelings. As a consequence, premature access to these drugs may constitute an additional risk factor for substance misuse among young people. Furthermore, most adolescents still have not developed the coping skills necessary to deal with difficult situations and are in close contact with friends and relatives who use drugs to cope with life stressors. According to international scientific literature on drug addiction, this psychosocial aspect is a problem of major concern in the prevention of substance misuse among adolescents (Hesselbrock, Hesselbrock & Epstein 1999). One could argue that the systematic exposure to ayahuasca could eventually predispose these adolescents to use or even abuse other psychoactive substances, but alternatively, it is also possible that affiliation with a religious group may play a protective role for substance misuse (Grob et al. 1999). The affiliation with a religious group implies adherence to a set of principles, norms and values involved with specific behavioral patterns that also include a person's relationship to alcohol and other drugs.

TABLE 2
Proportion of Recent Psychoactive Drug Users Among Adolescents using Ayahuasca Compared to Controls (N = 84)

Psychoactive Drug	UDV %	Control %	Statistic %
Alcohol	32.5	65.1	$x2 = 7.56; P = 0.006$
Amphetamines		12.2	$p = 0.087$ (trend)
Cannabis	10.8	25.0	
Cocaine/crack		7.5	
Hallucinogens		2.5	
Tranqilizers	2.6	2.5	
Sedatives	2.6	7.5	
Opiates		2.5	
Anticholinergics		2.5	
Tobacco	21.1	24.4	
Minor stimulants	26.3	24.4	
Solvents	2.6	5.0	
Steroids (AAS)	2.6	2.5	
Barbiturates		2.5	

In a comprehensive research investigation of ayahuasca in long-term adult members of the UDV conducted in the Brazilian Amazon city of Manaus in 1993, subjects appeared to have experienced a remission of severe psychiatric disorders, including drug and alcohol abuse, following their entry into this religion (McKenna, Callaway & Grob 1998; Grob et al. 1996). Given the methodological limitations of this pilot investigation, it is still unclear whether these preliminary findings can be attributable to the direct effects of ayahuasca or whether they are self-selecting factors for religious affiliation (Grob 1999).

In the present study, adolescents drinking ayahuasca within a religious context were overall comparable to the control group in terms of substance consumption profile, except for having a significantly smaller proportion of alcohol users. This phenomenon can be explained by the fact that alcohol abstinence is strongly recommended by the teachings of this religious community. Dobkin de Rios and Grob (1994) have argued that suggestibility under hallucinogenic experience is an underreported effect. For other substances, only slight differences could be observed between groups, most of them favoring ayahuasca-using adolescents. In the ayahuasca group, the observed higher proportion of minor stimulant users can be attributable to these adolescents' common practice of replacing alcohol with stimulant beverages in social settings, e.g., guaraná and coffee.

Ayahuasca drinkers were considered to be more confident, optimistic, outgoing, energetic, persistent, reflective, and scored higher than controls in measures of social desirability and emotional maturity than controls in the previously-mentioned study (Grob 1999). This probably reflects a strong sense of belonging to a structured religious community, a condition often considered a protective factor for substance use related disorders.

Among the limitations of the present study is the limited size of the sample, which did not allow us to evaluate the influence of distinct dimensions of religiousness on the outcome. Furthermore, since this is not a longitudinal study, only associations could be put in evidence, and no cause-effect relationship among events could be established.

Among UDV members, it can be seen that although some adolescents had used cocaine or crack in the past (lifetime use), they discontinued using this substance more recently (last year and previous month use). The promising role of ayahuasca in the treatment of addictive disorders, among other psychiatric conditions, still needs further investigation. However, since ayahuasca is considered by religious members to be a relatively safe substance, also potentially useful as medicine, future rigorous research represents a unique opportunity to advance present knowledge of human behavior.

Bibliography

Dobkin de Rios, M. & Grob, C.S. "Hallucinogens, suggestibility and adolescence in cross-cultural perspective." *Yearbook of Ethnomedicine* 3:113-32, 1994.

Grob, C.S. "The psychology of ayahuasca." In R. Metzner (Ed.)*"Ayahuasca; Hallucinogens, Consciousness, and the Spirit of Nature."* New York: Thunder's Mouth Press, 1999.

Grob, C.S.; McKenna, D.J.; Callaway, J.C.; Brito, G.S.; Neves, E.S.; Oberlander, G.; Saide, O.L.; Labigalini, E.; Tacla, C.; Miranda, C.T.; Strassman, R.J. & Boone, K.B. " Human psychopharmacology of Hoasca, a plant hallucinogen used in ritual context in Brazil." *Journal of Nervous and Mental Disorders* 184 (2): 86-94, 1999.

Hesselbrock, M.N.; Hesselbrock, V.M. & Epstein, E.E. Theories of etiology of alcohol and other drug use disorders. In B.S. McCrady & E.E. Epstein (Eds.) Addictions. New York: Oxford University Press, 1999.

McKenna, D.J.; Callaway, J.C. & Grob, C.S. "The scientific investigation of ayahuasca. A review of past and current research." *Heffter Review of Psychedelic Research* I: 65-77, 1999.

14: The Adolescent Study

Ayahuasca in Adolescence: Qualitative Results[1]

Marlene Dobkin de Rios, Ph.D.
Charles S. Grob, M.D.
Enrique Lopez, Psy.D.
Dartiu Xavier da Silveira, M.D., Ph.D.
Luisa K. Alonso, Ph.D.
Evelyn Doering-Silveira, M.Sc.

The following are the results of the qualitative data obtained on ayahuasca-using adolescents of the UDV (União do Vegetal Church) by Dr. Alonso, both in formal interviews and focus groups, as well as a control group.

Data was collected among 56 adolescent volunteers, ages 15 to 19 (a subset of the data based in the other UDV adolescent research articles appearing in this issue), from three cities in Brazil (São Paulo, Campinas and Brasilia). The control group was composed of volunteers from the same schools as the UDV teens. The goal of this study was to assess the effects of long-term use of ayahuasca on adolescent cognitive functioning. With this in mind, the use of qualitative data, in addition to neuropsychological testing, is a useful procedure to allow us to understand the social context in which the ayahuasca use occurs among the UDV adolescents compared to controls. From an anthropological point of view, data obtained through participant observation and interviewing tends to be the most important aspect of ethnological research and includes descriptions of religious beliefs, social organization, etc. This type of qualitative data about a society helps the ethnologist interpret the quantitative data and both are integral to ethnological research.

In addition to field notes, which were generated by de Rios and Alonso in direct

---

[1] This article was originally published in the *Journal of Psychoactive Drugs*; Jun 2005; 37, 2; p. 135-139. Reproduced with permission of the copyright owner, the Haight Ashbury Publications, San Francisco, California, Copyright 2005. This research was funded in part with a grant from the Heffter Research Institute, Santa Fe, New Mexico and from the Fundação de Amparo a Pesquisa do Estado de Sao Paulo (FAPESP), Brazil. Special thanks are due to Dr. Glacus Da Souza Brito and Dr. Otávio Castillo Campos Pereira, who served as liaison between the União do Vegetal Church and the Research Team.

observation, interviews and information obtained in focus groups with adolescents, appropriate categories for classifying data were developed and have been incorporated into the moral/ethical vignettes to follow. Since culture, society and human behavior are not just a random array of occurrences that develop without rhyme or reason, but rather as the result of interacting variables that influence the human condition, we have presented ethnological data in a correlative manner of two or more variables interacting together.

Anthropologists recognize that no aspect of culture and society can be completely explained by any single cause or independent variable and they thus rely on multidimensional hypotheses where many variables interact with one another, giving rise to a holistic perspective, and the attempt to demonstrate how sociocultural systems must be understood through the interconnections among these variables (see Scupin 1995). Please note that on some tables, multiple responses were possible and data may not agree with that presented by da Silviera and colleagues in this issue, due to a different sample taken from the adolescents queried.

TABLE 1
Characteristics of UDV and Control Adolescents

	UDV	Control	Chi Square Total
Teen's chores			
Household chores	29	25	0.726; p = N.S.
Outside employment	1	1	
No chores	0	6	
Total	30	32	
Live with parent(s):			
Both parents	23	19	0.106;p = N.S.
One parent only	5	9	
Total	28	28	
Who raised you?			
Parents	23	22	0.645; p = N.S.
One parent only	5	6	
Total	28	28	
Quality of home life			
Positive home life	27	22	0.021; p = <0.05
Tension at home	1	6	
Total	28	28	

	UDV	Control	Chi Square Total
Relationship with father			
Close	27	20	0.003; p = <0.05
Distant	1	8	
Total	28	28	
Friends drawn from			
School mates	11	27	0.000; p = <0.05
Neighbors	9	9	
Organizations	27	1	
Total	47	37	
Future expectations			
Higher education	27	27	0.180; p= N.S.
Professional career	25	25	
Marriage	23	18	
Travel	7	14	
Total	82	84	
Societal alienation and integration			
Perception of violence	10	17	0.012; p = <0.05
Corruption	7	14	
Total	17	31	
Moral and ethical values			
Importance of honesty	9	15	0.004; p = <0.05
Loyalty to family/friends	9	3	
Respect for others	23	17	
Love for humanity	3	6	
Having a goal in life	0	1	
Total	44	42	
Religious affiliations			
Roman Catholic	0	21	0.00; p = <0.05
Spiritist religious groups	6	2	
Atheist	0	4	
Personal	0	1	
Non UDV	0	0	
Total	6	28	
Prior drug experience			
None	24	24	0.513; p=N.S.
Marijuana	2	3	
Alcohol	2	1	
Total	28	28	
Sexual experience			
Virgin	13	13	1.000; p = N.S.
Non virgin	15	15	
Total	28	28	

Social Characteristics of UDV and Control Group Teens

Inquiry was made regarding teens' chores (see Table 1). There does not appear to be a significant difference between UDV and controls in this area. This suggests that UDV teens are just as involved and responsible as controls. However, it is important to note that six controls indicated they had no chores while UDV teens never reported lack of chores. This may suggest the UDV teens may be more responsible than the control group when it comes to having at least one chore to perform.

Demographic information was requested regarding the residence of the teens. There does not appear to be a significant difference between UDV and controls. This suggests that UDV teens are no different from controls with regard to social cohesion. Twenty-three of the UDV teens reported living with both parents, while 19 of the control teens reported than they lived with their parents. None of the UDV teens had parents who lived in different homes.

Teens were queried regarding who raised them. There does not appear to be a significant difference between UDV and controls in this respect. This suggests that UDV teens are raised similarly to control teens. All teens in both groups were raised by either both parents or by only their mother. None of the teens from either group reported being raised by their father.

The quality of home life was examined. There does appear to be a significant difference between UDV and controls. This suggests that UDV teens seem to have a better quality of home life compared to control teens. Twenty-seven of the UDV teens reported having a positive home life compared to 22 of the control teens. Six of the control teens reported having relatives who criticized them and tension at home. Only one UDV teen reported criticizing relatives with tension at home.

The teens were questioned regarding their relationships with their fathers. There does appear to be a significant difference between UDV teens and controls with regard to their relationship with their father. This suggests that UDV teens appear to have a closer relationship with their father compared to control teens. Twenty-seven of the UDV teens reported having a close relationship with their father compared to 20 of the control teens. Eight of the control teens reported having a distant relationship with their father. Only one UDV teen reported having a distant relationship with their father.

The teens were also asked about where their friends originated. There does appear to be a significant difference between UDV teens and controls with regard to where their friends were drawn from. The data suggests that UDV teens appear to overwhelmingly draw their friends from church members. They seemed to rely less on developing friend ships with schoolmates compared to control teens. Eleven of the UDV teens reported draw their friends from school mates compared to twenty-seven of the control teens. The UDV teens reported that they were hesitant to discuss their religious practices with schoolmates, who simply assumed they were only involved in the drug aspect of religion.

Future expectations and career options were queried. There does not appear to be a significant difference between UDV teens and controls. This suggests that UDV teens are likely to have similar future expectations as controls. However, it is important to note that only seven UDV teens indicated they wanted to travel compared to 14 controls. This may suggest that UDV teens are more likely to stay in close proximity to their home environment, since they are part of a social community.

The concept of societal alienation and integration within society was examined. There does appear to be a significant difference between UDV teens and controls with regard to social alienation. The data suggests that UDV teens appear to differ in the areas of perception of violence and corruption in society, with the UDV teens exhibiting greater optimism.

Moral and ethical values were also queried. There does appear to be a significant difference between UDV teens and controls with regard to moral and ethical values, even though the two groups differ in the different categories. Both groups were similar in choosing the value of respect for others as paramount. The control group strongly endorsed the importance of honesty, more so than the UDV teens, for whom loyalty to family and friends would appear to be an important value. There has been some reported stigmatization by UDV teens' peers.

The teens were asked about formal religious affiliation. There does appear to be a significant difference between UDV teens and controls in regard to religion practices. The control group was overwhelmingly Roman Catholic. Of the UDV group, six also belonged to Spiritist temples.

Experiences with drugs were examined. There does not appear to be a significant difference between UDV and controls. This suggests that UDV teens and controls are similar with regard to prior drug experiences. The majority of the teens in both groups reported having no prior drug experiences (24 in both groups). Only four teens from each of the groups reported having prior experiences with marijuana and alcohol.

Sexual experience of the teens was queried. There does not appear to be a significant difference between UDV teens and controls with regard to sexual experience. This suggests that UDV teens are just as experienced with regard to prior sexual history. Thirteen from each of the groups reported being virgins compared to 15 from both groups who classified themselves as non-virgins. It is important to note that 12 females from each of the groups reported being virgins, while 13 females of each group reported being non-virgins. Overall, with regard to gender both UDV and control groups were similar in their level of sexual experience.

TABLE 2: VIGNETTES			
	UDV	Controls	Chi Square Total
1. You are on a bus and an acquaintance sits down next to you. He offers to sell you some marijuana and he keeps insisting that you buy it and be like all the other kids.			
Leave without argument	2	5	0,065; P = N.S.
Leave denying interest	10	6	
Would buy for use in rock concert	0	1	
Total	12	12	
2. You are at a teen party and an acquaintance has a bottle of liquor that he wants to put in the drinks that people have without anyone seeing it. You tell him not to do this. He insists upon doing it.			
Convince the youth and tell parents	9	9	1.000; P = N.S.
Just tell parents	3	3	
Total	12	12	
3. You are at school and you see a classmate go into a teacher's office and begin to look through her handbag to take money.			
Confront thief	4	9	0.056; P = N.S.
Tell the teacher	8	1	
Lend the thief money	0	2	
Total	12	12	
4. You are with a group of four teens who go riding. Your friend parks his car and starts to have sex with the person next to him.			
Agree it is okay	0	2	0.301; P = N.S.
Leave car and go away	12	10	
Total	12	12	
5. You win a lottery for a small amount of money. You are faced with a decision about what to do with the money.			
Save money and/or pay off debts	10	4	0.001; P = <0,05
Give money or gifts to loved ones	1	3	
Spend it on self	1	5	
Total	12	12	
6. You are at home. Late one night, your friend calls you to Insist you sneak out of the house to go to a party.			
Reject offer	7	7	1.000; P =N.S.
Reject friend's offer/not tell their parents	5	5	
Total	12	12	

Responses to Vignettes

The six vignettes in Table 2 were designed to measure moral and ethical considerations of both the UDV and control teens. In modern day industrial societies, drug and alcohol use is often associated with excessive risk taking, impulsivity and often a disregard for safety and consequences. The authors believed that vignettes would permit an honest self-reporting by teens of their potential responses to conflict situations and their general level of maturity.

In response to the first vignette, UDV teens appear to be no different than controls in avoiding confrontation. This was also seen in their responses to the second vignette. Both alternatives in this case reflect a concern with the well being of others and a disinclination of the teens to back away from doing the right thing.

Regarding the third vignette, it appears that controls may be more confrontational. Results for the fourth vignette show that UDV teens find clandestine premarital sex to be distasteful and leave the scene just like controls.

Judging from responses to the fifth vignette, UDV teens are thrifty, responsible and think about the welfare of others.

Finally, concerning the sixth vignette, it is seen that UDV teens are realistic in not wishing to be antisocial and offend parents. This could be interpreted as a mature recognition of the importance of family in third world societies, both economically and socially. In this respect, the UDV teens are identical to the control group.

Limitations and Significance of the Study

Regarding the limitations of this small pilot study, the research is retrospective and, as such, is based on self-reporting. The sample was basically drawn from urban and not rural Brazil and was comprised of middle and upper middle class students. Ethnically, both subjects and controls did not fully represent the multiethnic diversity of Brazil.

The significance of the study, however, is in the examination of a modern use of a powerful hallucinogenic compound within a legal religious context. The young people, who participated in these ayahuasca religious ceremonies, usually with parents and other family members, appeared not to differ significantly from their non-ayahuasca-using peers.

This study and the studies to follow in this issue can do much to elucidate the full range of effects of plant hallucinogenic use within a socially-sanctioned, elder facilitated and structured religious context.

Conclusion

Overall, there appear to be few if any differences in responses between the UDV teens and the controls. However, the UDV group seems to be more responsible, respectful, and concerned about the welfare of others. They also tend to be less confrontational. There also appears to be a better quality of home life among the UDV teens when compared to their counterparts. The UDV teens tended to have closer relationships with their fathers when compared to controls. They also exhibit greater optimism than controls. They do not differ significantly with regard to virginity or drug use (other than ayahuasca used sacramentally).

We might expect that given the destructive consequences of youthful drug use in contemporary society that the UDV teens would lag far behind their peers in a number of different dimensions of sociability, honesty, studiousness, etc. In fact, it would be easy to assume at the outset of such a study as this that the UDV teens and the controls would differ in some significant fashion. In this sense, the qualitative data is quite revealing in that the teens appear to be healthy, thoughtful, considerate, and bonded to their families and religious peers.

Bibliography

Scupin, R. "Cultural Anthropology: A Global Perspective." Second Edition. Englewood Cliffs, New Jersey: Prentice Hall, 1995.

Methodology in the Study of the Use of Hoasca tea by Adolescents [1]

Luiza B. Nunes Alonso

Adolescence is a time of reconfiguring identity and the forming of new groups of belonging. It is a time characterized by physical and psychological changes, a time of creativity and even of aggression, often surprising to the family. To obtain the cooperation of adolescents in semi-structured interviews and focus groups demands caution of a scientific and ethical nature, as it relates to the epistemological approach, i.e. the manner in which we generate, share and justify knowledge.

Over a period of two years we conducted a study with 41 adolescents divided into two groups: users of the Hoasca tea in a religious context, and adolescents that do not make use of the tea and are not members of religious groups that use the tea. Adolescents between 14 and 18 years of age participated in our study, with equal numbers of boys and girls.[2]

Methodology

The first big question in studying the effects of the Hoasca tea in adolescence is the need for more than one scientific discipline in order to approach the subject, since it is an extremely dynamic phenomenon with different expressions.

---

[1] The feasibility of this study was possible through the unrestricted support of Dr. Glacus Brito, Dr. Otávio Castello and the members of the União do Vegetal, including the transcription done by Claudinelli Alvarenga Aguilar Daltro of the presentation given at the Hoasca Congress in May 2008. The helpful, friendly and prompt manner in which people and documentation were made available was a determining factor in conducting this study with the most absolute respect to scientific procedures. We are grateful to the Colégio Marista Arquidiocesano in São Paulo and to the Colégio Marista in Brasilia for the opportunity and permission to assemble the control groups. The following scientists contributed to this article: Charles S. Grob, Crisitiane Tacla, Dartiu Xavier da Silveira, Enrique Lopez, Evelyn Doering-Silveira, and Marlene Dobkin de Rios.

[2] All the adolescents, along with their parents, signed the Informed Consent, which was entered into voluntarily after a presentation regarding the objectives, methodology, and reasons for doing a study about the use of Hoasca tea in adolescence.

Conversations about drug use are not deemed to be criminal activities, nevertheless they cause mistrust in parents, fear of the unknown, nebulous and dangerous consequences at a time in life when one discovers that the world is not divided only into right and wrong. Beyond the legal and the criminal one realizes that there is also the ethical and the illicit; moreover, some social rules do not apply if one belongs to certain social groups.

Attempting to discuss sexuality in a society whose media stimulates, motivates and disdains those who are not sexually active causes adolescents to be defensive. Having to be sexually active is a mandate just as unfair as not being able to have sexual activity. Consequently, spontaneity is hidden when dealing with this subject.

What this means is that the study conducted was only exploratory, and the first of many to come. It was done with a small group and the results suggest the need for new studies with parents, teachers and adolescents who have little to no contact with religious or spiritual practices.

For this present study the qualitative research methodology was selected; which is a technique commonly used in human scientific research, specifically in sociology, anthropology and social psychology. In qualitative studies the most commonly used approach is through individual interviews, group discussions, and focus groups. The use of these techniques may seem, to those not in these fields, that qualitative research is essentially composed of listening to the opinions of others and then summarizing what was said. That is true, but it is not only that.

A qualitative study has three phases: considering what common sense says about the subject to be studied, collecting the data about what the modified common sense says, and investigating the field of related scientific possibilities through surveying bibliographical information.

When it comes to adolescents and the use of Hoasca, common sense says that any and every hallucinogenic substance could induce cases of aggressiveness or alienation. This means that to the common sense the use of the Hoasca tea involves personal and social risk. The common sense modified is the opinion or perspective informed by the proximity or familiarity with the object of the study. Therefore, those who are members of the União do Vegetal (UDV), a religious group that uses the Hoasca tea, have gradually developed a certainty that the ingestion of this tea does not cause any type of risk.

If the scientist were to conduct a study merely placing the common sense and the common sense modified in opposition to one another, he falls into a field of linear opposition that only considers the probability of a result that confirms one position or the other, meaning either a risk exists or does not. The scientist needs to enter into the field of building knowledge, the field of possibilities, open to there being something new, unexpected and sometimes even undesirable. In this study the social-scientist considered the common sense, found out about the existence of the common sense modified, and avoided the pitfall of the limitation of saying "yes, the use of the Hoasca tea is good, or no, the Hoasca tea is bad."

The elaboration of a generating question is fundamental, so that the researcher's attitude is not restricted to formalities or the mere application of data collection techniques and a pre-determined analysis model. To ask this question in a manner that raises aspects that are not apparent, demands knowledge of what has been previously written and a discussion of what in actuality will be investigated and how it will be researched.

As part of a broad research project, the first question raised was to verify whether or not the long-term use of the Hoasca tea effects the cognitive and affective functioning of adolescents. Within the qualitative realm this translated into the analysis of the use of the tea in relation to psychosocial aspects, effects on behavior and attitudes, and expectations of the adolescent members of the UDV in comparison with adolescents who do not participate in this religious society.

Epistemological Approach: or How the Knowledge of the use of the Hoasca tea by Adolescents was Built

Psychosocial aspects are related to values, ideas, beliefs, myths and vision of the future. Psychosocial variables occur in mental processing, in the way that we know ourselves, how we know others, and how we know our environment.

Knowing goes beyond being aware that something exists. Knowing is learning, doing, interacting and being. It is by means of a paradigm that a way of thinking and learning is configured. Contrary to what is imagined, knowing how to think is a learning process that involves learning how to think about ourselves, about others and about society, which has a direct impact on human products, that is, in language, in the capacity to make agreements and in the techniques that give us abilities.

The language used to express feelings, emotions, ideas and future perspectives, is not restricted to verbal communication. Speaking the same language means we are speaking of different modalities of expression within the same language. Through these modalities we know the social class and relational groups that identify an individual.

Making agreements, negotiating, articulating and interacting are essential conditions for life in a group and in a community. It is necessary to have a minimum of trust generated by the belief in common values. People carry out certain tasks, or not, based on informal and formal agreements. Human activities are characterized by agreements of interest and responsibility. No other living animal makes agreements.

Developing and knowing how to use different skills throughout life facilitates the transformation of our reality, which is the gap between theoretical knowledge and practice, the possibility of the conceptual domain to carry out an action in the realm of applicability. As a researcher, committed to the social reality in which I live, the challenge is to use accumulated knowledge in the interaction with reality. Without the reductionism of mere applicability, I must bear in mind the need to consider the actuality of an external reality, of a reality different from the one of my relational group, in order to study a group with other values and ideals. The objective is to establish a dialogue with the "different" without discrimination. It becomes necessary to reconfigure new connections to come closer to unfamiliar ideas, beliefs and myths, in order not to fall into the insensitive error of imagining that deep down the "different" is equal to that which is known. It is true that as human beings we have a lot in common, but there are differences that enrich us all culturally. Otherwise we repeat the classical error of reducing, for instance, the family life of the cave man to something similar to American suburban life in the fifties.

In the same way, in studying psychosocial aspects it is necessary to consider that these aspects are not static; on the contrary, they are in constant movement and are characterized by a dynamic that interacts with individual, group and social aspects. Therefore, more important than saying if the tea is good or bad for adolescents, is to understand the dynamic and the circumstances of when it can be bad or when it can be good. How much can it contribute to self-knowledge, to knowing others and the environment in which one lives, versus how much it can inhibit human development processes causing behaviors that result in personal, family and social suffering.

Techniques Used in the Qualitative Research

Data collection was done through in-depth interviews and focus groups. In-depth interview is a technique that involves an interviewer and an interviewee. It is conducted in a private space without the presence of other people and lasts for a determined period of time. The objective is to create the conditions for the interviewee to be able to reflect on topics and issues that are part of his/her daily life as an individual, a citizen, and a participant in different social groups, such as school, work, religious environments and recreational groups. It is common for the interviewee to realize that many subjects discussed had never before been articulated and therefore may experience, after going through the in-depth interview, a greater sense of self-knowledge.

There were twenty-four in-depth interviews conducted, twelve with adolescents from São Paulo and twelve with adolescents from Brasilia. In each city the interviews were conducted with six adolescents from the UDV and six that are not members of the UDV.

In a focus group there is a maximum of eight people. It is a more directed technique, with a clearly defined theme and a maximum duration of 50 minutes. Upon invitation the participants already know the theme of the discussion. The focus group is not geared towards consensus and the moderator must intervene when the opinions become polarized. It is important, however, to guarantee that all members participate, without judgment of right or wrong.

Twenty-eight adolescents participated in the focus groups. Sixteen were from São Paulo, 50% from the UDV and 50% from outside the UDV. In Brasilia, twelve adolescents participated, six from the UDV and six from outside the UDV.

In the in-depth interviews and focus groups, five vignettes were used to address topics related to social alienation, drug use, sexual activity, moral values and ethics. The vignettes are short stories that provide an opportunity for the adolescent to take a position regarding the attitude and behavior demonstrated in the story.

Content of the Instruments Used for Data Collection

In the in-depth interviews and focus groups, nine larger topics were addressed, with varying degrees of intensity. The first one was daily life: participation in domestic activities, if the participation was voluntarily or under pressure, interaction with other household members, how much time is spent at home and if there was any paid work activity.

The second topic was life within the family: if they lived with one or both parents, nature of the relationship with the one with whom they did not live (close or distant), siblings, if any, and sibling relationships, if there was any tension in the household, types of topics that could or could not be discussed at home; and if they could bring friends home.

Friends and friendship was the third topic: who the friends are in terms of gender, age, social class, educational level and specific interests, if they are neighbors, school friends, from a team or club, from work, and how friendship is defined.

Questions related to the future focused on expectations and plans: plans for the future; if going to college is part of the plan, if a career is already chosen, hopes of getting married or not, hopes of traveling alone, and at what point did they hope to realize a dream.

To address social integration and alienation, the perception of violence and corruption in today's society was discussed. Moral and ethical values such as honesty, loyalty to family and friends, respect for others and love for humanity, were approached in a general manner and in hypothetical situations.

Other topics addressed included religious affiliation, prior experience with drugs and sexual experiences.

This content was put together based on prior studies done with adolescents, particularly studies on issues of affinity groups. The questions were developed through the analysis of scientifically validated studies.

Preliminary Results of the Study

The results were grouped according to differences and similarities between the UDV group and the control group.

Differences: The differences are few. In general, the UDV group contributes more at home doing small household chores, such as making the bed, taking out the garbage, walking the dog, preparing a snack, washing the dishes, caring for a younger sibling, helping the mother with grocery shopping.

Another difference is that among the adolescents from the UDV who live only with the mother, the closeness and interaction with the father is greater than with the control group. In the UDV group the father is not seen or experienced as being absent.

On the subject of friends, the UDV adolescents invariably asked if the question was about "friends or *true* friends." To them true friends are not those in the neighborhood or at school. True friends are in the UDV.

In the control group there was a greater perception of the violence and corruption in society. These adolescents mentioned news reports from the media and expressed their positioning rather spontaneously and quickly, a behavior not observed in the UDV adolescents.

Among the five stories used in the vignettes, the one with the greatest difference between the two groups was one where a guy sees another student taking money from the teacher's purse at school. There was a greater assertiveness within the control group toward taking an action like calling an adult, scolding, talking gently to the person, and even offering financial help to the one taking the money. In all five stories the adolescents who were not in the UDV demonstrated a greater tendency toward interfering.

The control group demonstrated greater expectation of traveling for one or two years before finishing college, in particular among the females. The girls from the UDV demonstrated greater adherence to standards that are historically defined as feminine.

Similarities: Neither of the two groups routinely makes use of alcohol and drugs. In both groups, the boys mentioned that they had friends and acquaintances that used drugs, particularly during music concerts.

Participants of both groups agreed with the social and economic importance of the family as a place of protection and care. The majority of the adolescents from the control group live with both parents. Amidst the UDV adolescents, the number of those who live only with the mother or the father is slightly greater.

In general, the adolescents from both groups do not like confrontational situations, but for the ones in the control group, confrontation is more common, justified by an ethical perception of society and their function as citizens.

The majority of participants, both males and females, had no sexual experiences.

Both groups lived in environments where spiritual values are transmitted. In the UDV, it is done in a very explicit manner. The control group was composed of students from the Marista and Archidiocesano Schools (both private Catholic schools), environments where religious values are also taught in an explicit manner.

The scientific literature says that religious communities offer care, protection, safety and support to those who are members. In the UDV, the use of the tea is part of a ritual, as a sacrament. The tea is not consumed as something trivial, just for personal interest or need, like drug users would do. There exists a moment, a time, a specific place and a reason to drink the Hoasca tea. The reason for drinking the tea is based on values shared by the community. There is a fabric, an infrastructure that legitimizes the drinking of the tea for the person and their peers. The ceremony occurs within a structured religious context and in a socially acceptable environment, with the presence of parents and other caring adults. It is lawful to drink the tea. The adults have an important role because they are facilitators in an experience that may bring about self-knowledge, but also fear.

The context of the UDV is constantly referred to as a continuation of the nuclear family. The UDV is an extended family, which is demonstrated by the behavior of the adolescents who call the adults *"tios e tias"* (aunties and uncles) regardless of actual blood relations. The UDV is an environment of protection and orientation, mentioned often in the discourse of the UDV adolescents, to justify their lack of interest in meeting people who are not affiliated in the UDV. All the adolescents mentioned that the UDV is a reference in their lives that is as important as their parents.

The tea is consumed in an environment where the nuclear and extended family interacts, a space of affinity and high cohesion. The UDV adolescents said: *You are equal to everyone, even in being able to be different. I am UDV! Then, being UDV is being different from others.*

For a qualitative study to say that the tea does or does not do a specific thing is impossible, because the use of the tea in itself is not something that can be isolated as a behavior. The use of the tea cannot be excluded from its context and affinity groups. What this study permits us to conclude is that for the adolescents of the UDV the use of the Hoasca tea takes place within a religious and group context, with a strong emphasis on family values, such as participation in domestic life, tension-free family life, closeness with the father, future expectations approved by the UDV, explicit gender hierarchy and close friendships with those who share the same religious beliefs.

For the adolescents, the UDV functions as a social network of support and safety, an environment of tranquility and care.

Conclusions

Carrying out a study with adolescents on sensitive issues subject to judgment and prejudice, such as drug use, sexual activity and belonging to religious groups, can present a double challenge. One challenge can be the resistance of the adolescents to position themselves individually and not as part of a group, and the other is the discomfort of discussing topics that interest them, but that they do not find the space for discussing in a free and open format. The adolescents know that some topics are forbidden or taboo and they are not supposed to articulate doubts or questions about them.

The in-depth interviews and focus groups with the adolescents needed to provide an assurance of confidentiality beyond the privacy guaranteed to anyone who participates in a scientific study. In the beginning of the interviews and the focus groups, the interviewer and the participants made verbal contracts in which the researcher verbalized a commitment not to offer any individual information to parents, school coordinators or coordinators of the União do Vegetal, and that the reports would refer to the adolescents in general terms without specific details. It was also established that the researcher did not have the intention to behave professorially, judging right or wrong, and if that happened then the adolescents would be able to point out that it was happening. Before the data collection began, it was explicitly explained that the adolescent could end the interview at any time without explanation. There were no instances of terminations reported.

It was during the in-depth interviews, where only the interviewer and the interviewee were present, that some of the adolescents, both from the UDV and from the control group, asked questions about drug use such as marijuana and ecstasy. They were questions about the real effects of these drugs on the body.

With the exception of only one female in the control group, who quit in the middle of the data collection process due to an unexpected invitation to a party, all the adolescents were committed and cooperative.

Bibliography

Basset, Raewon; Beagon, Brenda L.; Ristovski-Slijepcevic, Svetlana and Chapman, Gwen E. "Tough teens: the methodological challenges of interviewing teenagers as research participants." *Journal of Adolescent Research,* vol. 23, no. 2, pp. 119-13, 2008 – DOI: 10.1177/0743558407310733.

Carvalho, José Jorge de. "A religião como sistema simbólico. Uma atualização teórica." *Série Antropológica,* 285. Brasília: DAN/UNB, 2000.

Da Silveira, Dartiu Xavier; Grob, C. S.; Dobkin De Rios, Marlene; LOPEZ, Enrique; Alonso, Luisa K.; Tacla, Cristiane and Doering-Silveira, Evelyn. "Ayahuasca in adolescence: a preliminary psychiatric assessment." *Journal of Psychoactive Drugs,* 37 (2), pp. 129-134, 2005.

Dobkin De Rios, Marlene and Grob, C. S.; (Eds.). "Introduction: Ayahuasca use in cross-cultural perspective." *Journal of Psychoactive Drugs,* 37 (2) pp. 119-121, 2005.

Dobkin De Rios, Marlene; Grob, C. S.; Lopez, Enrique; Da Silveira, Dartiu Xavier; Alonso, Luisa K.; and Doering-Silveira, Evelyn. "Ayahuasca in adolescence: qualitative results." *Journal of Psychoactive Drugs,* 37 (2), pp. 135-140, 2005.

Doering-Silveira, Evelyn; Lopez, Enrique; Grob, C. S.; Dobkin De Rios, Marlene; Alonso, Luisa K.; Tacla, Cristiane; Shirakawa, Itiro; Bertolucci, Paulo, H. and Da Silveira, Dartiu Xavier. "Ayahuasca in adolescence: a neuropsychological assessment." *Journal of Psychoactive Drugs,* 37 (2), pp. 123-128, 2005.

Doering-Silveira, Evelyn; Grob, C. S.; Dobkin De Rios, Marlene; Lopez, Enrique; Alonso, Luisa K.; Tacla, Cristiane; and Da Silveira, Dartiu Xavier. "Report on psychoactive drug use among adolescents using Ayahuasca within a religious context." *Journal of Psychoactive Drugs,* 37 (2), pp. 141-144, 2005.

Goulart, Sandra Lucia. "As religiões da Ayahausca e o tema das drogas: história e construção de identidade," *in:* Coggiola, Osvaldo (org.), *Caminhos da história.* São Paulo: Xamã Editora, pp. 79-87, 2007.

Henman, Anthony. "Uso del Ayahuasca en un contexto autoritario. El cas de la União do Vegetal en Brasil." America Indígena, 46 (1), pp. 219-234, 1986.

Labate, Beatriz Caiuby and Araujo, Wladimir Sena (orgs.). *O uso ritual da Ayahuasca.* Campinas: Mercado de Letras. (2a edição revisada e ampliada), 2004.

Macrae, Edward. "The ritual use of ayahuasca in three Brazilian religions," *in:* Coomber, Ross and South, Nigel (orgs.), *Drug Use and Cultural Contexts "Beyond the West."* London: Free Association Books, pp. 27-45, 2004.

Soibelman, Tania. *My father and my mother, show me your beauty: Ritual use of Ayahuasca in Rio de Janeiro.* (Master Thesis). California: California Institute of Integral Studies, 1995.

Adult Life Narratives of Experiences with Religious Orientation in Childhood and Adolescence[1]

Julia Maria Casulari Motta[2]
Edison Saraiva Neves[3]
Erica Monteiro de Almeida[4]
Janine Rodrigues[5]

This is the summary of a research project aiming to gather knowledge about the perspective of adults who attended activities at the núcleos of the UDV in their childhood or adolescence.

Religious orientation of children and adolescents is one possible aspect of the educational experience. A study of this process is a necessity, given that we live in a country (Brazil) where this practice is common in our culture.

Objective

To study how adults describe their religious experiences, within a religious entity, in childhood and adolescence.

---

[1] Excerpts from an article originally published in the Revista Brasília Médica 48 (4) – 2011 (Journal BSBM- Brasilia médica) http://www.ambr.org.br/portal/?page_id=11053. Reprinted by permission.

[2] Julia Maria Casulari Motta , Psychologist, doctor in Collective Health by State University of Campinas (UNICAMP). Research at LAPACIS-FCM-DMPS-UNICAMP, member of the Body od Counsel of the UDV – Núcleo Alto das Cordilheira, Campinas, Sao Paulo state. Correspondence: Rua Rosa de Gusmão 307, CEP 13.073-141, Campinas, SP. Fone/fax 19 3242-8461. Internet: juliacmotta@gmail.com.

[3] Edison Saraiva Neves MD, homeopathic doctor, Mestre of the UDV, national coordinator of Religious Teachings of the UDV.

[4] Erica Monteiro de Almeida, Art Educator, researcher and manager of the GTER (Religious Teaching Work Group of the UDV), member of the Body of Counsel of the UDV – Núcleo Grande Venture, Jarinu, Sao Paulo state.

[5] Bachelors in Law and Law Expert, master degree candidate in Sustainable Development, professor of Constitutional, Administrative, and Social Security Law, researcher and manager of the GTER (Religious Teaching Work Group of the UDV), member of the Instructive Body UDV – Núcleo Coroa Divina, Paraná state.

Method

Adults who had religious experiences in the União do Vegetal during the decades of the eighties and nineties were evaluated. Semi-structured interviews were conducted via the internet. A total of 301 questionnaires were sent to 26 centers of the União do Vegetal. One hundred seventy three narratives were studied (57, 6%).

Outcome

The need for integration of parents, institutions, and the young was observed in activities of religious and spiritual orientation. The importance of activities that promote and strengthen bonds of friendship among children and youth was considered, as well as activities that encourage professional development and form ethical participating citizens with critical conscience.

Conclusion

Religious and spiritual orientation is an important phase of human development that can influence the educational approach in order to create a better world actively engaged with building peace.

Introduction

At the present time an increasing number of religious organizations are attracting members from various social segments. Some of these religions are attending to the concerns of the economically and educationally underprivileged. Others attract members from diverse socio-political and economic backgrounds.

What is the most significant appeal of these religions? What family and individual needs do these religious practices endeavor to fulfill? How are the adults now who participated in a religious community during childhood or adolescence? How do these adults describe their religious and spiritual experiences in childhood and adolescence? What were the limiting factors that arose from these childhood experiences?

How do these experiences help the adult to face the adversities of life? Is it possible that the health of these adults relies on the added resource of early spiritual and religious experience?

In Brazil, there are many questions and fewer answers about this aspect of human development. This theme has received growing attention and even has a dedicated

---

[4] Raimundo Monteiro de Souza is a mestre of the Council of the Recordation of the Teachings of Mestre Gabriel.

national journal, Religion and Society, created in 1977 by the Center for Religious Studies (CER) and is presently published by the Institute for Religious Studies (ISER).

For children and adolescents learning occurs in their social networks, notably school and family circles. Beyond these circles, there are other social units that define more clearly the uniqueness of bonds, resources and limitations for their life choices.

Principles of psychology demonstrate that experiences from childhood and adolescence are well known to strongly imprint the individual personality. Exposure to ethical and moral criteria, fidelity and loyalty rules, and criteria for bonds with people and with nature help individuals to become more involved in processes of social transformation. Do children and adolescents who interact within a specific religious surrounding become more socially integrated? What will be their concept of citizenship? These are questions this project seeks to explore and elucidate.

In an article derived from his doctoral thesis about religious understanding and experience, based on the perspective of children, Pires suggests that it is possible to study the religious factor in the development of children based on their views.[6] He proposes that it is not necessary to interpret children's experiences but rather to study them, respecting their own process, which is not the same as that of an adult. To the child the symbolic content of religion is not at stake. On the contrary, what is at stake is the set of activities they participate in while in attendance at the religious community.

Who accompanies the children to the religious community, who relates to them during the time they are within the group, and what activities they do together: these are the important elements for the children. The playful process is central to learning ability and to sociability within this context.

Primitive societies and children follow an integrated process of building socialization and religious learning without separating the social and religious contexts. Within this context, to know is to live and to experiment. What counts is the experiential interaction itself, the experimentation, and not what the experience symbolizes. Interaction and playfulness hold an innate sense of delight, without need for other elaborations.[7]

According to Pires "as the child grows the practice becomes subordinate to its meaning." In other words, the feeling generated by the experience becomes the symbolized religious thought. It is no longer an experiential religiosity and it becomes religious thinking.

---

[6] Pires, F. Becaming Adult: an Anthropological approach about children and religion

[7] Julia Maria Casulari Motta. Jogos: repetição ou criação? Abordagem psicodramática. São Paulo: Ágora; 2002 *(Games: Repetition or creation? A Psychodrama Approach)..*

Therefore, the current research project is based on this premise that the direct study of children's religious and spiritual experience in the context of religious community has great value. This work presents and evaluates a wide range of knowledge on religious and spiritual development through the narratives of adults who participated in a religious community in childhood and/or adolescence.

Method

The basic question of this study was: how does an adult describe his/her religious experience, lived in their childhood or adolescence, within a religious realm? (In this case the Beneficent Spiritist Center União do Vegetal).

Men and women, between 18 and 35 years old, who were qualified for this study, had attended the community of the UDV in the eighties and nineties, independent from practicing the religion.

A semi-structured questionnaire was prepared to evaluate items related to the activities the participants engaged in at the religious entity:

(1) Activities you liked as a child

(2) Activities you did not like as a child

(3) Activities you liked when an adolescent

(4) Activity you did not like when an adolescent

(5) How would you be if you were responsible for activities with children?

(6) How would you be if you were responsible for activities with adolescents?

Contacts were used from the email list maintained by the religious entity, which at the time consisted of 691 participants. In each núcleo the management of distributing and collecting the questionnaires was done by volunteers that are usually responsible for such tasks.

Each researcher received and distributed the questionnaires and instructions via email to the volunteer participants. The responsible person at each núcleo collected the individual responses and assembled the answers into a summary table which was sent to the research coordinator. The research coordinator incorporated all the summary tables into a global response map.

Twenty six núcleos throughout Brazil participated in the states of: Amazonas, Rondonia, São Paulo, Minas Gerais, Goiás, Mato Grosso, Mato Grosso do Sul, Federal District, Tocantins, Paraná, Santa Catarina, Alagoas, Pernambuco, Paraíba, Rio Grande do Norte, Ceará, and Piauí.

Results

Three hundred and one questionnaires were distributed, mostly via email. The participants who did not have online access received printed questionnaires. There were 173 responses (57,6%). The main points of the narrative are presented below.

Activities You Liked as a Child

- The best activities were the ones that did not seem like school: having to stay quietly drawing or listening to stories being told without saying anything.
- The times when we could play freely without anyone directing the play, only coordinating.
- When the opinions of the children were considered in the decision making and the children's choices were respected.
- Everything that was useful to make friends.
- The most important were the friends and the fun games.
- I liked the outings away from the núcleo to meet other people and to see other places.
- One time we went to the theater, it was really cool, I still remember the play.
- Camping was always the best.
- Birthday parties of friends.
- One time we had a live Christmas nativity play. I was the donkey.
- I loved theater, fun activities.
- I made the best friends as a child at the UDV site and I have them to this day.
- When the adults talked in a good way with us; that is, when they also listened to us.

Activities you did not like as a child

- I did not like activities that I had to be seated listening to stories and had to draw afterwards. It was really boring because it seemed like school.
- When our parents had to be in a meeting and we had nothing to do except wait.
- When we went to other núcleos and did not know people, and the children there did not pay any attention to us; when we got scolded for making too much noise.
- When our parents left us at the núcleo with other responsible adults, and left to go do other things all day long.

- When our friends didn't go to the núcleo.
- When we had activities where something needed to be memorized.
- When activities seemed like school homework.
- When I did not want to go and my parents forced me.
- When I did not know at school what was my religion.
- When adults scolded me.
- When adults did not explain clearly things of nature, of the tea, of the tea preparation and we did not understand what was going on.
- When we went to other núcleos and the children there excluded those who were not from there.

Activities you did like as an adolescent

- Camping, youth gatherings, theater games, dance, art.
- When we went to visit other núcleos.
- All activities that promoted making friends and communication with other young people.
- Opportunities to make new friends.
- Polemic discussions in group dynamics, such as: sex before marriage, romance, the use of alcoholic beverages at parties, dance parties, illicit drugs.
- Activities that imposed nothing, like those that we read, made our own conclusions, shared information, enjoyed ourselves, and understood the message.
- When we learned about nature and about the tea.
- Visits to places where the Mariri and Chacrona were harvested to understand how the tea is produced.
- Sessions for young people where we could speak freely.
- The youth gatherings were always the best.
- Activities connected with nature and ecology.
- Opportunities to speak about falling in love, sex without guilt and relationships with other young people.

Activities you did not like as an adolescent

- I did not like youth gatherings that cost too much because the food and the lodging was more important than the youth being together to hang out and get to know one another.
- Long lectures where there was not freedom to interact with other young people.

- Circular dances or something slow and square.
- When our parents did not know what was going on in the group and left things up to the ones in charge.
- We lacked activities that taught us about money.
- We lacked activities that prepared young people to enter the job market.
- We lacked approaches that would assist parents to accept the choices made by their adolescents.
- We needed more interaction between the parents and those in charge for the youth group.
- The direction of the núcleo and the parents needed to be more aware of what was taking place with the adolescents.
- We lacked help for parents to assist them in accepting it when their adolescents did not want to go to the núcleo.
- We lacked anyone to work with the parents to help them accept it when their sons and daughters did not want to follow the UDV.
- Parents cannot push their parenting responsibilities onto other members of the UDV.
- When parents had activities at the núcleo and didn't know what to do with their children; we lacked activities at the núcleo to support parents who are engaged in activities there.

How would you be if you were responsible for activities for the children?

- I don't think that religious teaching for children needs to be like 'Sunday School'.
- If children are raised in a place where they feel captivated and safe, this is a lot more important in order for them to have the UDV as a reference in life and develop affinity with the path of the UDV.
- In some religious issues, I see that it is the role of the parents to explain to the child at a young age, discussing and stimulating the natural inquisitiveness of the child to discover and understand life.
- In my view, the UDV can have a role as a religious community that facilitates the development of children and adolescents by providing and strengthening friendships, groups and cycles in which children are captivated, through the experience of having happy moments, and have the opportunity to learn good values and how to overcome challenges.

- In childhood I heard few stories about Jesus; I feel it is important to present Jesus to children.
- We need to become aware that we live in different societies, we think differently from one another, and we educate our children differently.
- Directed activities must not take place on every escala with the children or the adolescents.
- I have observed that those in charge for activities with young people who are able to speak the same language as young people, have gained better results in the activities and have better fulfilled the objectives of the role.
- When possible organize different activities for children to have a choice, which could help the child develop more affinity with spirituality, learn how to make decisions and about the results a decision may bring; I would encourage initiatives to bring young people closer to one another and have them facilitate activities for the younger children.
- The importance of creative activities connected to nature to teach concepts of ethics, respect and citizenship without using school models.
- Work with parents so that they can collaborate in a team effort for planning with those who are responsible for activities for the young in order to have the family as the core structure of religious orientation for the children.
- Assist parents to find a better measure of equilibrium between family and religion.
- Make sure that activities are essentially creative and fun, preferably in group setting.
- Explain to the children what we do in the sessions, why we drink the tea, explain the objectives of the UDV and its spiritual guide.
- Promote outings outside of the UDV and promote more camping opportunities.

How would you be if you were responsible for activities for the adolescents?

- I feel it is important to avoid that our youth become square, church-mousy or fanatics for the UDV.
- If I were to one day orient the adolescents I would seek to find inspiration to do it in way that could awaken in them the substantiation that there is room for their perceptions so that they can afterward search for reality with sincerity.
- Sessions for the young ones are very important.

- I would promote activities where the natural interaction among adolescents could facilitate a more fluid awakening for spiritual life; abandon clichés and typical models of behavior and adopt activities that are more focused on awakening autonomy of world view. This could be more effective to inspire young people to focus on what is positive and on self-knowledge.
- It is important to have early youth interaction as the friendships encourage us to come to the UDV.
- There must be time for the children and adolescents to play freely, talk, and do what they wish.
- The children and the adolescents are the future of the UDV. The better the orientation the more loyal they will be to the teachings; the more they learn about ethics, morality and developing a good character at this phase of life the more they will have when they become the future leaders of the UDV. It is easier to cultivate, from an early age, transparency and simplicity in the way of thinking and doing things that could facilitate evolution.
- I see differences in a young person that was raised in the UDV and those who came later, in the way they understand the teachings, the way they act in life and the way they think about their family. The leaders are the mirror of the disciples, thus besides working well with young people, there needs to be uniformity in the members of the direction as to good character, ethics and morality to avoid problems in the future.
- Activities that teach them how to deal with money and finances, and the mainstream consumption, which is an evil that affects young people in general. I would also encourage activities to teach problem solving in life and how to be accountable as a member of society.
- Education on illicit and licit drugs.
- Work with the parents to participate alongside their sons and daughters.
- Assure that fanaticism, rigidity, and forced participation does not take away freedom of choice; activities that unleash the talent young people have.
- Respect for the timing of each person and not impose teachings like 'catechism' or like it is school.
- Young people in the UDV are not different from other young people.
- How to speak of the UDV to people they don't know.
- Sessions and youth gatherings are always important because they develop a sense of responsibility, interest, and motivation in life.

- Activities that assist young people to understand the value of charitable works.
- I would like that everything be done the same as it was done when I was a child here in the UDV.
- Work with parents to help them understand their accountability for the religious education of their children, that it is not only the responsibility of the institution.
- Parents used to 'deliver' their children as if taking them to school.
- Activities in which the design does not come from top to bottom but ones in which young people have input about the planning, and most importantly that they spontaneously participate and are not forced to do so.
- Activities that develop a leadership spirit.
- Activities that include financial management education.
- Align the work with young people with the direction of the núcleo.
- Young people in the UDV don't drink, don't smoke, and don't do some other things that may make it seem to the youth of the UDV that they are not 'enjoying life' or that they are 'square,' thus there is an essential need for dynamic activities that encompass responsibility, adequate to their surroundings and with a lot of fun. We can expand our activities to more social contexts.

Discussion

This study was the first in which the researchers used the format of interviews via the internet. The researchers state that they have no knowledge of other religious experience narratives studies developed in this format in Brazil. This investigation had as a goal to test this instrument and determine the response potential of the studied subjects, provide experience for the UDV religious teaching study group, generate conditions to develop future studies based on this preliminary study and to produce knowledge for this field.

For this purpose some theoretical concepts were used, such as the concept of Paulo Freire which states that in order to investigate it is necessary initially to learn how to ask questions.[8] This implies understanding that the process begins with tolerance of what is different and is completed by accepting answers that do not correspond with what was expected, i.e., not included in the original intention of the questions.

---

[8] Freire, Paulo & A. Faundez (1989). *Learning to Question: A Pedagogy of Liberation.* New York: Continuum. Por uma pedagogia da pergunta. Rio de Janeiro: Paz e Terra; 1985:27.

To begin a study project is to select a question from among many that can be asked about a theme. It may be a theoretical or a theoretical-practical question. It is important that the central question be clearly defined, simple and well considered, have interesting content to motivate all involved, not be leading to an answer, and instead encourage reflection so that it can be beneficial to the participants.

For this study, sufficiently clear questions were selected to facilitate email communication for the participants and to allow them to feel connected with the researchers. Questions were chosen that could motivate them to share their memories with others. The intention was for the participants to benefit from their narrative by reviewing their own history. It is believed that when people describe their own history they get in touch with new aspects of the narrative. To recount is, therefore, an instrument of transformation.

It was necessary for the researchers to prepare themselves in order to grow their capacity for tolerance of different answers. Many responses were surprising. There was no opportunity for discussion, for responding to the concerns by offering new questions, to create clarification. As this was a preliminary first study, it was decided to have only a single contact for the interview.

Regarding the narrative memory, it is found in the work of historian Walter Benjamin that memory functions not only to search for times gone by, but it also allows people to visit the past in search of the future. Through a journey into the past, memory provides the possibility, of reactivating a social commitment. This could also be called a political commitment, in the sense of contributing to the social welfare, in the individual and collective present. Memory is the capacity to be in contact with the unconscious, voluntarily and involuntarily. To Benjamin, memory is the unique resource of collective participation and the possibility of being a creator of a better world; by visiting the past one can see what one could have done differently. One's history could have been another history. Memory and narrative history allow men and women to have a human existence by proclaiming the world, because it is not through silence, but through the word that one becomes oneself – and dialogue is the bond among men.[10]

The guiding question of this investigation was: "How do you describe your religious experience within the realm of the UDV in childhood or adolescence?" The other questions unfolded from this initial question.

---

[10] Julia Maria Casulari Motta, Psicologia e o mundo do trabalho no Brasil: relações, história e memórias. São Paulo: Ágora; 2005. (Psychology and the World of Work in Brazil: Relations, History and Memories)

Through the percentage of received answers, the researchers consider this study to have attended the subjects' need to be heard in their narratives and that the narratives contribute to the collective effort of gathering knowledge about childhood and adolescence in this community.

The majority of participants stated that they had more good memories than uncomfortable memories. Some courageous statements made important consideration and reflection possible. About 10% of the respondents said that they would not change anything as they had good experiences. The majority, despite considering their experiences as good, propose adjustments to the approach with children and adolescents.

Many of the participants in the study are presently fathers and mothers of children who attend the UDV activities. This is a driving factor in their willingness to participate in the study and explains the profusion of creative ideas for activities in the section "if you were responsible for activities." Only three replies came from people who are no longer members.

It is interesting to note that 90% of the participants responded that they would make changes in the activities they experienced when young, despite having considered them to be good experiences. This indicates interest, availability, and discernment about the planning that took place at the time when they were children or adolescents. The factor most mentioned was the small degree of collaboration in the planning of activities between parents, activity coordinators and the direction of the núcleo.

Clearly the participants strongly recommend that activities for children and young adults be planned with participation from parents, coordinators, and adolescents voicing their opinions and being taken into consideration. At the same time they suggest that young people have the freedom to choose, decide, and give input, and that work be done with parents to accept choices their sons and daughters make to follow other religions.

As parents today, they speak of their own needs, and can see their weaknesses as parents. When a role is learned a counter-role is also learned. Therefore, having lived the role of sons and daughters, they also learned at the same time the role of father and

---

[15] Marisa Mendes Machado, attorney, General Coordinator of the Legal Department of the CEBUDV from 1982-1998, and a Counselor in the UDV.

[16] Flavio Mesquita De Silva, a researcher from Brazil, is a doctorate candidate at Fielding Graduate University studying the impact of cultural dialogue, cultural design, and creating a culture of peace in a multi-generational context. He is former President of the UDV's General Directorate (2009-2012).

mother. They do not want to repeat the mistakes of their parents. The strongest change factors referred to the relations between parents, children and the institution. One of the concerns expressed was not to allow "squareness", fanaticism, and rigidity to take over flexibility, fraternity, and possibilities for tolerance of differences. For these participants the goal of a model for spiritual orientation includes: learning how to deal with money, preparing for a professional future, becoming a participating citizen that relates well with nature, with others and with spirituality.

They perceive that the most important activities are those that encourage friendship bonds among the children. Being able to make friends was a determining factor in "if the activity was a good one and if it was a good day at the núcleo." Hanging out, playing games, making art, being together, getting to know each other, discovering possibilities of having fun, and being chosen to do something, all of these were the memorable religious experiences in the lives of the children and adolescents. The reflexive vision of the narratives confirms this as a promising field for other studies. This preliminary investigation will guide a future and wider investigation which will confirm or challenge the present findings. The subjects will, possibly, feel more open to express their opinions and to re-evaluate their life experiences since this is an internal study, all pointing to the positive results of this preliminary phase. The participants proposed participation and availability, as well as signed their narratives, affirming commitment to what they wrote.

In conclusion, the hope that bringing new knowledge about religious and spiritual orientation at an important phase of human development may provoke new reflection about the art of educating children and youth on the path to creating a better world – the active building of peace.

Conflicts of Interest

The authors have nothing to state.

Bibliography

Carter, B. Mcgoldrick M. "As mudanças no ciclo de vida familiar: uma estrutura para terapia familiar." Porto Alegre: Artes Médicas, 1995.

Pires, F. "Tornando-se adulto: uma abordagem antropológica sobre as crianças e religião." Relig Soc., 30:143-64, 2010.

Motta, J.C. "Jogos: repetição ou criação? Abordagem psicodramática." São Paulo: Ágora, 2002.

CEBUDV. "Consolidação das leis do Centro Espírita Beneficente União do Vegetal." Sede Geral, Brasília, 3.ª edição, 1994.

Gentil, L., Gentil H. "O uso de psicoativos em um contexto religioso: a União do Vegetal." In: Labate, B. and Araujo W. (orgs.) "O uso ritual da Ayahuasca." Campinas: Mercado das Letras, São Paulo: FAPESP, p. 513-24, 2002.

Motta, J. C., Gentil L. "Memórias: uma breve narrativa baseada no acervo de depoimentos com mestres da origem da União do Vegetal." UDV, 2009 (mimeo).

Brito, G. "Farmacologia humana da Hoasca: chá preparado de plantas alucinógenas usado em contexto ritual no Brasil." In: Labate, B. and Araujo, W. (orgs.) "O uso ritual da Ayahuasca." Campinas: Mercado das Letras; São Paulo: FAPESP, p. 577-604, 2002.

Grob, C.S., McKenna, D.J., Callaway, J.C., Brito, G.S., Neves, E.S., Oberlaender, G., et al. "Farmacologia humana da Hoasca: efeitos psicológicos." In: Labate, B. and Araujo, W. (orgs.) "O uso ritual da Ayahuasca." Campinas: Mercado das Letras, São Paulo: FAPESP, p. 605-30, 2002.

Santos, R.G. "The pharmacology of ayahuasca: a review." Brasília Med., 47:187-94, 2010.

Freire, P., Faúndez, A. "Por uma pedagogia da pergunta." Rio de Janeiro: Paz e Terra, p. 27, 1985.

Benjamin, W. "Obras escolhidas." Volume I. Magia e técnica, arte e política. Ensaios sobre literatura e história da cultura, 2.ª ed. São Paulo: Brasiliense, 1986.

Motta, J.C. "Psicologia e o mundo do trabalho no Brasil: relações, história e memórias." São Paulo: Ágora, 2005.

PART II
Hoasca and Society

Objectives of the União do Vegetal as a Brazilian and International Religious Group[1]

Edson Lodi Campos Soares
Cristina Patriota de Moura

Introduction

The Beneficent Spiritist Center União do Vegetal (UDV) is a religion of Christian foundation composed of almost 14 thousand members, with more than 150 *núcleos* (centers) and authorized distributions of the Vegetal officially recognized in Brazil and overseas. Since its founding by José Gabriel da Costa (Mestre Gabriel) on July 22, 1961, the UDV follows the principle of working for the development of the human being in a spiritual, moral and intellectual sense. This spiritual principle is based on the belief that it is possible to build a more just and peaceful world.

José Gabriel da Costa was born on February 10, 1922, in the small township of Coração de Maria, in the state of Bahia, Brazil. As a young man he joined the rubber army and migrated to the state of Rondônia, where he worked as a rubber tapper. In the Amazon forest, Mestre Gabriel came into contact with the Hoasca tea and started to conduct sessions is his home in the rubber-tapping region of the forest where he lived, and later in the city of Porto Velho. He worked as a rubber tapper, brick maker, truck driver and nursing assistant, struggling to support his family with the help of his wife, Raimunda Pereira da Costa, Mestre Pequenina.

The Hoasca tea, according to the teachings of Mestre Gabriel, is to be used as a vehicle for mental concentration by those who ingest it of their free and spontaneous will. The rituals that he created, initially with only the participation of family members and a few disciples, encourage the participation of the participants through questions asked to the Mestre who is directing the session. The teachings are transmitted orally, from "mouth to ear," in the escala (scheduled) sessions, which take place on

---

[1] This article is an edited excerpt from the article originally published in the book edited by Henrik Jungaberle and Beatriz Labate, The Globalization of the Use of Ayahuasca, Gottingen-Bern-Wien-Oxford, Hogrefe, Editora Mercado de Letras, Campinas/SP – Brazil, 2004.

the first and third Saturday of each month. The doctrine of the UDV includes the belief in reincarnation and in spiritual evolution, with special reverence to the teachings of Jesus Christ, whom Mestre Gabriel recognized as "the Divine Master."

The disciples must work toward spiritual evolution through their moral development, with the Christian value of loving others as their main objective. The UDV has Light, Peace and Love as a symbol for peace and human fraternity. This symbol encourages the disciples to work for a healthy equilibrium between the different aspects of their lives, including profession, family, and religion. There are three classes of members: Mestres, Counselors and Disciples, organized in a hierarchy with different degrees of commitment in relation to the UDV and to the individual work of spiritual development.

The UDV started with a small group in Porto Velho and is today an institution with núcleos officially recognized in all Brazilian states, as well as in the United States and some countries in Europe. The UDV has grown and established itself as a religion, acquiring public recognition through appropriate legal channels, both in Brazil as well as overseas.

Although discretion is a principle of the UDV, on several occasions UDV members have taken legal action in order to secure the right to the communion of their sacrament, the Hoasca tea, or the Vegetal. This article describes the main steps taken by the UDV to formally gain legal recognition, principally in Brazil. These actions have contributed to the UDV being legally recognized as a religion, gaining the guaranteed right to use Hoasca in its religious rituals and receiving the title of *"Utilidade Pública Federal"* (Institution of Public Benefit) granted by the Brazilian Federal government.[2]

The Beginnings of the UDV and the First Steps toward Legalization

The name of the UDV, at the time when its first bylaws were composed, was simply "União do Vegetal." It was then legally registered as "Associação Beneficente União do Vegetal" (Beneficent Association União do Vegetal), and in 1971 it became the Centro Espírita Beneficente União do Vegetal (Beneficent Spiritist Center União do Vegetal). The fact that the organization was initially registered as Beneficent Association União do Vegetal, and then later changed to a Spiritist Center, is related,

---

[2] For more information about these achievements of the UDV see the texts by Santos, Machado and Lima, in this book. Regarding the institutionalization process of the UDV overseas, see articles by Bronfman, Boyd and Prades, and Marin, in this book.

among other things, to the ongoing search for better institutional positioning in different political contexts.

Since the beginning, the UDV has taken the initiative of demonstrating, to those not familiar with its practices, that the Vegetal (Hoasca) "is proven harmless to the health." These words of Mestre Gabriel have been in the bylaws of the Beneficent Spiritist Center União do Vegetal since they were filed in 1971. Of equal importance is the doctrine transmitted in the sessions of the UDV, whose precepts are aligned with the ethical and moral values of the greater society. As a religious institution, the UDV aims for the physical, mental and spiritual equilibrium of its members, individually and in interpersonal relationships.

The first contact between the UDV and government officials took place in Porto Velho in the late sixties. It is important to note that, at that time, a military dictatorship was in effect which imposed many restrictions on the citizens' right to gather or to form associations. It is also important to keep in mind that throughout Brazilian history there had been several instances of violent repression against religious groups, officially justified by a mix of political, economic and spiritual allegations. In the sixties, Rondônia was a territory under the direct supervision of the Federal Government, even though the majority of its terrain was covered by dense forest where the population was composed of various indigenous tribes and migrants from different Brazilian regions who worked as rubber tappers for powerful landowners, in indentured servitude. Porto Velho was a center for important medical, commercial and military activities in a frontier region.

The use of Hoasca tea, also called Yagé, Caapi, and Cipó (in addition to other names) was common in those remote parts, and was seen mainly as an inconsequential indigenous and "caboclo" (mestizo) practice. Nonetheless, when the UDV started to establish itself as a religious group with regular meetings in urban areas, it attracted attention from the local authorities. The urban members of the UDV felt the necessity to formalize their organization, which led to the writing of the first bylaws in 1967. Although the Association had not yet been registered, the members elected their first directorate, with a president, treasurer, secretary and other positions.

First Reactions from the Authorities

The use of the Hoasca tea and periodic group meetings faced prejudice and arbitrary measures by a resistant chief of police in Porto Velho who, on one occasion, even arrested Mestre Gabriel. An account of that event was published in the Alto

Madeira Newspaper in October of 1967 with the title "Conviction of the Mestre." Mestre Gabriel was arrested for interrogation and set free the following morning. He then explained to his disciples the mission of the UDV, reminding them of the symbol of peace and human fraternity held by this religion: Light, Peace and Love.

This incident showed the necessity to formalize the Association by registering with the local authorities. Therefore, the first Statute of the União do Vegetal was registered in 1968. This is an important landmark for this religious institution.

In 1970, the chief of police of the Rondonia Territory publically declared that the União do Vegetal would be closed down. Mestre Gabriel did not close the UDV, but out of respect to the local authorities, he did not permit adventicios in the sessions and continued the sessions only with people who were already members.[3] Raimundo Monteiro de Souza, Mestre Monteiro, who at that time was the president of the Association, hired an attorney to defend the rights of the UDV and contacted the Federal District and Territories Justice Court. As per legal counsel, the members composed a new Statute that explicitly addressed the use of the Vegetal and changed the name of the religious institution to Centro Espírita Beneficente União do Vegetal, a term that placed the UDV amidst other religious groups with an emphasis on its spiritual objectives (not to be confused with political ones).

The UDV was registered in June of 1971, referring to the use of the Hoasca tea in its religious practice with the words that still remain today: "The associates of the Center, of their free and spontaneous will, drink a tea, Hoasca, which is the union of two plants, the Mariri and the Chacrona, proven harmless to the health" (CEBUDV 1971).

In July of 1971, the Bishop of Porto Velho criticized the UDV in his sermon during Sunday mass. Mestre Gabriel responded in an article published on July 16th in the Guaporé newspaper with the title "Velando Enquanto Dorme" (Keeping Watch While Sleeping). The article said that once a person had been a member of the UDV for more than 60 days, he was no longer obligated to spend time in places that could be harmful to a man's moral development. It also said that the UDV aims to combat the use of narcotics and alcohol.

Since the disincarnation of Mestre Gabriel in September of 1971, UDV leaders have worked to establish the Center's legal and respected status, for which its founder strived tirelessly. With the UDV expanding to all regions of Brazil, as well as to the US and Europe, the Center has always provided all the information requested by the authorities and has achieved the right to practice its sincere religion. The leadership

---

[3] Adventicios are those who drink the Vegetal for the first time in the UDV.

of the UDV, along with other institutions who use the Hoasca tea as a sacrament, has striven to establish ethical principles to guide the use of the tea.

During the seventies and eighties there were several occasions on which the UDV had to defend itself from hostile action lead by institutions and individuals connected to the government. In 1982 the General Headquarters of the UDV was transferred to Brasilia, where it remains to this day. At that time, the UDV had already grown from Porto Velho to Manaus, São Paulo, Rio de Janeiro and some states of the Northeast.

The Exclusion of the Banisteriopsis caapi from the List of Proscribed Substances

Almost three years after the transfer of the General Headquarters to Brasilia, the UDV again had to take legal action to secure the right to its religious practice. On June 24, 1985, the UDV petitioned the Federal Narcotics Council (CONFEN), through its legal representative Luis Felipe Belmonte dos Santos, to have the *Banisteriopsis caapi* (mariri) removed from the List of Proscribed Substances of the *Divisão Nacional de Vigilancia Sanitária de Medicamentos -DIMED* (Brazilian National Health and Drug Administration). The DIMED had included the vine on its list of proscribed substances through Ordinance no. 2/85, alleging that it contained *dimethyltriptamine* (DMT). This was an error because the mariri does not contain DMT; this substance is found in the *chacrona* (Psychotria viridis). Nonetheless, the UDV suspended the use of the Vegetal, following the orientation of its founder who taught his disciples to always respect the law and government authorities, until it was certain that its members would not be prosecuted. This demonstration of respect, cordiality and good will assisted the UDV in justifying the legal use of the Vegetal before the Brazilian government. The UDV also offered to cooperate with scientific studies on the effects of the tea on its members during its rituals. The petition sent to the CONFEN stated:

> The petition for the re-examination of this matter, to include its sociological, chemical, pharmacological, anthropological, cultural and constitutional-legal aspects, is based on the fact that the said substance is used in the preparation of a tea that is used by various religious entities, one of them being the Centro Espírita Beneficente União do Vegetal, an institution with 2000 members, that is recognized as an organization of Public Benefit in several locations (CONFEN 1985).

Consequently, as a result of this initiative by the UDV, CONFEN created a study group to examine the production and use of the substances derived from the *Banisteriopsis caapi* and the *Psychotria viridis,* with respect to its medical, sociological, anthropological and general health effects (CONFEN 1985). The UDV cooperated fully with the study group composed of scientists and representatives from other ayahuasca religions, providing information and permitting observation of its rituals.[4]

On February 4, 1986, CONFEN issued Resolution 06/86, excluding the *Banisteriopsis caapi* from the list of proscribed substances, basing its decision on the constitutional right of religious freedom. This decision gave legal backing for the UDV and other groups to continue practicing their rituals. Nevertheless, the study group continued its work and the decision was only published in August of 1992, with the inclusion of a clause providing for the review of the matter in the case of the occurrence of new facts (Sá 1987, 1992).

Meanwhile, the UDV participated, along with other religious institutions, in the writing and signing of the Letter of Principles of Ayahuasca Using Entities. The objective of this Letter was to ensure the responsible use of the tea. This was an important step in establishing alliances with other groups who have the same commitment to religious responsibility and spiritual work that benefits the spiritual development of the human being. Everything seemed peaceful, but the issue was not yet resolved. In 1995 the CONFEN issued the minutes of its 3rd Ordinary Meeting that recommended banning the use of the tea by minors, based on a complaint made by the mother of a minor who attended another ayahuasca group. The consequence of this was felt in some states and municipalities where local judges prohibited the use of the Vegetal by children.

In 1996 the UDV once again took legal action against the CONFEN, requesting re-examination of the matter as well as scientific studies with UDV adolescents. Despite all the efforts and cooperation of the UDV, the government published its findings, recommending that the "tea not be used by minors, even if accompanied by parents or guardians, regardless of dosage or ceremony." Once again such a recommendation was not based on empirical observation or scientific research and was successfully challenged by the UDV and other Ayahuasca using entities, as described in the next section.

Traditionally, the UDV had permitted children, under the supervision of their parents, to drink the Vegetal in small quantities, increasing their participation as they grew older. Participation was always voluntary and the UDV required the

---

[4] For more information regarding the action of the CEBUDV before the CONFEN see article by Santos, in this book.

authorization of the parents or legal guardians for every minor who participated. Presently, children under 12 years old are permitted to participate in five specific sessions per year; children 12 and over are permitted to participate in the rituals once a month; children 14 and over have authorization to participate in two sessions per month. Once they become 18, if they wish, they may associate with the UDV.[5]

The Continuation of the Legalization Process and Institutional Challenges

In 1998 the CONFEN became extinct and its activities were removed from the realm of the Brazilian Justice Department. In that same year the Conselho Nacional Antidrogas – CONAD (Brazilian National Anti-Drug Council) was created, along with the Secretaria Nacional Antidrogas – SENAD (Brazilian National Anti-Drug Office). These new departments were now connected to the Gabinete de Segurança Institucional da Presidência da República (Cabinet of Institutional Security of the Presidency). The members of the UDV closely accompanied these institutional changes, while continuing to insist on their right to the free exercise of religion and providing the information necessary to prove the harmlessness of the tea.

Meanwhile, in 1999, the UDV received a request from the University of California at Los Angeles, in partnership with other universities, to begin a research project with adolescents who drink the Hoasca tea in the UDV.[6] During the study and until its conclusion, the UDV kept the CONAD and the Ministério Público Federal (Federal Prosecutor) informed on the procedures and the results. Finally, on August 17, 2004, CONAD's council approved the recommendation by the Câmara de Assessoramento Técnico-Científico (Chamber for Technical and Scientific Advisory), guaranteeing the right of minors to participate in the religious rituals which include the communion of the tea. This document, published in November 2004, states that: "the participation by children and pregnant women in the religious use of Ayahuasca shall remain a matter of parental discretion, in the adequate exercise of parental rights" (CONAD, Resolution 5/2004).[7]

Another measure in the same resolution was the formation of the Multidisciplinary

---

[6] For a detailed description of the recognition process of parental rights in the religious orientation of minors, see article by Machado, in this book.

[7] See da Silveira et al. 2005; Dobkin de Rios et al. 2005; Doering-Silveira et al. 2005a, 2005b, in the section The Study on Adolescents, in this book.

[8] See article by de Machado, in this book.

Working Group (GMT) for the surveying and accompanying of the religious use of Ayahuasca, acknowledging that "the administrative and social control of the religious use of Ayahuasca can only be structured adequately with the inclusion of the knowledge held by the groups who use the tea." The GMT, a group composed of representatives of entities who use the Ayahuasca tea and members of the scientific community, met several times between 2004 and 2006. The members of the GMT elected Dr. Dartiu Xavier da Silveira Filho, a medical doctor and Professor at UNIFESP (Federal University of São Paulo), to be the president of this group and Edson Lodi Campos Soares, coordinator of institutional relations of the UDV, as vice-president.[8] The final document issued by the GMT was approved in 2006, though it was only published in the Official Registry of Brazil in January of 2010. It reflects many of the principles that have been adopted by the UDV since its creation by José Gabriel da Costa.

The Final GMT Report and the Responsible Use of the Vegetal in the UDV

In this section we present the deontological principles defined in the final GMT report and compare these principles with some of the practices already existing in the UDV. In the conclusion of the report that was approved in 2006, we find the following text:

The Multidisciplinary Working Group approved the following deontological principles for the religious use of Ayahuasca:

1. The Ayahuasca tea is the product of the decoction of the Banisteriopsis caapi vine and the leaf of the Psychotria viridis; its use is restricted to religious rituals in locations approved by the respective leadership of entities who use the sacrament, and its use is prohibited in association with illicit psychoactive substances;

2. The entire process of production, storage, distribution and consumption of Ayahuasca is part of the religious use of the beverage; commercialization is forbidden as is the perception of any benefit, in cash, in goods or in kind, by way of payment, whether for production or for consumption, apart from contributions for the maintenance and regular operation of each entity, according to their traditions or statutory provisions;

3. The responsible use of Ayahuasca presupposes the extraction (harvesting) of the sacred plant species to be used in the religious rituals. Each instituted

---

[8] For the Curriculum Vitae of Doctor and Professor Dartiu Xavier da Silveira Filho, see http://buscatextual.cnpq.br/buscatextual/visualizacv.do?metodo=apresentar&id=K4787797T9

entity should seek to become self-sustainable within a reasonable period of time, developing its own cultivation of the plants, to meet their needs and to prevent the depredation of native forest species. The extraction of the plant species from the native forest must comply with environmental regulations;

4. The entities shall avoid offering tourist packages associated with the advertisement of the effects of Ayahuasca, apart from legitimate exchanges of members of these entities within their respective communities;

5. With the exception of the constitutional right to information, it is recommended that the entities avoid advertisement of Ayahuasca, and in their public manifestations they should always be guided by discretion and moderation with respect to its use and in the description of its properties;

6. The practice of *"curandeirismo"* (folk healing practice) is prohibited by Brazilian legislation. The healing and medicinal properties of Ayahuasca – which the entities know and attest to – require the responsible use of the tea and must be understood from a spiritual perspective, avoiding any and all advertising that may cause misunderstandings by the public and the authorities;

7. It is recommended that the groups who practice the religious use of Ayahuasca be constituted as legal organizations, led by responsible individuals who are experienced in recognizing the sacred plant species, the cultivation, preparation and use of Ayahuasca, and the conducting of the rituals;

8. Each religious entity is responsible for exercising strict control over the system for admitting new members, including conducting interviews with those interested in the ingestion of Ayahuasca, to prevent it from being given to people with mental disorders or people under the influence of alcohol or other psychoactive substances;

9. It is also recommended that a registration form be maintained with each participant's information, and that participants be informed ahead of time about the principles of the ritual, start and end times, and protocols, including the necessity for the person to remain at the facility until the end of the ritual and the effects of the Ayahuasca subside;

10. In complying with the deontological principles herein defined, each entity, and likewise its members, is accountable for upholding ethics and mutual respect, in relations with one another, be they institutional, religious or social (CONAD 2010, pg. 59).

The Beneficent Spiritist Center União do Vegetal, of its own accord, maintains the following procedures:

1. The religious use of the Vegetal

    The Vegetal is the sacrament in the sessions of the UDV. Its use is strictly religious, for the effect of mental concentration. Experienced individuals are responsible for the distribution of the Vegetal and the participants are required to remain at the facility of the UDV for a minimum of four hours after the ingestion of the tea, the period in which they participate in the session (the religious ritual). The Vegetal is used exclusively in sessions and with the transmission of the UDV's spiritual doctrine. The Cadre of Mestres is responsible for the use of the tea in each núcleo and authorized distribution.

2. Non-use of illicit substances

    Other than the Vegetal, the UDV does not use psychoactive substances in its rituals. Its members are urged to avoid the use of any substance that may incur chemical dependency, including licit substances such as alcohol and tobacco.

3. Production and distribution

    The Vegetal is prepared in the exact amount needed to attend to the ritualistic needs of the Center. The cost of transportation and production are shared among the members, without profit or the sale of surplus.

4. Dissemination of information

    The UDV is not secretive, but it is discreet. There is no advertising about the use of the tea. The Direction of the Center only engages in activities that expose the UDV's practices in order to provide clarification to those interested in understanding its activities.

5. Therapeutic use

    The UDV believes that the Vegetal has therapeutic properties, but does not believe in an isolated therapeutic use outside of the religious context. There are no specific rituals dedicated to healing.

The final report of the GMT is considered an important accomplishment confirming the steadfast commitment of the UDV to guarantee its sacramental rights and to confirm the words of its founder that "the Vegetal is proven harmless to the health." Throughout many years the members of the UDV have endeavored to gain official recognition, not only regarding the right to drink the Hoasca tea, but also to establish itself as a socially respectable religious group, wherever it is present. In this way the institution has not only grown numerically and geographically, it has also acquired a series of departments that organize and promote voluntary activities among the membership. The departments and commissions of the UDV are: Medical and Scientific Department (DEMEC), Legal Department, Institutional Relations Commission, Scientific Commission, Communications Commission, Plantation Department, Charitable Works Department, Memory and Documentation Department. There are also two legally independent associations that are connected to the UDV: The *Casa da União,* a philanthropic association, and the *Novo Encanto Association for Ecological Development* (www.novoencanto.org.br), an environmental NGO with offices in various regions of Brazil.[9]

More recently, the UDV and the associations connected to it have organized several projects aiming to promote social and environmental improvements for individuals, local populations, natural resources and society in general. Due to these initiatives the institution has been awarded the title of *"Utilidade Pública Federal"* (Institution of Federal Public Benefit), which has been maintained since 1999. This is an important acknowledgement by the Brazilian Government that is granted each year through careful examination and the inspection of annual reports. One important initiative of the UDV is the program called Luz do Saber (Light of Knowledge), which provides literacy classes for adults. This program started in 2002 in the state of Mato Grosso, and since then has successfully taught 2000 adults in 27 locations throughout Brazil.[10] Another initiative is the *Festival Água no Terceiro Milênio* (Water in the Third Millennium Festival), which has taken place in several Brazilian cities: Brasilia, Pocinhos (Mina Gerais), Caxambu (Minas Gerais) and Campo Grande (Mato Grosso do Sul), and also in Spain. The objective of this event is to educate the local population on the preservation of valuable hydrological resources.[11]

The UDV has also organized national and international conferences aimed at sharing information on the accumulated knowledge within its sphere of action, particularly the Fourth UDV Congress and the Second International Hoasca Congress, which took place in Brasilia on May 9-11, 2008, with 1,200 registered participants and was also broadcast live on the internet.

In retrospect, we see that the UDV has already come a long way from the small group gathering in the rubber-tapping forests, and then in Porto Velho, led by the migrant Bahian man who worked as a rubber tapper, nursing assistant and truck driver, always caring for his family and working voluntarily on behalf of the well-being

---

[9] See the section Preservation and Improvement of the Landscape and the Environment, in this book.

[10] See text by Lima in this book, regarding the charitable works of the UDV.

[11] See article by Abes, in this book.

of his disciples. José Gabriel da Costa never received money from the religious institution he created, having always worked for the benefit of humanity. The members of the UDV seek to maintain the example of Mestre Gabriel as a guide to be followed all the time.

The global expansion of the use of the Hoasca tea through the UDV is also a means for other cultures to come into contact with the linguistic and cultural dimensions of Brazil. Presently, the UDV in Brazil is working for the recognition of the use of the Hoasca tea as an immaterial national heritage. This status gives the phenomenon of the Hoasca religious rituals its proper place as a cultural expression born of the inhabitants of the forest, that has also manifested in the urban environments of Brazil, as a religious practice that significantly contributes to people's spiritual, physical and mental well-being.

Bibliography

Alto Madeira. "Convicção do Mestre." *Jornal Alto Madeira,* October 6, 1967.

Bronfman, Jeffrey. "The early history of the UDV in the United States, and the foundation of American Law," *in:* Jungaberle, Henrik and Labate, Beatriz (eds). The globalization of the use of Ayahuasca, Gottingen-Bern-Wien-Oxford: Hogrefe, 2004.

Carta De Princípios das Entidades Religiosas Usuárias do Chá Hoasca. Rio Branco, November 24, 1991. (Mimeo)

Costa, José Gabriel da, *et al.* "Velando Enquanto Dorme." Jornal *O Guaporér.* Rondônia, July 16, 1971.

CEBUDV – Centro Espírita Beneficente União Do Vegetal. "União Do Vegetal. Hoasca: Fundamentos e Objectivos." Brasilia: Departamento de Memoria e Documentação da União do Vegetal, 1989.

CEBUDV – Centro Espírita Beneficente União Do Vegetal. "Regimento Interno." 1971. (Mimeo).

CEBUDV – Centro Espírita Beneficente União Do Vegetal. "Regimento Interno." Centro Espírita Beneficente União do Vegetal. Consolidação das Leis. 4a ed. Brasilia: Sede Geral, 2003.

CONAD – Conselho Nacional Antidrogas. *Resolução no. 5, de 4 de novembro de 2004.* Brasilia: Diário Oficial da União, Poder Executivo, 8 de novembro, Seão I, p. 8.

CONAD – Conselho Nacional Antidrogas. *"Ayahuasca."* Relatório Final, Grupo Multidisciplinar de Trabalho (GMT), 23 de novembro, 2006. (Mimeo)

CONAD – Conselho Nacional De Politicas Sobre Drogas. *Resolução no. 1, de 25 de janeiro de 2010.* Brasília: Diário Oficial da União, Poder Executivo, 26 de janeiro, Seção I, p. 57-60.

CONFEN – Conselho Federal De Entorpecentes. Petição do Centro Espírita Beneficente União do Vegetal ao CONFEN protocolada sob o no. 019547, de 23 de julho, 1985.

CONFEN – Conselho Federal de Entorpecentes. Resolução no. 6, de 4 de fevereiro de 1986. Brasília: Diário Oficial da União, Poder Executivo, 5 de fevereiro, Seção I, p. 2054, 1986.

CONFEN – Conselho Federal De Entorpecentes Ata da 3a Reunião Ordinária do Conselho Federal de Entorpecentes – *CONFEN,* realizada em 2 de junho de 1995. Brasília: Diário Oficial da União, Poder Executivo, 11 de agosto, Seção I, p. 12121, 1995.

Da Silveira, D. X.; Grob, C. S.; Dobkin De R. M.; Lopez, E.; Alonso, L. K.; Tacla, C. and Doering-Silveira, E. "Ayahuasca in adolescence: a preliminary psychiatric assessment." *Journal of Psychoactive Drugs,* no 37, vol. 2, pp. 129-134, 2005.

DIMED – Divisão Nacional De Vigilância Sanitária De Medicamentos. Portaria no. 02, 08 de março de 1995. Brasília: Diário Oficial da União, Poder Executivo, 13 de março, Seção I, p. 4421-4434, 1985.

Doering-Silveira, E.; Lopez, E.; Grob, C. S.; Dobkin De R. M.; Alonso, L. K.; Tacla, C.; Shirakawa, I.; Bertolucci, P.H. and Da Silveira, D. X. "Ayahuasca in adolescence: a neuropsychological assessment." *Journal of Psychoactive Drugs,* no 37, vol. 2, p. 123-128, 2005a.

Doering-Silveira, E.; Grob, C. S.; Dobkin M. De R.; Lopez, E.; Alonso, L. K.; Tacla, C.; And Da Silveira, D. X. "Report on psychoactive drug use among adolescents using Ayahuasca within a religious context." *Journal of Psychoactive Drugs,* no 37, vol. 2, pp. 141-144, 2005b.

Dobkin M. de R.; Grob, C. S.; Lopez, E.; da Silveira, D. X.; Alonso, L. K.; and Doering-Silveira, E. "Ayahuasca in adolescence: qualitative results." *Journal of Psychoactive Drugs,* no 37, vol. 2, p. 135-140, 2005.

Lima, F. A. S. and Tófoli, Luís Fernando (In press). "Mental Health Recommendations and Providences Concerning The Religious Use of Hoasca (Ayahuasca): A Case Report of an Experience of Epidemiologic Surveillance," In Jungaberle, Henrik and Labate, Beatriz C. (Eds.). *The Globalization of The Uses of Ayahuasca,* Göttingen-Bern-Wien-Oxford: Hogrefe.

Prades, José Vicente Marin (in press). "Legal Recognition of the Centro Espírita Beneficente União do Vegetal (CEBUDV) in Spain," in: Jungaberle, Henrik and LABATE, Beatriz C. (eds.). *The globalization of the uses of Ayahuasca,* Göttingen-Bern-Wien-Oxford: Hogrefe (in press).

Sá, Domingos Bernardo Gialluisi da Silva. "Relátorio Final do Grupo de Trabalho." Conselho Federal de Entorpecentes, 1987.

Sá, Domingos Bernardo Gialluisi da Silva. "Findings." Ministério da Justiça: Conselho Federal de Entorpecentes, 02 de junho, 1992.

The Legalization of the Hoasca Tea with the CONFEN

Luís Felipe Belmonte dos Santos

The history of the institutional legalization of the use of the Hoasca tea started in 1967 when Mestre Gabriel and José Rodrigues Sobrinho were called to provide an explanation to the authorities.[1] Soon thereafter, M. Monteiro, despite being a government employee, took legal action in order to defend the use of the Hoasca tea.[2] We then remained for a long time in the pending status determined by the chief of police from Porto Velho: the authorities could not prohibit but also could not authorize the sessions.

Spiritual authorization has always existed, given the benefit that the Vegetal provides to us. We have always had and experienced cases of rehabilitation, social integration, life improvement, and physical, psychological, material and spiritual equilibrium. In accordance with the Christian doctrine professed by the UDV, "a tree is known by its fruit." Judging by the fruits of this União, we are certain that this seed of goodness, planted by Mestre Gabriel, is yielding a tree with strong roots. Nonetheless we have had to work for many years, with the help of many people, to be recognized and legitimized by governmental authorities.

The process of the legalization of the Vegetal in Brasilia started when we received permission from the Juvenile Court on September 18, 1981, to have minors 14 years and older attend sessions at Núcleo Estrela do Norte. The commissioners of the

---

[1] This event is explained in the article "Convicção do Mestre" (Conviction of the Mestre), published in the Alto Madeira Newspaper, issued on October 6, 1967 (CEBUDV 1967) read in every Escala (scheduled) session of the UDV, which take place on the first and third Saturdays of every month. Due to this incident there was the need to register the UDV with the local authorities, and at that time the first Statute was also registered in 1968.

[2] This incident with M. Monteiro (Raimundo Monteiro de Souza) took place in 1970, when the Beneficent Association União do Vegetal was already registered. The chief of police of the Rondonia territory wanted to close down the União do Vegetal, and M. Monteiro, who was then the president of the Association, contacted the Court of the Federal District and of the Territories and, following legal counsel, composed a new Statute and changed the name to the present one: Centro Espírita Beneficente União do Vegetal. For more information see the article by Campos Soares and Moura, in this book.

court came to observe the session in order to inform the judge. We were mostly young people back then; however, the testimony of our brother Cesar Gonçalves carried much weight. He was a respected white-haired gentleman who gave support to our cause in his statements to the authorities, affirming the benefits he was receiving from the União do Vegetal. The permission was granted and we had the approval of public authorities. Nonetheless, on March 13, 1985, the DIMED - Brazilian National Health and Drug Administration-issued Ordinance 02/85, including the plants and the Vegetal on their list of proscribed substances.

We only became aware that the circulation of the plants and the tea made from them had been prohibited while filing a commonly required form of the Brazilian Internal Revenue Service, at the end of President Figueiredo's term (March 15, 1985).

To clarify, the DIMED had the legal duty to list the substances whose use had been proscribed in the country, for the purpose of criminal incidence, as provided for in the existing Narcotics Law at that time.

Once certain that we had indentified the source of the problem, we went to the Federal Police to request an explanation regarding the origin of the prohibition. Present were Edson Lodi, José Mauro Fagundes, Flávio Mesquita, Marcos Coutinho and myself, and we explained the beneficent work that was being conducted by the União do Vegetal. The Deputy Chief of the Repression Section heard us out, but affirmed that there was a law in effect that needed to be followed, and that if the law needed to be changed we needed to take the matter to the appropriate authorities. In other words, it was already prohibited so they were no longer able either to prohibit or to authorize.

As a precaution, the direction of the UDV decided to suspend the session activities at the Center for some time, for a few basic reasons: 1) to demonstrate respect for the law, within the principle of captivating the authorities, according to what was recommended by our Mestre Gabriel; 2) to demonstrate that the Hoasca tea does not cause dependency in anyone. We were criticized by some, but time proved the wisdom of that measure because this approach was seen by the authorities as a sign of our respect and generated, in them, a sense of urgency to provide a solution to the issue.

We then contacted the Federal Attorney General, Dr. Sepúlveda Pertence, who guided us to contact Dr. Técio Lins e Silva, recently appointed as the president of the Federal Narcotics Council, which had not yet had its members appointed.

When he was informed of the situation, Dr. Técio was surprised to learn of the prohibition, as he himself knew people who used the tea and they were all well-mannered people. He promised to find out what had happened.

At that time, the Beneficent Spiritist Center União do Vegetal was still organizing its Medical and Legal Departments, but there were people interested in defending our interests. The doctors who were members of the Center already were seeing the necessity of having studies conducted on the tea, and the topic had already been discussed at the Convention of the Direction of the Center in April of 1985.

When the tea was prohibited, we did not yet have studies on the tea, except for one study that was not very conclusive from Swedish researchers (Rivier and Lindgren 1972). But we had three things in our favor: 1) the word of Mestre Gabriel, that the tea was inoffensive to the health; 2) the evidence of so many people making use of the tea for so many years; 3) the legal certainty that we would not have to prove that the tea was good, but that the authorities would have to demonstrate that it wasn't, if they could.

On June 24, 1985, we submitted our petition to CONFEN requesting that they revise the prohibition, and urging them to examine the subject in its "sociological, chemical, pharmacological, anthropological, cultural and constitutional-legal aspects." This petition was accompanied by a statement from the medical doctor Edison Saraiva, dated June 14, 1985, which demonstrated that the prohibition was scientifically unfounded, citing the "complex pharmacology of the plant products in its totality as a decoction." The petition was also accompanied by a statement from the respected General Fidélis Chaves Silveira, who had always supported us, after seeing the extraordinary transformation that the União do Vegetal had brought about in his son, today Mestre José Mauro.

It is important to note the impact of the members of the Center in this effort, doctors and authorities who provided declarations and signed petitions in support of the União do Vegetal at a time when the Vegetal was banned, exposing themselves publically, for a common goal which was to assure our right to fully exercise our religious choice.

Soon thereafter, Dr. Técio Lins e Silva called to inform us that no study on the Hoasca tea was found in CONFEN's files. This gave us great tranquility, because it proved that DIMED's action of including the Vegetal on the list of proscribed substances was legally invalid because the due process was not followed. The protocol of due diligence, in this case the prior conference of the appropriate agency- the CONFEN, which is essential for such an action to be valid, had been neglected. DIMED had issued an action that was not based within the law.[3]

Consequently, there was a way to resolve the situation from a strictly legal perspective, as the evidence showed that the ordinance was invalid. But the DIMED not being able to prohibit was not enough, we needed recognition and authorization. Until then there had been no studies on the subject of the Hoasca tea, but now there would be.

Precisely because there were not yet any conclusive medical or scientific studies on the subject, we requested that the subject be examined in its sociological, chemical, pharmacological, anthropological, cultural and constitutional-legal aspects.

The British speak of the importance of the right person, at the right time, in the right place. Dr. Técio Lins e Silva was precisely this. His sensibility, humanistic understanding and legal insight, as well as that of Dr. Domingos Bernardo Sá, were fundamentally instrumental for our rights, not only human rights, but also sacred rights, to be secured.

When the members of CONFEN were appointed, its President issued a Resolution creating a Working Group and determining that the study of this subject take into consideration medical, sociological, anthropological, and general health aspects.[4] Consequently, any decision made by the CONFEN would need to be based not only on chemical aspects, but on all the other aspects considered fundamental for a decision to be in accordance with the main principle of Public Administration: attend to social interest, and balance principles of social order while safeguarding the right to freedom of worship. The decision on the subject was linked to the study of all of the aforementioned areas of scientific knowledge.

In Brazilian Administrative Law there are two types of legal action: discretionary and conditional. Discretionary acts are those adopted by the Public Administration

---

[3] The CONFEN Resolution No. 6, February 4, 1986, mentions this legal inconsistency of DIMED Ordinance 02/85, which included the mariri and the chacrona on the list of proscribed substances. The text of the Resolution reads: "Considering that through DIMED's Ordinance No. 02/85, the "Banisteriopsis caapi," referred to as "vine of chincrona or chacrona or mariri," was included on the list of proscribed products, it was, however, not in observance of the provision in the 1st paragraph of Article 3 of Decree No. 85,110, September 2, 1980, in that it was without the prior hearing of CONFEN, the agency responsible for policy guidance and technical supervision over the activities monitored by the Sistema Nacional Divisão de Prevenção, Fiscalização e Repressão de Entorpecentes (National System of Narcotics Prevention, Monitoring and Enforcement) (CONFEN Resolution no. 6)

[4] CONFEN's Resolution No. 04, July 30, 1985, instituted the Multidisciplinary Working Group (GMT) for the evaluation of the Vegetal in its multiple aspects. The GMT was composed of the following people: Dr. Antonio Carlos de Morais (vice president of CONFEN and president of the GMT), Dr. Suely Rozenfeld (DIMED), Professor Isac Germano Karniol (Associação Médica Brasileira- Brazilian Medical Association), Professor Sergio Dario Seibel (Ministry of Social Health and Welfare) and Dr. Paulo Magalhães Pinto (Dvisão de Repressão de Entorpecentes do Departamento da Policia Federal- Division of Narcotics Repression of the Federal Police)..

exercising the criteria of convenience and opportunity. The conditional acts, as the name implies, are dependent upon determining valid motives for their issuance, thus the requirement of a study on the medical, sociological, anthropological and general health aspects of the tea assured that only after a thorough assessment of all these aspects could a valid policy decision be made. The Public Administration was constrained to conduct the study of this subject according to the approach and presuppositions provided in the Resolution. This was already a great victory.

Furthermore, in the case of a prohibition or when any norm restricting rights is issued, it is a legal imperative that the motives and intentions of the said prohibition or restriction be stated, in order for the act to have validity. In the case of prohibiting the use of the Hoasca tea, this had not occurred. Moreover, by the rule of competence, it was CONFEN's responsibility to identify the substances of proscribed use in Brazil, and then forward it to DIMED for issuance. In other words, DIMED's responsibility was only to pronounce and it was CONFEN's responsibility to decide. This also was not done.

This being the case, Dr. Técio Lins e Silva, in the name of the truth, made sure that the Resolution stated that no study regarding the tea existed in the realm of CONFEN, which characterized the inclusion of the Hoasca tea in DIMED's list as invalid.[5] This alone would, at the least, secure for us the *writ of mandamus* for the defense of legal right and clear against any measure intended to hinder our spiritual work. We did have some localized problems with the authorities, specifically in Manaus, in the state of Amazonas, and Boa Vista, in the state of Roraima; nevertheless, we prevailed.

Remember that at that time there were no studies on the subject nor did the authorities have the knowledge that exists today. What we had was the prohibition, the prejudice from a large majority of society and a small number of people that believed in the cause they were defending.

There is a principle in law that is universal: the principle of Natural Law. According to this principle, that which is harmful must be combated and that which is beneficial must be liberated and encouraged. Within this premise, and within the word of the Mestre, we were certain that we had the key to our victory. We knew, as all of us who drink this tea know, of the benefit we have received for so many years.

---

[5] Resolution no 4, of July 30th, 1985, which instituted and designated the Working Group, affirms in the considerations that "there are no records at CONFEN about studies related to these plants" (CONFEN, Resolution No.4).

With the serene, prudent, firm and secure leadership of the General Representative Mestre, at that time, M. Monteiro, we joined together to work towards obtaining our victory: the liberation of the use of the Hoasca tea.

At the beginning of the activities of CONFEN's working group, we were faced with the determination, from some sectors, to uphold the ban of the tea, because, according to precautionary warnings from the federal police, a new synthetic drug could be created that could cause social harm. There was also the preoccupation of how the use of the tea would impact urban centers. As we know, there are people who, mistakenly, only see solutions to the ills of humanity in the criminal code and in repression. I thought about how small the possibility was, almost nonexistent, that these problems could occur.

It is important to note that in the wake of this concern of the authorities, a moment came when we received a direct communication from CONFEN representatives, that the ban would be maintained. This caused us to take action. After some considerations, we proposed that before any decision was made, visits should be made to the religious societies that used the tea, so that the reality of the rituals and its participants could become known. At that time there was also a change in the membership of the Working Group, a shift in the chairmanship took place, and Dr. Domingos Bernardo Sá, a renowned jurist, was appointed to preside over the group. The proposal for visitation was then accepted.[6]

A *"preparo"* (ritual preparation of the tea) was scheduled at Núcleo Pupuramanta in Rio de Janeiro, and the members of the Working Group went there to see what we were doing. They all participated in a session, along with the UDV members present, directed by M. Monteiro. The members of CONFEN were visibly impressed by the Christian principles and the doctrine of the União do Vegetal, and by the words and the life of Mestre Gabriel, as it was told to them. In addition to the visit to the UDV, they also visited other Hoasca groups.

Other studies by the Working Group followed and at several instances we were present to answer questions, provide information, and provide any type of assistance that could contribute toward a favorable solution of this matter.

It is also noteworthy that while the CONFEN was studying the Hoasca tea, there

---

[6] CONFEN's Resolution No. 7, July 9, 1986, altered the composition of the Working Group, replacing Dr. Antonio Carlos de Morais with Counselor at Law Domingos Bernardo Gialluisi da Silva Sá. Also this same Resolution included the following advisors in the Working Group: Francisco Cartaxo Rolin, João Manoel de Albuqerque Lins, João Romildo Bueno, Gilberto Alves Velho, Regina Maria do Rego Monteiro de Abreu and Clara Lúcia de Oliveira Inem.

were two people whose presentations before the Minister of Justice were important and decisive. Mestre Mario Piacentini and Mestre Cel. Eurico Pascoal, members of the UDV, went in person to give their testimony to Minister Oscar Dias Correa, then Minister of Justice.[7, 8]

Consequently, we received a favorable opinion from CONFEN, first with the reports from Dr. Isac Germano Karniol and Dr. Segio Dario Seibel, in the Working Group presided over by Dr. Domingos Bernardo G. de Sá, and later with the confirmation of the liberation, contained in the report from Dr. Domingos Bernardo himself, based on the statement from Prof. Carlini, assuring the constitutional right to freedom of belief, with the liberation of the Hoasca tea.[9]

This subject was addressed several more times by CONFEN, and the liberation became definitive, but the compositions of the government and of the CONFEN changed and so our struggle continued.[10]

What is certain is that good spiritual orientation, a just cause, the force of the União, a firmly defined objective and much dedication were, and are, the pillars in the building of our victory.

---

[7] Mario Piacentini (1916-2009), founding member of Núcleo Samaúma, the first núcleo of the União do Vegetal outside of the north region of Brazil in 1972 (CEBUDV 2006).

[8] Eurico Pascoal, deceased, was a colonel of the military police in the state of Minas Gerais. He became the president of the Military Justice Court of the state of Minas Gerais, which has honored him by naming the Cadeira 16 of the Academia Mineira de Direito Militar do Estado de Minas Gerais (Minas Gerais State Military Law Academy) after him (each core requirement of the law degree is named after a historical figure). See page 13 in http://www.tjmmg.jus.br/images/stories/downloads/academia/amdm.pdf. In the UDV, Eurico Pascoal as a member of the Cadre of Mestres. He was also a founding member, along with Mario Piacentini, of Núcleo Rainha das Aguas, in Caldas (Minas Gerais).

[9] Eliseo Araujo Carlini, medical doctor and retired professor of psychopharmacology of the Escola Paulista de Medicina – UNIFESP (Sao Paulo Medical School), member of the Brazilian Academy of Sciences. See <http://www.abc.org.br/~ecarlini>.

[10] The text of Machado, in this book, explains the continuation of the fight for the religious rights of the CEBUDV.

Bibliography

CEBUDV – Centro Espirita Beneficente Uniao Do Vegetal. "Convicção do Mestre." *Jornal Alto Madeira,* Porto Velho, Rondônia, edição de 6 de outubro, 1967.

CEBUDV – Centro Espirita Beneficente Uniao Do Vegetal. "90 anos, Mestre Mário: o homem com uma estrela no coração." *Jornal Alto Falante* (edição comemorativa). Brasília: Sede Geral, edição de 4 de abril, 2006.

CONFEN – Conselho Federal De Entorpecentes. *Resolução n. 04, 30 de julho de 1985.* Brasília: Diário Oficial da União, Poder Executivo, 5 fevereiro, Seção I, p. 2054, 1985.

CONFEN – Conselho Federal De Entorpecentes. *Resolução n. 06, 4 de fevereiro de 1986.* Brasília: Diário Oficial da União, Poder Executivo, 10 julho, Seção II, p. 3568, 1985.

DIMED – Divisão Nacional de Vigilâncial Sanitária de Medicamentos. *Portaria n. 02, 8 de março de 1995.* Brasília: Diário Oficial da União, Poder Executivo, 13 de março, Seção I, pp. 4421-4434, 1985.

Rivier, Laurent and Lindgren, Jan-Erik. "Ayahuasca, the South American hallucino genic drink: an ethno-botanical and chemical investigation." *Economic Botanic,* vol. 26, p. 101-129, 1972.

The UDV Action Before CONFEN and CONAD

Marisa Mendes Machado

The minutes of the 5th Ordinary Meeting of the Brazilian Federal Narcotics Council (CONFEN), approving the opinion of the council's advisor, Domingos Bernardo Gialluisi da Silva Sá, of June 2, 1992 (SÁ, 1992), were published in the Official Registry of Brazil on August 24, 1992. The opinion reiterated the final report of the activities developed by the Working Group created by CONFEN Resolution no. 4, which contained, among other recommendations, that the tea and the plants from which it is composed remain excluded from the country's lists of proscribed substances and that the re-examination of this matter should only take place in the event of new facts.

Despite this, three years later on August 11, 1995, a new CONFEN resolution was published in the Official Registry of Brazil, which unfortunately was restrictive. The council had approved the declaration of one its members, José Costa Sobrinho, recommending the prohibition of the use of the tea by minors.

This declaration was in response to a petition sent by "Mrs. Alicia Castillo, requesting that measures be taken with regard to the Santo Daime sect, related to her daughter Veronica Castillo Jamil" (Sobrinho 1995). As a result of that petition, the process of examining the use of Hoasca tea was re-opened. We verified that the complaint, made by a distressed mother, was indeed the cause of CONFEN's restriction of the use of the Hoasca tea by minors. The decision was not preceded by any substantiation, investigation, research or survey regarding minors who use the tea. The decision, contained in the minutes of an ordinary meeting of CONFEN that took place on August 11, 1995, was based solely on the opinion of Mr. José Costa Sobrinho, an advisor to the Council:

> It is recommended that the use of the tea by minors be prohibited, considering that they are in a phase of development and structuring of their personalities, with consequent limitation to their capacity for discernment, and also

considering the Statute of the Child and Adolescent, specific legislation that guarantees their rights.

Quickly the repercussions of this opinion, approved as a resolution of CONFEN without any scientific basis, began to be felt. In the following months, the regular operation of the UDV was affected by this restrictive decision. The legal team of the UDV had to take action in juvenile courts in the cities of Boa Vista, Roraima; São Roque, São Paulo; Joaçaba, Santa Catarina; and Ilhéus, Bahia.

It became necessary for the UDV Legal Department to take continuous action to defend the Center before the CONFEN. Eventually, in 1996, the UDV presented a petition requesting that the Council re-examine the matter through adequate studies of the use of the tea by minors who are children of the members of the institution. We requested that the restrictive resolution be modified and we presented proposals. These proposals were in alignment with the practices of the UDV, which traditionally watches over and cares for its children and youth. We formalized the recommendation for parents and guardians to accompany minors attending sessions. Also, guidelines were made explicit with respect to the frequency of ingestion and the quantity ingested, always paying attention to the minor's age.

The UDV's petition was added to the CONFEN's agenda. In prior conversations with the members of the council, a perceptible tendency to not attend to the UDV petition was noticed. Then something happened that is noteworthy: when the time arrived on the agenda for the matter to be addressed, the president of CONFEN at that time, Mr. Mathias Flach, had to leave and turned the chairmanship of the meeting over to the vice-president, Dr. Domingos Bernardo Sá. Besides being a renowned jurist, Mr. Bernardo Sá is aware of the struggle for the recognition of the sacred right of the religious use of the Vegetal, a right that clearly is also extended to minors for them to follow their parents' religion. I was witness to the clarity with which Mr. Bernardo Sá positioned himself regarding this matter. Some council members questioned the necessity for the re-examination of the matter, since to them, the opinion of Mr. José Costa Sobrinho was sufficient. Mr. Bernardo Sá firmly defended the UDV petition for re-examination and Mr. José Costa Sobrinho was appointed to be the record keeper of the reopened case. Later Arnaldo Madruga Fernandes replaced Sobrinho as record keeper.

The process of clarification continued for months as we presented our statements, much documentation, and the studies that had been conducted. We provided the necessary access so that the adolescents of the UDV could be studied, interviewed and evaluated. The president of the UDV at that time, Edison Saraiva Neves, and the General Representative Mestre, Mestre Raimundo Monteiro, placed themselves at the disposition of the authorities, demonstrating transparency in the organization and in the operations of the UDV.

Despite all of our cooperative efforts, on July 8, 1997, a new determination was published in the National Official Registry of Brazil, restricting the use of the Hoasca tea by minors. The opinion of Mr. Arnaldo Madruga Fernandes recommended, "that the use of the tea called Ayahuasca by minors under 18 (eighteen) years of age be avoided, even if accompanied by parents or guardians, regardless of dosage or ceremony" (CONFEN, July 8, 1997).

There was no scientific foundation or any specific research backing up this decision of the CONFEN. Once again the council had approved the opinion of an advisor, Arnaldo Madruga Fernandes.

Why?

The CONFEN records contained a query by the judge of the Juvenile Court in Boa Vista, Roraima. The judge wanted to know if the "CONFEN proscribed the substances *Banisteriopsis caapi* and *Psychotria viridis*" (Process CONFEN no. 08000.017948/96-21). The answer was negative. The second question had the objective of finding out if "there was a working group responsible for studying these plants and any possible harmful effect caused when ingested by adolescents" (Process CONFEN no. 08000.017948/96-21). The answer was: "CONFEN had established a commission for the study of this matter (Process CONFEN no. 08000.017948/96-21), and later disbanded it, because issues of greater importance had priority at that moment" (CONFEN, July 8, 1997).

Twice, therefore, this serious matter was decided upon by the Federal Justice Department without any prior investigation, study or research. Furthermore, this federal agency explicitly admitted to not considering this matter to be important.

The UDV proceeded by petitioning the Federal Justice Department to institute a civil investigation "for the purpose of recommending to CONFEN what is established in the law, in the best interest of guaranteeing the fundamental right to freedom of religious practice, family integration and the right of children and adolescents whose parents are followers of the UDV" (MPF Process no. 08100.004392/97-84).

A petition was also presented to CONFEN, demonstrating the illegality of the restriction and informing the agency of the petition that was sent to the Federal Attorney General for Citizen's Rights.

One more noteworthy item regarding the role of Mr. Domingos Bernardo de Sá must be added. He was not present at the CONFEN meeting when the opinion of Mr. Arnaldo Madruga was approved. However at the next meeting he expressed his opposition to the deliberation. The entire content of his words of opposition was added to the record and we were able to see that he vehemently rose up against what he considered an arbitrary decision, an "undue and forceful intervention by the State into the framework of family relationships."

A few years went by until the solution arrived.

In 1998, CONFEN, which was an agency of the Brazilian Justice Department, was extinguished. On June 19 of the same year the National Anti-Drug Council (CONAD) was created, along with its executive secretariat, the National Anti-Drug Secretariat (SENAD). The CONAD is an agency of the Department of Institutional Security of the National Presidency. The first president of the CONAD was the Chief-Minister of the Department of Institutional Security of the National Presidency, General Alberto Mendes Cardoso. The first secretary of the SENAD was Dr. Walter Maierovich.

We started our work with the CONAD and SENAD requesting a legal certificate validating CONFEN's decision to exclude the Hoasca tea and the plants from the proscribed substance list. There was no answer. The alleged reason was that for many months all the documents and materials related to the Hoasca tea that came from the extinct CONFEN in 40 sealed boxes had remained closed. The presence of the UDV's legal department became constant at the new CONAD/SENAD offices.

When CONFEN was replaced by CONAD/SENAD, the issue of minors was still pending. No study or research had yet taken place. This was the reason why, in 1999, the UDV accepted the request from the University of California (UCLA) to conduct a scientific study to examine the profile of minors who use the Hoasca tea within the União do Vegetal.[1] We presented UCLA's research protocol to the Department of Justice and to CONAD, and requested that both departments accompany this study. Meanwhile, the Federal Attorney General for Citizen's Rights case was still in process. There was no response on the part of CONAD or the Attorney General's office regarding the study, but the UDV did its part: we informed them on each development phase of the study, through to the final favorable result.

Our interaction with the CONAD and SENAD, since the beginning, has been

---

[1] This research protocol was the origin of the Ayahuasca in Adolescence Study published in this book.

carried out with the usual approach of cooperation with the legal authorities. In November 1998, the UDV participated in the 1st National Anti-Drug Forum organized by SENAD, and also in the 2nd National Anti-Drug Forum in November 2001.[2] Both events engaged Brazilian public authorities and civil society with the objective of establishing a national anti-drug policy. The UDV was present at both events representing our institution within the Religious Institutions Subgroup. The UDV was the only Hoasca society that was officially present at both occasions. I was present at the 1st Forum, representing the UDV, along with Ruy Fabiano, a journalist and member of the UDV who was at that time the coordinator of the Religious Institutions Subgroup. Mr. Fabiano was invited to be a part of the 1st Forum's organizational team and later chosen to coordinate the Subgroup composed of many institutions that also use the tea. The secretary at that time, Walter Maierovich, and Minister Alberto Cardoso himself, were particularly attentive to the work being developed within the Religious Institutions Subgroup. The coordinator, Mr. Fabiano, maintained both of them abreast of the developments and he introduced me to SENAD's Secretary, who wanted to discuss the religious use of the Hoasca tea.

It is important to mention that in addition to me (Marisa Mendes Machado) and Mr. Ruy Fabiano, more than 70 UDV members were present, participating in other Subgroups, who had traveled from various regions of Brazil: educators, jurists, journalists, doctors, and other professionals. I can affirm that the UDV made a significant contribution to the 1st National Anti-Drug Forum.

We also collaborated with the National Anti-Drug Council and with SENAD in the Hoasca tea regulation process in order to establish appropriate controls for the use of the tea, to prevent abuse and irregularities.

I consider it noteworthy that the UDV has always presented itself institutionally before the authorities, and before society as a whole, defending the responsible use of the Hoasca tea within a religious context. SENAD's secretary, General Paulo Roberto Uchôa, demonstrated his commitment when he expressed a special interest in including the community of sacramental tea users.[3] During that time, I witnessed him stating this interest several times with the UDV's Coordinator of Institutional Relations, Mr. Edson Lodi, the UDV's President, Mr. James Allen, and the General Representative Mestre of the UDV, Mestre José Luiz de Oliveira. Federal Congressman João Magno also gave us his support.

---

[2] Both forums took place in the city of Brasilia.

[3] Paulo Roberto Uchôa, General of the Brazilian Army Division, was appointed secretary of SENAD in late 2001.

The government has always been able to count on the UDV's participation in relations with other religious communities that use the tea. The UDV has historically cooperated with the SENAD in order to facilitate closer contact with these societies. The UDV gave significant support when the SENAD proposed to do a survey, through a questionnaire, to acquire information on these societies. Members of the UDV acted as the interface necessary to establish contact between the Public Authorities and the leadership of these groups who use the tea religiously. We supported and collaborated at meetings with these leaders in Acre and in Brasilia, with the presence of the SENAD's secretary and other authorities. The agenda of the meetings was the shared commitment to the responsible use of the tea in order to acquire greater legal security.

What is the objective of the UDV in facilitating government regulation of the use of the tea? The answer is: greater legal and institutional security in the religious use of the Vegetal.

This long history of struggle and cooperation with the authorities, which also include other incidents not mentioned here, had a consequence: it kept the issue of minors on the agenda of matters to be better defined by the National Anti-Drug Council, until August 17, 2004, when CONAD's entire council approved the opinion of its Technical and Scientific Advisory Council, recognizing the legitimacy of the religious use of Ayahuasca.

This thorough opinion deserves to be known and studied. Its content covers the entire history of the legalization process for the religious use of the Hoasca tea in Brazil. It is based on the Federal Constitution, the Civil Code, the Convention on Children's Rights, and on the decisions of CONFEN that excluded the tea and its plants from the list of proscribed substances.

The opinion was approved and issued by CONFEN in Resolution No. 5 on November 4, 2004, and published in the Official Registry of Brazil on November 10, 2004.

Resolution No. 5 declared the following about the issue of minors: "the participation in the religious use of Ayahuasca (…) shall remain within the parents' criteria, in the appropriate exercise of family rights." Finally, a definitive pronouncement had come from the Public Authorities regarding the legality of the use of the Vegetal by our children and adolescents.

Resolution No. 5/2004 constitutes one more victory in the long struggle for legalization of the religious use of the Vegetal. It states that "the administrative and social control of the religious use of Ayahuasca can only be adequately structured with the inclusion of the knowledge accumulated by the groups that use the tea (...), therefore the Multidisciplinary Working Group has been instituted."

This Multidisciplinary Working Group had the following objectives: to promote the national registering of all institutions that use the tea religiously, to conduct a survey and accompany the religious use of Ayahuasca, as well as to experimentally research its therapeutic use. The Group must also establish a preventive plan of action to avoid the inappropriate use of the tea.

The Beneficent Spiritist Center União do Vegetal has been present and active in this endeavor. We continued cooperating with the authorities, working toward well being for all. Representing our institution we had Edson Lodi, the UDV's Coordinator of Institutional Relations, as the vice-president of the Multidisciplinary Working Group.

After many months of work, on November 23, 2006, the Multidisciplinary Working Group presented its final report, detailing important aspects of the responsible use of the Hoasca tea.[4] The Group affirms and sanctions the exclusively religious use of the tea, non-commercialization, production sustainability, and non-publicity. In addition, the therapeutic use of the tea shall only be permitted in the case of duly accredited professionals and for scientific research. The procedures for the admission of new members and use by minors and pregnant women are to be defined. In the case of pregnant women the responsibility lies with the women themselves.

In regard to minors, the main topic of this text, the Multidisciplinary Working Group stated the following in its final report:

> In light of the lack of sufficient scientific evidence and taking into account the secular use of Ayahuasca, which showed no adverse health effects, and the terms of the CONAD Resolution 05/2004, the use of Ayahuasca by minors (under 18 years of age) shall remain subject to the approval of the parents or guardians, in the appropriate exercise of their parental rights (Article 1634 of the Civil Code). (GMT Report/Resolution CONAD no. 5/2004)

Here we have the record of yet another victory.

---

[4] This report was published in the Official Registry of Brazil on January 26, 2010. See CONAD, Resolution No. 1.

Bibliography

CONAD – Conselho Nacional Anti-Drogas. Resolução n. 5, *de 4 de novembro de 2004*. Brasília: Diário Oficial da União, Poder Executivo, 8 de novembro de 2004, Seção I, p. 8, 2004.

CONAD – Conselho Nacional Anti-Drogas. Resolução n. 1, de 25 de janeiro de 2010. Brasília: Diário Oficial da União, Poder Executivo, 26 de janeiro de 2010, Seção I, p. 57-60, 2010.

CONAD – CATC. Câmara de Assessoramento Técnico e Científico sobre o uso religioso da ayahuasca, 17 de agosto, 2004.

CONFEN – Conselho Federal De Entorpecentes. Resolução n. 04, 30 de julho de 1985. Brasília: Diário Oficial da União, Poder Executivo, 8 de agosto, Seção I, p. 11397, 1985.

CONFEN – Conselho Federal De Entorpecentes. *Relatório Final*. Brasília: Grupo de Trabalho sobre Uso Religioso da Ayahausca, 1987.

CONFEN – Conselho Federal De Entorpecentes. Ata da 5a Reunião Ordinária do Conselho Federal de Entorpecentes, realizada em 2 de junho de 1992. Brasília: Diário Oficial da União, Poder Executivo, 24 de agosto, Seção I, p. 11467, 1992.

CONFEN – Conselho Federal De Entorpecentes. Ata da 3a Reunião Ordinária do Conselho Federal de Entorpecentes, realizada em 2 de junho de 1995. Brasília: Diário Oficial da União, Poder Executivo, 11 de agosto, Seção I, p. 12121, 1995.

CONFEN – Conselho Federal De Entorpecentes. Ata da 3a Reunião Ordinária do Conselho Federal de Entorpecentes – em conjunto com o Conselho Estadual de Entorpecentes de Alagoas, realizada em 16 de maio de 1997. Brasília: Diário Oficial da União, Poder Executivo, 8 de julho, Seção I, p. 14299, 1997.

Sa, Domingos Bernardo Gialluisi da Silva. *Findings*. Brasília: Ministério da Justiça; Conselho Federal de Entorpecentes, 2 de julho, 1992.

20: The UDV Overseas

The Struggle for the Religious Freedom of the UDV in the United States of America

Jeffrey Bronfman

Respected members of the General Representation of the UDV, mestres, counselors, disciples and distinguished guests; it is with a sense of honor and gratitude that I stand before you today to speak some of my experience representing the União do Vegetal in the United States where I reside. A lot has happened over the course of my life (particularly over the past 9 years) that brings me to this moment as a speaker, and participant at this Congress presenting the UDV and its people.

What I have been asked to share with you today specifically relates to a truly historic accomplishment in the area of law and civil liberties, resulting from a legal action that positioned our religion against the full power and authority of the Federal Government of the United States. An authority that was, at that time, arguably, the wealthiest, most influential, politically powerful nation on this earth.

In an article published in 2004, Jose Augusto Padua (a professor of political history at the Federal University of Rio de Janeiro, and former director of Greenpeace International here in Brazil) described this challenge as "a true struggle of David against Goliath - with the UDV having won at all the stages of the confrontation acting with notable competence, seriousness and confidence in its rights as well as in the honesty of its purpose".

I wish to share with you today some of how I experienced these events as a disciple of the UDV who found himself at the center of this great social political, legal (as well as personal/spiritual) challenge.

Upon the request of the organizers of this event I have brought with me Dr John Boyd who, over the 9 years that I have known him professionally, has become a trusted personal friend and who was an essential part of the team of lawyers and experts that assisted and has represented the UDV in this legal action.

Mr. Boyd is a senior partner in the law firm of Freedman, Boyd, Hollander Goldberg and Ives in Albuquerque, New Mexico. He graduated with highest honors from the Law School of The University of New Mexico in 1973, and has practiced civil litigation in the United States for 35 years. His specialties include civil rights law particularly related to issues involving freedom of religion, freedom of the press, and freedom of speech where he (for more than 12 years) has been listed as one of the "best lawyers in America".

Mr. Boyd will be speaking as scholar in the area of law discussing the details of our legal action against the Government of the United States from his perspective as a lawyer (and representative of the US legal system) who is not a member of the UDV. I will be following, speaking a little bit about our case from a more sociological and spiritual perspective, as member of this religious society. Subsequently I will informally interview John to bring out some additional points that I believe you may find to be of interest. We hope to allow time for a few questions from the floor as well.

Beginning on that memorable afternoon of May 21st, 1999 (when agents of the United States Customs service and Federal Bureau of Investigation conducted a raid on my personal office - which also served as the administrative offices of the UDV) - a new era of my life began. It has been a period of profound learning about the abuses and just application of governmental power, and the nature of the higher laws and spiritual forces that truly conduct our lives. Through this process I have learned much about the power of the word, of friendship and of the goodness that comes to many - when a few unite in peace, in faith and in service to a Higher Power.

Subsequent to the Drug Enforcement action against the UDV back in 1999 I wrote a letter to the authorities representing the United States Department of Justice in the area of Criminal Prosecution (and the Division of Dangerous Drugs) introducing myself and the UDV and pledging our full cooperation in the institutional investigation of our religion. In the letter I submitted I said-

> *On Friday the 21st of May, the US Customs Service arranged for the delivery and then seizure of a shipment of tea made from two plants indigenous to the Brazilian Amazon. This tea is a sacrament fundamental and essential to the religion that I follow, the União do Vegetal. The effect of the use of this tea, within our rituals, is increased mental clarity and inner peace. Our members are kind, humble people, working for the good, developing virtues and living under the symbol of our union which is Light, Peace and Love.*
>
> *We seek a relationship of mutual understanding, cooperation and peace with your office. I offer to you, as representatives sworn to uphold the constitution of*

this country, my commitment - in any way I can - to help you understand my religion and the sacred, mysterious tea that we use in our communion. I am at your service, along with our church leadership in Brazil and the United States, to answer any and all questions in this regard.

Eighteen months later, when our efforts to reach an accommodation with these officials (and thereby avoid an extended court battle) were largely ignored I presented myself and the UDV to the Federal Justice System in the following way, through our initial court filing:

I consider it an honor and privilege to be in the position of introducing my religion o the government and people of the United States. I see the UDV as a Light in this world, bringing wisdom, understanding, hope, comfort and peace into the lives of its practitioners. The UDV was reestablished on this earth in a time and place of great suffering, and poverty. It appeared among people who lived in near slavery in almost unimaginably harsh and difficult living conditions in Brazil in the 1950's. Today its goodness has reached the society of the greatest influence and political power in the world, a country of unprecedented material and technological accomplishment.

The bringing of this institution of goodness and spiritual wisdom into our society has been conducted with great care, respect and humility. It is because I have believed and trusted in the noble principles on which this country was founded that I have accepted this mission under substantial personal strain, and considerable legal risk. I have done so because I believe in the beauty and truth of this religious practice, and the good it can bring to our country and to the world.

Sadly, despite the UDV's efforts to realize a cooperative, respectful relationship with the constituted authorities in the United States, representatives of the United States Department of Justice have taken an aggressive, hostile, deceptive approach to combating the UDV's request for religious accommodation in the United States Courts. In the process there has been produced a public legal record of thousands of pages of transcripts, scientific research studies and expert testimony over a period of now almost 10 years since the case first began.

As Mr. Boyd has explained, the UDV's notable success before the Federal Courts in the United States has been a result of the excellent legal representation we have received, and the founding principles of American jurisprudence which protect religious liberty as the most fundamental of basic human rights. It is also, as I would submit to you today, a consequence of the integrity of our membership, and our fidelity in following the doctrine which is the foundation of our religious faith.

In recreating the UDV in the Amazon Forests between Brazil and Bolivia in 1961 Mestre Gabriel established his religious work based upon certain principles, through which we aspired to conduct ourselves in all of communications with, and responses to, the constituted authorities of our country.

The principles of transparency, respect for the law and responsibility with the distribution of our sacrament were evidenced in the initial correspondences and efforts to negotiate a peaceful settlement I have already cited. The foundation of the UDV's teachings related to the importance of honesty and integrity within our use of our word, was subsequently a guiding principle in every legal document that we prepared.

It is important to note that the sincerity of the UDV's members was never questioned in court by the United States Government. This fact was further evidenced over a period of 5 and half years (while we awaited a court order granting us the legal right to exercise our faith) where we still met once or twice a month at our places of worship, without the use of our sacrament. In these same places where we had once received Holy Communion with God through Hoasca, we conducted our same rituals drinking only water - the basis of not only our own existence, but in reality, of all life.

Water, of course, is also the element within which our sacrament is ritually prepared. It is in water, we are taught, that the sacred plants are united and known to release their mysteries. It is in water, as well, where we are baptized, reborn and renewed.

In Santa Fe, New Mexico (actually an area of desert in the Southwest United States) where I reside, some of our disciples travel as much as four or five hours by car to be able to attend our ceremonies. Almost all of our members continued to do this for five and a half years without being permitted to use the vegetal; clearly demonstrating the value of our religious faith to our personal lives, and the fact that we were in no way addicted or harmed by our prior use of Hoasca.

To the contrary, since the time that our religious rights were restored by the United States Supreme Court, our members have enjoyed greater health, happiness and well being through the use of this sacred, life transforming tea.

Our Núcleo, in the city where I reside, had received the name of Núcleo Santa Fe within the União do Vegetal. The force of this name, and who we were as disciples before it, was both a challenge as well as a source comfort for us during the five and a half years where we came together and drank only water.

We kept this faith alive however by working with what we had. We still had the documents and laws of the UDV, which are read at the beginning of every session. We still had the teachings and the doctrine that had been brought by Mestre Gabriel and brought to our country by the Mestres he had instructed in the continuation of his sacred work.

Through these teachings we had learned that within the faithful practice and constancy within our duties that we would be free from all dangers. We had the dates within in our religious calendar that commemorated important moments in our Mestre's life that were occasions to come together. We also had one another, and the important friendships and relationships that we had established with our guides and teachers here in Brazil.

Perhaps more than anything else, we gratefully had this structure, securely established in this country, where those of us who were able to could visit once or twice a year, in order to receive the communion of our religion and renew ourselves within this fraternity.

When our Mestre Gabriel was still incarnate, there was an incident where he was briefly imprisoned by the local authorities in Porto Velho for conducting religious works with the Vegetal. At the time, after being placed in liberty, the Mestre advised all of those who wanted to accompany him in His mission, of how we needed to conduct ourselves - in Light, in Peace and Love. It was these words, repeated in sessions of the UDV ever since, that guided our conduct in the United States. As we have translated them within our documents, the Mestre said:

"We might be censured by all, but we cannot censure anyone; we might have enemies, but we cannot be anyone's enemy; we might be offended by all but we cannot offend anyone; we might be judged by all, but we cannot judge anyone; we might be revolted by everyone, but we cannot revolt nor be revolted by anyone."

This counsel, from our spiritual guide, served as a reference to us in every document we submitted to the U.S. Courts for their evaluation. Every word, presented by our lawyers, was carefully evaluated to be sure that it was true and correct within our Mestre's Doctrine; a doctrine that instructs us with respect to the right use, and subsequent effect of our word.

So through this process we have learned a lot about ourselves, about faith, about trust, and about how good can triumph over evil, with Light Peace and Love. We have learned that the principles upon which this religion was established are true, and that the one whose word we follow was truly a man of peace, a man of wisdom and a man of God.

It is, as I said in my opening statement, a privilege for me to be standing before you today. It is my sincere wish, for the disciples of this União that our example in the United States could serve as a source of inspiration and faith to you of the talent and authority of the guide that we are following. It is also my wish that the Brazilian Authorities present here today can also, through our example, perhaps realize the cultural treasure of the legacy of Jose Gabriel da Costa, and the way he instructed us in how to work with this sacred tea within the União do Vegetal.

The Legal Victory of the UDV in the United States Supreme Court: A Personal Statement

John Boyd

On May 21st, 1999, Jeffrey Bronfman contacted my law partner to ask her to defend the UDV against charges of unlawful trafficking in a controlled substance, Hoasca. At that time, Mr. Bronfman was in the front of establishing União Do Vegetal in the United States.

Agents of the Drug Enforcement Administration and other agents of the United States Government had just raided the UDV's offices in Santa Fe. They had executed a warrant to seize the UDV sacramental *Hoasca*, and any other evidence relating to UDV's allegedly unlawful conduct. They not only seized UDV's Hoasca, they seized all of UDV's documents and computers.

My partner, Nancy Hollander, or I had ever heard of the UDV or Jeffrey Bronfman or any of the other members of UDV whom we have had the privilege of representing now for nine years. It has been an extraordinary legal journey. I have no doubt that it has been a painful, but thus far triumphant personal journey for Jeffrey and the other members of UDV.

My law partner, Nancy Hollander, had made a career out of representing people accused of serious crimes. Over the twenty-five years of my practice, I had often represented clients needing to assert their rights under the First Amendment to the United States Constitution. That Amendment protects free speech, forbids the government from establishing religion and protects the right to the free exercise of their religions.

When Nancy and I met with Jeffrey and other members of the UDV, we learned about the history of UDV, its beliefs, and the role of *Hoasca* in the UDV faith. The government's position, at first, was that these were simply people who were engaged in clear and repeated violations of the Controlled Substances Act, which, among many other things, forbids any possession of dimethyltriptamine, a naturally-occurring chemical found in one of the plants that are brewed to make Hoasca.

Nancy Hollander and I spent the next few months attempting to persuade the prosecutor's office that this was not a situation that merited criminal prosecution; that these were people who were practicing their religion legitimately; that this religion was entitled to the respect of the government, not harassment and prosecution. It is fair to say that the lawyers within the Department of Justice who became involved ranged from dismissive and hostile to bewildered. None of them, however, took the view that the UDV was a legitimate religion, that its use of *Hoasca* should be protected and respected. Some took the view that the UDV's members should be prosecuted and imprisoned. Others expressed the view that the UDV's members were simply misguided amateurs who should not be prosecuted so long as they agreed never to possess or use Hoasca again.

Thus the UDV and its lawyers were left in a state of uncertainty, but it was a state of uncertainty that could have no happy outcome if it remained. UDV's members might be prosecuted even if they never practiced their religion again. On the other hand, they would certainly be prosecuted if they again practiced their religion. Either way, the power of the United States Government would be devoted to making sure that UDV's adherents never practiced their religion again. The government's view was that there would be no religious exception made for UDV's use of *Hoasca*. As the representative of our government argued seven years later in the Supreme Court, "not one drop" should be tolerated.

Our "First Amendment" to the United States Constitution protects freedom of speech and freedom of religion, including protection of the "free exercise" of religion. Of course, throwing virgins into a volcano would not find protection under this amendment. On the other hand, taking a day out of school to attend an annual religious ritual would of course be protected. The question for all of us - the members of UDV, Nancy and me, and the prosecutors – was where does the use of *Hoasca* fall within this range? Is it protected by the amendment or not?

Another certainty is that if you are in a disagreement with a prosecutor over whether your conduct is lawful or not, the prosecutor has the advantage. He holds the keys to the prison and the believer whose religious exercise is challenged holds nothing but his or her belief.

Fortunately, a few years before these events, the United States Congress had passed a law called "The Religious Freedom Restoration Act." This act laid out a procedure under which a group such as the members of the UDV could go to court to determine whether their conduct should or should not be legally exempt, under principles of the free exercise of religion, from laws that could be used to suppress particular religious conduct. Congress' intent in passing the law was to prescribe a manner in which federal courts must address any claim that the government is unlawfully interfering with a person's right to his or her free exercise of religion.

Under this Act, the religious adherent must first establish that the government is imposing a burden on the person's free exercise of religion. In this case, that was easy for the UDV to show. The government was threatening to throw UDV's members in prison for many years if they dared to follow their religious beliefs by taking the *Hoasca* sacrament. It was, in fact, almost a medieval choice: give up your religion or go to the dungeon.

Under the Religious Freedom Restoration Act, once a person shows that the government has burdened his or her sincere exercise of a genuine religion, the government must carry a double burden. First, the government must show that the burden serves a compelling governmental interest. Courts have held that a "compelling interest" is an interest of the "highest order." Second, it must show that there is no less restrictive a means by which the government's compelling interest may be served. Applying those principles to the UDV, once the UDV showed the Court that its religious exercised was burdened by the Controlled Substances Act and the government's threat of prosecution, the government would be required to prove not only that applying the controlled substances act to the UDV served a compelling governmental interest, but that the government's interest could not be served by some less restrictive means that would permit the UDV to practice its religion without compromising the compelling interest that the government claims.

A key to understanding this act is that it is not enough for the government to show that it has a general interest in suppressing the use of non-prescription "drugs." Instead, the government must demonstrate that it has a compelling interest in suppressing UDV's use of *Hoasca*.

On November 21, 2000, we filed suit under the Religious Freedom Restoration Act, alleging that the government was unlawfully interfering with UDV's member's right to the free exercise of their religion.

After having investigated the UDV for many months, the government knew that it had no good faith basis to argue that UDV was not a genuine religion or that its members were not burdened by the threat of imprisonment. Once the government made those concessions, the burden was on the government to prove its compelling interests, if any. It offered three. First, it argued that it had a compelling interest in protecting the health and safety of the members of the UDV by preventing them from drinking *Hoasca*. Second, it argued that it had a compelling interest in eliminating the risk that Hoasca might be diverted to recreational use. Third, it argued that it had a compelling interest in adhering to the 1971 Convention on Psychotropic Substances which, according to the government, forbade the United States from permitting any importation of *Hoasca*. After it failed to prove that any of these concerns were real, it alleged a fourth compelling interest; the need for uniform application of the Controlled Substances Act to all persons.

Under the procedures of American courts, cases can take years to be resolved. When a plaintiff is seeking to obtain a court order forbidding someone else from doing something that will harm the plaintiff, the procedures permit the Court to act at the beginning of the case to prevent the harmful conduct if the court feels that the plaintiff is likely to prevail at the end of the case. This is called a "preliminary injunction."

We filed suit and moved for a preliminary injunction. The federal court held a hearing that lasted two weeks, during which both sides called witnesses to support their position. The testimony was for the most part from experts for the UDV and experts for the government who provided their views regarding the health and safety issue and the "risk of diversion" issue.

After the judge heard the two weeks of testimony, he ruled that the government had failed to show that there was any risk to the UDV members' health and safety and ruled that the government had failed to show that there was any likelihood that UDV's *Hoasca* would be diverted to recreational use. In short, there was no evidence of any significant health risk and the evidence showed that UDV was careful to protect its sacrament and that it was in any event very unlikely that anyone would be interested in taking it for recreational purposes. I believe it is fair to say that it meant a great deal to the trial judge that UDV is well-established and well-respected in its home country of Brazil. Without this legitimacy, I believe the outcome of the case might well have been different. A highpoint of the hearing was the testimony of Mestre Jose Luis de Oliveira, including his colloquy with Judge Parker, a religious man, regarding the Christian beliefs of the UDV.

After the judge entered a preliminary injunction against interference with the UDV's religious use of Hoasca, the government immediately appealed to the regional court of appeals that sits in Denver, Colorado. The government also immediately sought and obtained a stay of the injunction. This meant that UDV's members were still unable to practice their religion in the United States because they still risked prosecution.

On appeal, the government argued that the Court of Appeals should overturn the trial court's decision; that the fact that *Hoasca* contained DMT, and that DMT was a "Schedule 1 controlled substance" should be sufficient to permit the government to forbid its use by anyone, including any religion. The government also quibbled over the evidence regarding health and safety and other aspects of the trial court's decision.

Although there are 13 judges on the 10th Circuit Court of Appeals, only three judges hear any case, unless the case is considered so important that it should be heard by all thirteen judges, after the panel of three has reached its result. The panel of three which heard the government's appeal ruled, 2-1, to sustain the trial court's decision. The government then took the extraordinary step of requesting that all 13 judges of the Court of Appeals reconsider the decision by the three-judge panel.

The Court agreed to hear the case again, this time with all thirteen judges participating. This is a rare occurrence. This case had clearly become a matter of great importance, at least to the government. Of course, it had always been a matter of great importance to the members of the UDV.

The thirteen judges fragmented into small groups, each with a different view of the case. Those groups, however, could be divided into two; those who wanted to sustain the trial court's decision and those who wanted to overturn it. The result was that eight were in favor of sustaining the trial court and five wanted to reverse the trial court and dismiss UDV's case entirely.

I invite you all to review those opinions, which are available on line at www.udvusa.com. It would take me far too long here to explain them.

The government appealed to the Supreme Court, which has the authority to accept appeals and consider them or to simply reject them. It accepts less than 1% of the appeals that come to it from the lower courts. It accepted the government's appeal, but dissolved the stay that had been in place since September of 2002. As a result, for the first time since 1999, our clients were free to practice their religion.

As many of you know, our Supreme Court unanimously affirmed the trial court's decision. It held that the trial court had correctly applied the Religious Freedom Restoration Act and had correctly concluded that the government had failed to demonstrate any compelling interest in criminalizing UDV's religious conduct.

The case, however, is not over. You recall that I explained that the government took its appeal after the trial court entered a preliminary injunction against interference with the UDV religion. The court has not yet made that injunction permanent, and we are now back before the Court, continuing to wrestle with the government.

The government has said that it has no further evidence regarding health and safety, risk of diversion, or international treaties. Instead, the government is now taking the position that even though the UDV may be able to lawfully possess *Hoasca*, it must now comply with all regulations that govern any company that imports, packages and distributes a controlled substance. Those regulations are as thick as a phone book. The government's position is that UDV must now apply to the Drug Enforcement Administration for exemptions from any of them. Thus UDV will have to have a license from the Drug Enforcement Administration. Anyone who will be involved in handling Hoasca would be subject to a background check and licensing. UDV would be required to state the exact amount of DMT contained in any container of *Hoasca*. There are hundreds more regulations. Our position is that UDV is exempt from these regulations. So this is the new battleground.

We argued this before the trial court two weeks ago. We are awaiting a decision. The government's view is that if it can ensnare the UDV in its regulatory morass, it is likely that there will be some misstep that will permit DEA to withdraw UDV's license and effectively prevent UDV from continuing to practice its religion. The government believes that once UDV is subject to licensing by the DEA, UDV will be subject to discretionary control by the DEA and that any appeal that UDV might want to take from an adverse agency decision will not go to the trial court in New Mexico where this case has unfolded for the last 8 years, but will instead go to a different court entirely. If the government accomplishes this, then it will be in a position to argue that any court must provide only the most deferential review of the agency's conduct. It has been clear to any participant in the UDV litigation that the government lacks any sense that it has a duty to respect and accommodate the UDV religion and its followers. The government is institutionally incapable of grasping this because its institutional outlook is that we must all be in line and we must all obey all laws and the government cannot tolerate deviation. Our Supreme Court, luckily, ridiculed the government's argument: "The Government's argument echoes the classic rejoinder of bureaucrats throughout history: If I make an exception for you, I'll have to make one for everybody, so no exceptions."

After almost eight years of litigation, after winning in each court, and seeing the government employ every device to prolong the litigation and now, after it has lost in three courts, begin its latest trick to defeat this religion, I have learned that this case is about more than the freedom of 130 UDV members in the United States and the many thousands of members here. At its core it is about the relationship between citizens and their government.

In the papers the government recently filed regarding the applicability of the Drug Enforcement Administration's Regulations and regulatory procedures to UDV, the government made a statement that will be seen to be quite ironic, in retrospect, if the UDV prevails entirely, as I believe it will. The government stated, "the UDV misapprehends the relationship between the government and the governed." Perhaps. But so far, the misapprehension is of the government, not UDV's.

Legal recognition of the UDV in Spain and brief considerations on legal recognition in other European countries

José Vicente Marín Prades
Patricia Lúcia Cantuária Marín

The objective of this article is to analyze the process of legalization of the UDV in Spain and to present brief considerations on the legal situation in Europe. We will present a general summary on the norms that govern European law as it relates to religious issues, as well as a brief analysis of the specific legal situation in some European countries in addition to Spain: United Kingdom, France, Germany, Holland and Italy.

Legal Recognition of the UDV in Spain

DATE	HISTORICAL TIMELINE
04/01/2000	Preliminary studies for the registering of the UDV in the Religious Entity Registry of the Justice Department of Spain
05/05/2001	Registration of the Centro Espírita Beneficente União do Vegetal (similar to corporate filing with a local public regulation board)
07/11/2001	Petition of registration in the Justice Department's Religious Entities Registry. Began seeking an attorney that specializes in religious matters
12/26/2001	Justice Department denies petition for registration
2004	Attorney contracted
04/13/2005	Centro Espírita Beneficente União do Vegetal – Núcleo Inmaculada Concepción is constituted as an entity
05/20/2005	Petition for registration of Núcleo Inmaculada Concepción in the Religious Entities Registry
11/11/2005	Justice Department denies petition for registration
03/31/2006	Appeal to the National Court.
10/04/2007	Favorable decision from the National Court.
01/16/2008	Attorney General accepts the decision.
06/19/2008	The UDV is registered in the Registry of Religious Entities.

[1] See: http://dgraj.mju.es/EntidadesReligiosas/NCindex.htm Centro Espirita Beneficente União do Vegetal 1475-SG/A.

Preliminary Studies for the Registration of the UDV in the Registry of Religious Entities of the Justice Department of Spain

On April 1, 2000, the initial studies began for the recognition of the UDV in Spain. The initial technical evaluation indicated that the Center should be registered with the Spanish Justice Department.

The Registry of Religious Entities (RER) is a department of the Spanish Justice Department, created by Royal Decree 142/1981 on January 9, in accordance with Article 5 of the Organic Law of Religious Freedom.[2,3] Within the hierarchy of the Justice Department it is under the General Direction of Religious Matters and is governed by the General Sub-direction of Registry and Institutional Relations. The registration in this registry has a constitutive character, which recognizes the religious entity's civil status as an organization. Those permitted to enter the registry are:

- Churches, Smaller Minority Religious Sects and Religious Communities
- Orders, Congregations and Religious Institutes
- Religious Associations constituted within Churches and Confessionaries
- Respective Federations
- Canonical Foundations

Presently, the Registry of Religious Entities of Spain's Justice Department contains 12,369 Catholic entities, 2,046 minor religious groups (among them the Santo Daime) and 301 canonical foundations.[4] With the registration the entity becomes a corporate entity, which permits the institution to enter into legal contracts (as a buyer, seller, etc.), to be the principal party before the Courts, etc.

The registered entities, according to Article 6 of the Organic Law of Religious Freedom, have full autonomy and are able to create their own organizational regulations, bylaws and human resources guidelines. They are also able to appoint their religious leaders and maintain relations with other religious organizations, both domestic and international. The Register of Religious Entities is a public register and any citizen may access it. It is organized into three sections:

---

[2] Royal Decree 142/1981, January 9, on the Organization and Functioning of the Registry of Religious Entities. Published in the Official Bulletin of the State (Boletín Oficial del Estado - BOE) on January 31, 1981.

[3] Organic Law 7/1980, July 5, on Religious Freedom. Published in the Official Bulletin of the State (Boletín Oficial del Estado - BOE) on July 24, 1980.

[4] The Santo Daime is registered as: Iglesia del Santo Daime de España (Cefluris, Centro Eclectico de la Fuente de Luz Universal, Raimundo Irineu Serra de España). Registry number 689-SG. Date of registration 10/07/2003. See: http://dgraj.mju.es/EntidadesReligiosas/NCindex.htm

- Special Section: Churches, Smaller Minority Religious Sects and Communities that have a cooperation agreement with the Government. Among them are the Catholic Church, the Evangelical Federations and Religious Entities of Spain, the Federation of Israelite Communities of Spain and the Islamic Commission of Spain.
- General Section: Churches, Smaller Minority Religious Sects and Communities that do not have a cooperation agreement with the Government.
- Foundations Section: Canonical Foundations of the Catholic Church.

The favorable decision on the consumption of Hoasca Tea

It is important to emphasize that in the chain of events that led to the legal recognition of the CEBUDV in Spain, a judicial decision was made that determined that the article of the Spanish penal code that defines drug trafficking, does not apply to the Vegetal, given the quantity of DMT it contains.

On October 20, 2000, Judge Maria Tereza Palácios issued a report filing of the lawsuit filed against two Brazilian citizens who entered Spain with 10 liters of Hoasca tea.[5] The detention took place due to an infraction against public health since the ayahuasca tea contains DMT, a substance included on Schedule I of the 1971 Convention of Psychotropic Substances.

The Scientific Police (forensic unit) analyzed the samples and found that the concentration of pure DMT was 0.087%.[6] According to the National Institute of Toxicology, the amount of DMT considered hallucinogenic, when administered intravenously, is 75 to 1000 milligrams, meaning that an oral dosage would be at least 10 times greater. The judge, in her legal opinion, affirmed that "according to these findings we can conclude that the apprehended substance, given its concentration and liquid state, appears to be a product that is incapable of harming the legal well being protected by Article 368 of the Penal Code." The referenced Article addresses cultivation activities, production, or trafficking that can aid the illegal consumption of toxic drugs, narcotics or psychotropic substances.

In addition to the analysis of the Scientific Police, demonstrating that the amount of DMT was insufficient to be considered a drug, the Judge added the following as favorable facts:

---

[5] Previous Diligences 60/2000, of October 20, 2000. Da. Ma. Teresa Palácios, judge of the Central Court Circuit 3, Madrid, Spain.

[6] Information contained in the report filing.

- Those involved were ongoing consumers
- The place of consumption is a private location (temple), where unknown third parties are not permitted to participate.
- The consumption was to take place immediately.

Moreover, the legal decision cites the jurisprudence of the Supreme Court that considers self-consumption when a group of people create "a common fund with the purpose of acquiring the substance that will be consumed by the entire group." Here, it is worth noting that the UDV produces the tea by hand and in the exact measure to supply the needs of the congregation.

Notarized Registration of the Centro Espírita Beneficente União do Vegetal

Registration in the Registry of Religious Entities is accomplished by request of the entity through submitting an application that includes the founding bylaws/articles of incorporation, duly notarized, and the document of "foundation and establishment" in Spain, duly registered (art. 3 of Royal Decree 142/1981).

To fulfill this requirement, the Articles of Incorporation of the UDV, which included the Statutes, were registered on May 5, 2001, as a "corporate not-for-profit entity". The document specifies its objective of meeting the requirement for registration in the Register of Religious Entities.

At this time the following offices were established:
- President: Miguel Romero Vera
- Vice-president: Juan Manuel Fernández Prieto
- Treasurer: Joana de Oliveira Souza
- Second-treausurer: Antonio Pasto Millet
- Secretary: Zeneide do Nascimento Zouza
- Second-secretary: Asunta de Hormaechea Arenaza
- Official Orator: Piedad Ortíz Fernández de Alba

Request for registration of the CEBUDV in the Spanish Justice Department's Registry of Religious Entities

On July 11, 2001, Mr. Luiz Sendino Penalva submitted the application requesting that the Centro Espírita Beneficente União do Vegetal be registered in the Justice Department's Registry of Religious Entities (RER). On December 26, 2001, the Justice Department denied the registration.

It is important to mention that according to Law 30/1992 of November 26, 1992, which governs Administrative Proceedings, the maximum period for a response to the petitioner is six months from the date of the request.[7] Once this period expires Article 42 of Law Decree 30/1992 is then applied and the registration becomes mandatory, through the principle of "administrative silence." This was the case, for example, of the registration in the RER of the "Iglesia del Santo Daime de España." To clarify, registration accomplished by means of "administrative silence" also gives full rights to the registered entity.

The legal principles of the resolution from the Justice Department, in summary, were:

1. The fact that the registration in the RER gives the Entity corporate legal status and that the Organic Law of Religious Freedom (LOLR) recognizes the right that religious entities have to create specific legal bylaws different from other entities of common rights.

2. The resolution is based on the LOLR and on RD 142/1981: "the existence of a type of entities that are more complex and important than others, from which the others are derived." Consequently, Churches, Smaller Minority Religious Sects, and Religious Communities must fulfill the common requirements: a proprietary doctrine, rituals and ceremonies that constitute worship, existence of locations for worship and religious purposes, worship ministers or religious leaders, religious purposes that respect freedom of religion and a significant number of adherents.

3. "Even though in the documentation submitted it is clear that the petitioners seek to establish an entity whose nature is of a Church or Smaller Minority Religious Sect, this factor was not sufficiently accredited." Certainly we have here an entity that does not possess the character of a Smaller Minority Religious Sect, on the contrary, its goals are closer to the category of 'diffusion of humanistic values', which are not considered religious purposes according to the third article of the Organic Law of Religious Freedom."[8]

---

[7] Law Decree 30/1992, November 26, 1992, Regímen Jurídico de las Administraciones Públicas y del Procedimiento Administrativo Común (Legal Ruling Principles of Public Administration and Common Administrative Procedures), in the Boletín Oficial del Estado-BOE (Official State Bulletin), on 12/27/1992: http://www.boe.es/aeboe/consultas/bases_datos/doc.php?id=BOE-A-1992-28641 (last visited on March 3, 2012).

[8] Spain, Justice Department: "General Direction of Religious Matters Denial Resolution." Dezember 26, 2001.

Constitution of the entity Centro Espírita Beneficente União do Vegetal – Núcleo Inmaculada Concepción

After the denial of the request for registration in the RER, a search for an attorney who specialized in religious matters began, and subsequently Mr. Dionísio Llamazares Fernández was retained.

This attorney put together an informative report in which he recommended that a new entity be constituted. After a favorable review from the Legal Department of the UDV, issued on August 6, 2004, the name Centro Espírita Beneficente União do Vegetal-Núcleo Inmaculada Concepción was approved.

On April 13, 2005 this new entity was constituted, registered in public records, with the following officers:
- President: Juan Manuel Fernadez Prieto
- Vice-President: Miguel Antonio Romero Vera
- Secretary: Maria Reyes Garcia Romero
- Treasurer: Maria del Carmen Luzardo Cabrera

The statutes were also adapted, following the counsel of the attorney, taking into consideration some requirements of the Spanish code of law.

New Request for Registration in the Registry of Religious Entities

On May 20, 2005, after the new entity had been created, Mr. Juan Manuel Fernandez Prieto submitted the request for Centro Espírita Beneficente União do Vegetal - Núcleo Inmaculada Concepción to be registered.

On November 11, 2005, this request was also denied for the same reasons that it was denied in 2001, as the new documentation presented was considered insufficient to characterize the UDV as a religious entity. Within the right to appeal the decision through administrative means *(recurso de reposicion* – administrative appeal) or judicial means *(recurso contencioso-administrativo* - contentious administrative appeal), the administrative option was chosen and an administrative appeal to the Department of Justice was filed on December 20, 2005. This appeal attempted to contest the decision of the Justice Department that stated it was the same entity, and cited precedents of the jurisdiction of higher courts in favor of religious freedom (National Court, Supreme Court, and Constitutional Court). For example, on February 24, 1999, the National Court *(Audiencia Nacional),* had decided in another case that "the registration cannot be denied based on the argument of lack of doctrine or liturgy, or specific religious purposes, or be based on a lack of significant numbers of members."

The administrative appeal *(recurso de reposicion)* was denied on January 26, 2006, with the Justice Department insisting on the issue of the identity of the entities: "even if the petitioner insists on demonstrating to the contrary, the identity appears clear in the subject, the purpose of the request and the name of the entity; regarding the statutes, though there has been some changes, it is possible to affirm, without any risk, this is simply an attempt to adapt to the circumstances of each moment."

Once the resources of the administrative approach were exhausted, a contentious-administrative appeal was filed with the National Court.

Appeal to the National Court

The National Court is based in Madrid and has four divisions:
- Appeals
- Criminal
- Contentious-Administrative
- Social

The National Court's jurisdiction encompasses crimes against the Royal House and Higher Departments of the Nation and of the Government, among others.

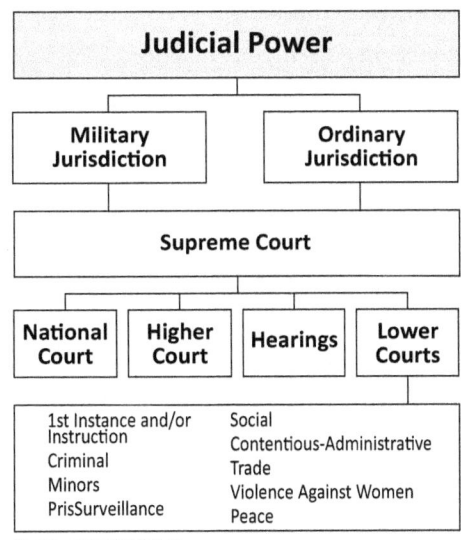

Source: www.mjusticia.es

The "Contentious-Administrative" sector of the National Court addresses contentious-administrative appeals against resolutions and acts of State Ministers and Secretaries. Since the denial of the registration in the Registry of Religious Entities is within the jurisdiction of the Justice Department, delegated to the General Direction of Religious Matters, this is the appropriate judicial department in which to file the appeal.

On March 31, 2006, the contentious-administrative appeal was filed (201/2006) which contained identical arguments to the prior appeal.

Favorable Decision from the National Court

On October 4, 2007, the National Court issued its favorable decision, annulling the resolution of the Justice Department and "recognizing the right of the petitioner to be registered in the Registry of Religious Entities."

Eight months later, on June 19, 2008, the registration of the Centro Espírita Beneficente União do Vegetal, Núcleo Inmaculada Concepción was recorded in the Registry of Religious Entities.[9]

This confirms that, in Spain, it was necessary to persevere through the administrative obstacles (which twice rejected the request for registration in the Registry of Religious Entities) and also to seek judicial remedy in order to secure the legal recognition of the CEBUDV as a religion and to guarantee its members the right to practice.

Spain's recognition of the UDV as a religion sets a precedent that can be used in favor of the UDV in the effort for recognition in other European countries. In addition, Spain is a signatory of the European Human Rights Convention, which guarantees the right to a religion and to a religious practice. Therefore, this recognition by Spain can be used by the European Human Rights Court as a favorable argument in other similar cases.

Europe

In Europe there are various norms related to religious freedom, including:[10]
- Final Minutes of the Conference on Security and Cooperation in Europe (Organization for Security and Cooperation in Europe, Madrid, September 9, 1983).

---

[9] See: http://dgraj.mju.es/EntidadesReligiosas/NCindex.htm Centro Espirita Uniao do Vegetal. Registration Number 1475-SG/A (last visited in March, 2012)

[10] These norms are listed on Spain's Justice Department website, see: http://www.mjusticia.gob.es/cs/Satellite/es/1215197982464/Estructura_C/1215198071682/Detalle.html (last visited March, 2012)

- Final Minutes of the Conference on Security and Cooperation in Europe (Vienna, January 19, 1989).
- Letter from Paris to a New Europe (Organization for Security and Cooperation in Europe, November 21, 1990).
- Recommendation of the European Council's Committee of Ministers on European Prison Regulations (February 12, 1987).
- European Parliament's Resolution on common actions of member States of the European Community regarding the diverse legal violations committed by new organizations under the cover of religious freedom (European Union – European Parliament, May 22, 1984).
- Declaration no. 11 of the Final Minutes of the Amsterdam Treaty on the statutes of non-confessional churches and organizations (European Union, October 2, 1997).
- European Union's Charter of Fundamental Rights (European Council, December, 2000)

The European Union's Charter of Fundamental Rights states civil, political, economic, and social rights within a single text.[11] It is a compilation of the rights that are already existent in the member countries of the European Union. Article 22 of this document affirms that "the Union respects cultural, religious and linguistic diversity."

Among the rights incorporated in the Charter of Fundamental Rights are the rights established in the European Convention on the Rights of Man, commonly known as The Convention for the Protection of Human Rights and Fundamental Freedoms.[12] Article 9 of this Convention states:

1. Everyone has the right to freedom of thought, conscience and religion; this right includes freedom to change his religion or belief and freedom, either alone or in community with others and in public or private, to manifest his religion or belief, in worship, teaching, practice and observance.
2. Freedom to manifest one's religion or beliefs shall be subject only to such

---

[11] European Union, Charter of Fundamental Rights, signed on December 7, 2000. See http://www.europarl.europa.eu/charter/pdf/text_en.pdf (last visited March 3, 2012)

[12] Council of Europe, European Convention on Human Rights (Convention for the Protection of Human Rights and Fundamental Freedoms) adopted on November 4, 1950, in effect since September 1953. This convention was created based on the Universal Declaration of Human Rights of 1948. For the text of the European Convention on Human Rights see: http://www.echr.coe.int/ECHR/EN/Header/Basic+Texts/The+Convention+and+additional+protocols/The+European+Convention+on+Human+Rights/ (last visited on March 3, 2012).

limitations as are prescribed by law and are necessary in a democratic society in the interests of public safety, for the protection of public order, health or morals, or for the protection of the rights and freedoms of others.

All countries mentioned in the present article are signatories of this Convention.[13] Lawsuits against the member countries of the European Convention on Human Rights for infringement of human rights may be initiated by other member countries or by individuals who are citizens of member countries. To file a lawsuit the person has to be the direct victim of the infringement and have exhausted all other legal recourses.[14]

United Kingdom

The United Kingdom is a signatory of international agreements that guarantee religious freedom and/or prohibit religious discrimination and incitement of religious hatred. The country does not have a formal constitution. Constitutional rights can be found in different parts of the ordinary code of law as well as in not written sources.[15]

Among these laws is the Human Rights Act, in which the rights from the European Convention on Human Rights were incorporated with the objective of guaranteeing religious freedom and protection against religious discrimination.[16] With the adoption of the Human Rights Act, British judges have to take into consideration the decisions of the European Court on Human Rights.[17]

Article 9 of the Human Rights Act, titled "Freedom of Thought, Conscience and Religion" states that:

1. Everyone has the right to freedom of thought, conscience and religion; this

---

[13] See http://www.coe.int/lportal/web/coe-portal (last visited March 3, 2012)

[14] The victim has only six months from the date of a final decision on the national level to file a lawsuit in the European Court of Human Rights. After this period, a lawsuit will not be accepted by the court.[13] See http://www.coe.int/lportal/web/coe-portal (last visited March 3, 2012)

[15] A constitution that is not 'written', or not codified, is the result of the evolution of the legal system throughout the centuries. In the Westminster Tradition which originated in England, a constitution that is not codified includes written segments adopted from Parliament as well as sources that are not written, such as legal cases that constitute precedents for future cases, customs, traditions and royal prerogatives.

[16] The Human Rights Act was adopted by the United Kingdom Parliament on November 9, 1998 and took effect on October 2, 2000. See http://www.legislation.gov.uk/uksi/2000/1851/contents/made (last visited March 3, 2012)

[17] The European Court of Human Rights must not be confused with the Court of Justice of the European Union, whose headquarters is in Luxembourg. The European Union is composed of 47 member countries. The European Court of Human Rights was idealized by the European Convention on Human Rights to monitor compliance by the member countries of the Council of Europe. The European Court on Human Rights was created in 1959 and is based in Strasbourg. For the Council of Europe member list, see: http://www.coe.int/lportal/web/coe-portal

right includes freedom to change his religion or belief and freedom, either alone or in community with others and in public or private, to manifest his religion or belief, in worship, teaching, practice and observance.

2. Freedom to manifest one's religion or beliefs shall be subject only to such limitations as are prescribed by law and are necessary in a democratic society in the interests of public safety, for the protection of public order, health or morals, or for the protection of the rights and freedoms of others.

Therefore, it is seen here that everyone has the right to freedom of thought, belief and religion, and the right to put their thought and beliefs into action. Consequently, the British public authorities cannot prohibit someone from practicing his/her religion, publicly or privately, without a good reason, according to what is stated in the law. Public authorities can only interfere with the freedom of thought, belief and religion if they can provide evidence that such a measure is necessary and proportional to protect:

- Public safety
- Public order
- Health and morality
- Rights and freedom of others

A "proportional" response to a problem can be considered an action that is not more than what is necessary to address the situation. That is, adequate and not excessive. In addition to the Human Rights Act, the United Kingdom also adopted the Equality Act, which states that a religion or belief must be recognized as being convincing, serious, congruent and compatible with human dignity.[18]

In conclusion, the UDV does not fit into the restrictions on religious freedom established by the law, and according to the Human Rights Act, everyone has the right to practice a chosen religion.

France

On November 18, 1999, the French police seized a quantity of Hoasca tea and, as a consequence of this seizure, six people were convicted for "international use and trafficking of narcotics."[19]

---

[18] The Equality Act was adopted in 2006 by the United Kingdom Parliament and amended in 2010. See: http://www.legislation.gov.uk/ukpga/2010/15/contents (last visited on March 3, 2012). For more information about the Human Rights Commission, see: http://www.equalityhumanrights.com/legal-and-policy/

[19] All the information contained in this section is based on the site http://en.wikipedia.org/wiki/Santo_Daime (last visited March 3, 2012)

After an appeal filed on November 4, 2004, the Court of Appeals issued a decision revoking the first ruling and ordering that the Vegetal seized be restituted. Consequently, on May 3, 2005, a commission from the French Agency for Safety of Health Products (an agency of the Health Department) published a decision in the Official Registry of France, signed through delegation by the minister and by the general health director, including the main components in the ayahuasca tea *(Banisteriopsis caapi and Psychotria viridis)* on the schedule of narcotic substances.[20] In July of 2005, a new petition was filed with the Health Department, requesting that these components be removed from the list, but in February of 2006, the Health Department denied the request.

In December of 2006, a petition was filed with the State Council alleging abuse of power by the Health Department. On January 4, 2008 the State Council rejected the petition. At this time, as a result of these events, the communion of the Vegetal is prohibited in France.

Germany

DMT is among the substances that are prohibited from entering the country.[21] When a substance is considered a "drug" consumption (in theory) is legal; however, possession is illegal. Since consumption without possession is impossible, therefore, in practice, consumption is also illegal.

Germany does not have a registry of religious entities as Spain does. There are only special contracts, called "Staatsvertrag", between the Republic of Germany and the Catholic Church, the Evangelical-Lutheran Church, and the Central Jewish Assembly.

It is noteworthy to mention that on May 16 to 18, 2008, a Conference took place in Heidelberg, Germany, in which the subject of the legal use of the Vegetal, among other subjects, was addressed *(The globalization of Ayahuasca: an Amazonian psychoactive and its users.)* The UDV was invited to participate and was represented at this conference.[22]

---

[20] This decision is available in the Official Journal of the French Government, search page http://www.journal-officiel.gouv.fr/frameset.html, in French, search by date May 3, 2005, see item 18 (Arrêté du 20 avril 2005). (last visited March 3, 2012)

[21] The information about Germany was provided by professor Henrik Jungaberle, from the University of Heidelberg, Germany: http://www.klinikum.uni-heidelberg.de/index.php?id=2613

[22] The conference schedule is available at: http://www.bialabate.net/wp-content/uploads/2008/10/2008-aya-conference-schedule.pdf (last accessed on March 5, 2012)

Holland

On October 6, 1999, Geraldine Fijneman, the person responsible for the Santo Daime in Amsterdam, transported and stored in her home approximately 17.5 liters of Vegetal to be used in Santo Daime rituals. On March 23, 2001, Geraldine appeared before the court in Amsterdam, accused of possession and transportation of a substance that contains DMT.[23] DMT is listed in the Opium Act and in the International Convention of Psychotropic Substances.[24]

The Court heard testimony from an anthropologist, a historian, a theologian, and professor Dr. F. A. Wolff, who describe the origins of the Santo Daime in Brazil and the use of psychoactive substances by some religions without any harmful effects to the health. It is interesting that, like Brazil's CONFEN/CONAD, the Court examined the matter beyond its chemical aspect.[25] The court weighed its duty to prohibit DMT against the right to religious freedom and the fact of there being no harm to the health in ayahuasca rituals. On May 21, 2001, the District Court of Amsterdam acquitted Ms. Fijneman, deciding that her constitutional right to religious freedom must be respected.[26]

Italy

Italy is a member country of the European Convention of Human Rights that guarantees religious freedom in Article 19 of its Constitution:

> Everyone has the right to practice freely their religious belief in any manner, individually or with others, to promote and celebrate rituals, in public or in private, as long as it is not offensive to public morality.[27]

---

[23] Holland, Opium Act, 1928. The updated version of this law and its amendments can be found at: http://www.cannabisbureau.nl/en/doc/pdf/Dutch%20Opium_Act_30556.pdf (last accessed on March 5, 2012)

[24] The International Convention on Psychotropic Substances, adopted at the United Nations Conference in Vienna that took place January 11, 1971 through February 21, 1971. See: http://www.unodc.org/pdf/convention_1971_en.pdf (last accessed on March 5, 2012).

[25] See the 'UDV in Brazil' section in this book.

[26] This decision, number 13/067455-99, can be viewed at http://www.santodaime.it/Library/LAW/Olanda/amsterdamcourt01_english.htm (last accessed on March 5, 2012)

[27] Constitution of the Italian Republic *(Costituzione della Repubblica Italiana)* adopted on December 22, 1947, entered into effect on January 1, 1948. See Article 19: http://www.quirinale.it/qrnw/statico/costituzione/costituzione.htm#P1T2 (Last visited on March 5, 2012) "Tutti hanno diritto di professare liberamente la propria fede religiosa in qualsiasi forma, individuale o associata, di farne propaganda e di esercitarne in privato o in pubblico il culto, purché non si tratti di riti contrari al buon costume."

Furthermore, Article 8 of the Italian Constitution states that all smaller minority religious groups are equal before the law and have the right to organize themselves according to their own statutes, in accordance with the Italian code of law.[28]

Law Decree no. 1159, June 24, 1929, states the following in Article 1:

> The State permits different sects of the Roman Catholic Apostolic Religion, as long as the principles and rituals are not contrary to public policy or morality.[29]

In Italy there is a registry of religious entities (Registro delle Confessioni Religiose), and the Department of the Interior, more specifically the division of General Direction on Religious Affairs (Minstero dell'Interno, Direzione Generale Affari dei Culti), is responsible for processing the petition for registration.[30] After the institution is recognized as a religious entity, negotiations begin in order to establish an agreement between the Government and the institution. Once the agreement is signed it must be approved by the Italian Parliament.

After an investigation that lasted eight months (an operation called "Mistica"), in March of 2005, the Financial Police arrested 24 members of the Santo Daime in the city of Perugia, in the central region of Italy.[31] In this investigation the police confiscated 40 liters of ayahuasca in Assisi and in the central and northern counties.[32]

The Italian Court in Perugia initiated penal proceeding no. 8531/04 R.G. and the case was eventually dismissed due to a lack of evidence:

---

[28] See http://www.quirinale.it/qrnw/statico/costituzione/costituzione.htm#P1T2 "Tutte le confessioni religiose sono egualmente libere davanti alla legge. Le confessioni religiose diverse dalla cattolica hanno diritto di organizzarsi secondo i propri statuti, in quanto non contrastino con l'ordinamento giuridico italiano.I loro rapporti con lo Stato sono regolati per legge sulla base di intese con le relative rappresentanze."

[29] Italy. Law Decree 1159 of July 24, 1929, published in the *Gazzeta Ufficiale* (Official Journal) on July 16, 1929. See Article 1: http://www.interno.it/mininterno/export/sites/default/it/sezioni/servizi/legislazione/religioni/legislazione_500.html (last visited on March 5, 2012)

[30] See: http://www.governo.it/Presidenza/USRI/confessioni/ (last visited on March5, 2012)

[31] The *Guardia di Finanza,* meaning "Financial Guard", is an Italian law enforcement agency under the authority of the Minister of Economy and Finance and is part of the Italian armed forces. The Guard is essentially responsible for dealing with national border control, military police, public safety, anti-terrorism police, customs authority, anti-drug smuggling and financial crime. See http://www.gdf.it/GdF/it/Home/index.html (last visited March 5, 2012).

[32] On March 18, 2005, news of this arrest appeared on these sites: http://noticias.uol.com.br/ultnot/afp/2005/03/18/ult34u120853.jhtm and http://noticias.terra.com.br/imprime/0,,OI490612-EI306,00.html

After several appeals alleging a total absence of crime, which were rejected by the Court of Perugia, the Supreme Court *(Suprema Corte di Cassazione)* convened in October of 2005 to deliberate on the case *(Corte Suprema di Cassazione – VI Sez. Penale, sentenza no. 44229/05 del 10/06/2005, v. allegato)*. The Supreme Court determined that the evidence was insufficient to prove a crime and said that the beverage utilized in the religious context could not be considered a drug, since it is a natural derivative of plants from the Amazon forest and is not a man-made product fabricated with the objective of increasing its effect. Given all this, the presiding Judge of the Court of Perugia ordered the case to be dismissed due to the absence of proof of a crime (Court of Perugia, sentence no. 1391/05 of o4/04/2006).[33]

Conclusion

Due to the need to adapt to the laws of a country, it is not always possible to reproduce the legal/organizational model of the CEBUDV in Brazil in other countries. There is also the orientation of Mestre Gabriel to "respect the laws of the country." This respect for the laws of the country, we may take to mean more generally, "to respect the laws of each country." In order to be able to respect, we need first to know the laws of each specific country.

The statement from the legal department of the CEBUDV regarding the legalization procedures in Spain, on August 6, 2004, states: "Complying with the laws of the country where the UDV is located is also an established procedure. It is also a factor of institutional stability that this compliance be maintained both in Brazil and overseas, wherever authorized distributions and núcleos are created by the Center."

We can observe that, even though there are religious freedom laws in Europe, there is a wide margin of interpretation in the application of these laws in each country. This, in some cases, can cause the process of legal recognition to take longer, since the law may impose restrictions upon religious freedom, as is the case with France with respect to public health. Furthermore, in order to have access to the European Court of Human Rights it is necessary to exhaust all legal options available in one's country, which can take years.

---

[33] Translation of the original text available at: http://tribes.tribe.net/daime/thread/bfe572ab-5754-4d58-b09b-ab84bd843842#cff15449-83f5-46dc-bce4-4cc14d5b31d3. Website for the Perugia Court: http://www.tribunalediperugia.it/ (last visited April 16, 2012)

Bibliography

Equality and Human Rights Commission http://www.equalityhumanrights.com/human-rights/what-are-human-rights/the-human-rights-act/freedom-of-thought-belief-and-religion/ (Last visited on September 15, 2012).

Heidelberg Conference, conference schedule available at: http://www.bialabate.net/wp-content/uploads/2008/10/2008-aya-conference-schedule.pdf (Last visited on September 15, 2012).

Council of Europe; European Convention on Human Rights (Convention for the Protection of Human Rights and Fundamental Freedoms), adopted on November 4, 1950, in effect since September 1953. See: http://www.echr.coe.int/ECHR/EN/Header/Basic+Texts/The+Convention+and+additional+protocols/The+European+Convention+on+Human+Rights/ (Last visited on September 15, 2012).

Decision of the French Department of Health: Official Journal of the French Government, http://www.journal-officiel.gouv.fr/frameset.html, in French, search by date May 3, 2005, see item 18 (Arrêté du 20 avril 2005). (Last visited on September 15, 2012).

Information on the Santo Daime in France: http://en.wikipedia.org/wiki/Santo_Daime (Last visited on September 15, 2012).

Law 30/1992, November 26, 1992, *Regímen Jurídico de las Administraciones Públicas y del Procedimiento Administrativo Común* (Legal Ruling Principles of Public Administration and Common Administrative Procedures), published in the *Boletín Oficial del Estado-BOE* (Official State Bulletin), on 12/27/1992: http://www.boe.es/buscar/doc.php?id=BOE-A-1992-26318 (Last visited on September 15, 2012).

Organic Law 7/1980, July 5, on Religious Freedom. Ley Orgánica 7/1980, de 5 de julio, de Libertad Religiosa. Published in the Official State Bulletin (BOE) on July 24, 1980: http://www.boe.es/buscar/doc.php?id=BOE-A-1980-15955 (Last visited on September 15, 2012).

List of religious entities registered in Spain: http://maper.mjusticia.gob.es/Maper/DetalleEntidadReligiosa.action?numeroInscripcion=1475-SG/A#bloqueBuscadorProcesos (Last visited on September 15, 2013).

List of Member Countries of the Council of Europe: http://www.coe.int/lportal/web/coe-portal (Last visited on September 15, 2013).

Department of Justice – Spain *(Ministério de Justícia):* http://www.mjusticia.gob.es/cs/Satellite/es/1200666550194/DetalleInicio.html (Last visited on September 15, 2013).

The Equality Act was adopted in 2006 by the United Kingdom Parliament and amended in 2010. See: http://www.legislation.gov.uk/ukpga/2010/15/contents (Last visited on September 15, 2013).

The Human Rights Act was adopted on November 9, 1998 by the United Kingdom Parliament and became effective on October 2, 2000. See: http://www.legislation.gov.uk/ukpga/1998/42/contents (Last visited on September 15, 2013).

Royal Decree 142/1981, January 9, 1981, on Organization and Administration of the Registry of Religious Entities. Published in the Official Bulletin of the State - BOE, on January 31, 1981: http://www.boe.es/aeboe/consultas/bases_datos/doc.php?id=BOE-A-1981-2368 (Last visited on September 15, 2013).

University of Heidelberg (Germany): http://www.uni-heidelberg.de/ (Last visited on September 15, 2013).

Constitution of the Italian Republic, adopted on December 22, 1947, in effect since January 1, 1948. See http://www.quirinale.it/qrnw/statico/costituzione/costituzione.htm#P1T2 (Last visited on September 15, 2013).

Italy, Law Decree 1159 of July 24, 1929, published in the *Gazzeta Ufficiale no. 164* on July 16, 1929. See: http://www.interno.it/mininterno/export/sites/default/it/sezioni/servizi/legislazione/religioni/legislazione_500.html (Last visited on September 15, 2013).

Religious *Confissiones* in Italy: http://www.governo.it/Presidenza/USRI/confessioni/ (Last visited on September 15, 2013).

Guardia di Finanza (Financial Police): See http://www.gdf.it/GdF/it/Home/index.html (Last visited on September 15, 2013).

Ayahuasca confiscation in Assisi: News of this arrest appeared on the following sites: http://noticias.uol.com.br/ultnot/afp/2005/03/18/ult34u120853.jhtm (Last visited on September 15, 2013).

Court of Perugia: http://www.tribunalediperugia.it (Last visited on September 15, 2013).

Casa Regina della Pace report on the legal case in Italy: http://tribes.tribe.net/daime/thread/ (Last visited on September 15, 2013).

The UDV and the Historic Hoasca Institutions

Edson Lodi Campos Soares

The ritual use of Hoasca, this mysterious tea that unites us as spiritual brothers and sisters, is an ancient practice that, throughout the history of specific Amazonian peoples, continues to have rich meaning, connected to a great variety of cultural traditions. The tea itself, which we call Hoasca, has received different names. When we use the term Historic Hoasca Institutions we want to emphasize the efforts of the spiritual guides who brought the use of the tea into urban contexts, even if initially it was restricted only to specifically "caboclo" communities, as in the case of the first members of "Alto Santo."[1]

Raimundo Irineu Serra, Daniel Pereira de Matos e José Gabriel da Costa are known to their disciples as Mestre Irineu, Mestre Daniel and Mestre Gabriel. These men are important references in their respective communities. They had their first contact with the Daime or Vegetal, which are the same as Hoasca, in very informal places, which at the time did not follow a firm line of conduct. These Mestres organized rituals, brought together congregations, and taught Christian principles, combined with elements that are connected to the enchanted beings of the forest. These rituals have assisted, and continue to assist, a growing number of people from the most diverse walks of life, in dealing with life's anxieties, bringing encouragement, comfort and direction in the sense of spiritual evolution.

We therefore consider the institutions that these leaders built to be pillars of institutionalization and of the recognition by the national population and Brazilian Government of the legitimacy of this practice with its ritual variations. These institutions are the *Centro de Iluminação Cristã Luz Universal (CICLU- Alto Santo)* (Universal Light Christian Illumination Center CICLU – High Saint), represented here at this Congress by a dear friend of so many journeys searching for goodness,

---

[1] The word caboclo generally refers to a rural or forest dweller of mixed ancestry; Brazilian Native and African ancestry.

Antonio Alves; the *Centro Espírita e Culto de Oração "Casa de Jesus – Fonte de Luz,"* ("House of Jesus – Fountain of Light" Spiritist Center and Prayer Worship, known as Barquinha (Little Boat), represented here by our brother Francisco Araújo, and the Centro Espírita Beneficente União do Vegetal.[2]

Having the responsibility for speaking on behalf of the União do Vegetal, I will provide a brief narrative about our Mestre Gabriel. José Gabriel da Costa was born in 1922, to a large family as one of 14 siblings, in the county of Coração de Maria, near Feira de Santana in the state of Bahia, the son of Manuel Gabriel da Costa and Prima Feliciana da Costa. His relatives told stories indicating that, even as a small child, Jose Gabriel da Costa already stood out as someone special. In 1944 he joined the "rubber army" and went to Rondônia to become a rubber tapper. In 1947 he married Raimunda Ferreira da Costa, known as "Pequenina."

From 1950 to 1958, the Mestre and his family went three times, back and forth, from the seringais (rubber-tapping forests) to the town of Porto Velho. On the third time, when they were preparing to return to the forests, Mestre Gabriel told his wife and children that they were going to find a "treasure." In 1959, in an area of the *seringais* called Seringal Guarapari, José Gabriel da Costa drank the Vegetal for the first time, receiving it from the hands of a rubber tapper named Chico Lourenço. Mestre Gabriel always showed respect and consideration toward the one who facilitated his re-encounter with the treasure that he later affirmed to have known for thousands of years.

On July 22, 1961, the União do Vegetal was created, a religion whose name was given by Mestre Gabriel. Before that time the tea was known by several names: cipó, yajé, mariri, and Daime.

With regard to the Daime, it appears that there was in the region of Porto Velho a group connected to Mestre Irineu, led by a Mr. Virgílio. Mestre Gabriel had a good relationship with Mr. Virgílio, having participated in sessions, with some of his own disciples, on more than one occasion. He also received visits from members of that center, and also made a "chamada" (religious chant) in a session of the União do Vegetal using a *"daime"* that he had received as a gift. This chamada received the name *"Correi Para Onde Tem Sombra"* (Run to Where There is Shade) and is part of the compilation of chants used in our rituals.

Mestre Gabriel and Mestre Irineu both disincarnated in the same year of 1971. As a gesture of friendship, Dona Peregrina, the widow of Mestre Irineu, affectionately known as Madrinha Peregrina, went to Porto Velho to visit our Mestre Pequenina, the widow of Mestre Gabriel.

The founder of the UDV always worked to maintain good relationships, not only with other Hoasqueiro leaders, but also with the general population and local authorities. He needed, nonetheless, to face some difficulties in order for the use of the Vegetal to be related not only to indigenous people and other traditional peoples of the forest, but to become accepted in wider circles with legal status and part of the national scope and order.

The trajectory of the União do Vegetal, since its beginnings, has been toward an increasingly formal organization, without losing sight of its original doctrine and caboclo roots. We have always promoted initiatives to clarify to those who are not yet familiar with our practices, demonstrating that the Vegetal is "proven harmless to the health." This statement has appeared in our documents since 1971, when the bylaws of the UDV were registered. Equally important is the "straight doctrine" which is in accordance with ethical and moral values shared with the most respectable sectors of the greater society. The UDV, as a religious institution, aspires for its members to be physically and psychologically equilibrated individuals, as well as socially integrated members of society.

Initially, the *"Associação Uniao do Vegetal"* (União do Vegetal Association) was created. Mestre Hilton Pereira Pinho composed the first "Internal Rule" (bylaws) with 16 articles, authorized by Mestre Gabriel, but not yet registered in the public record. These bylaws were simply called União do Vegetal.

On June 23, 1967, one of the disciples, Mestre Cruzeiro (presently known as Mestre Florêncio) traveled to Manaus. He distributed the Vegetal to his family members there on July 29, authorized by Mestre Gabriel. This is the beginning of the núcleo in Manaus, which later received the name of Núcleo Caupuri. Mestre Gabriel made the commitment to visit Manaus, and Mestre Florêncio to visit Porto Velho, once a year. At the inauguration in Manaus in 1971, Mestre Gabriel prophesied that from Manaus, the UDV would circle the world.

From the beginning, the Mestre and his disciples struggled against opposition to the use of the Hoasca tea. Despite being "proven harmless to the health," its use encountered prejudice and arbitrariness. A police officer in Porto Velho even detained Mestre Gabriel for questioning. This incident was published in the Alto Madeira Newspaper in October of 1967, in an article titled "Conviction of the Mestre." The Mestre was detained and released the next day, and explained afterwards to his disciples the mission of the UDV, reminding them of the symbol of Peace and Human Fraternity adopted by this religion: "Light, Peace and Love."

After that incident, the need to legally register the UDV was evident. Mestre José Luiz de Oliveira and Mestre Hilton Pereira Pinho were already composing the bylaws of the Beneficent Association União do Vegetal and showed them to Mestre Gabriel, who read them; made necessary changes, and then approved them. They continued the process by forming the first Directorate on November 1, 1967, and legally registered the first bylaws in March of 1968.

In 1970 there was another strong persecution by the authorities, when the chief of police of the territory of Rondônia, Mr. Rodolfo Ruiz (equivalent to the state secretary of public safety) verbally declared that the União do Vegetal was closed. Mestre Gabriel did not close the UDV, but, abiding by the public authorities, he stopped attending to *adventícios* (those drinking the Vegetal for the first time) and continued having sessions with the members. Mestre Monteiro, who at the time was the president of the UDV, retained an attorney, Dr. Jerônimo Santana, to defend the legal rights of the members. Confident of his duty before the União do Vegetal, he proposed to file a petition with the Court of Justice of the Federal District and of the Territories (the court that had jurisdiction over the territory of Rondonia at that time). As a result of the decision of the Court, a new set of bylaws were composed, in which the use of the Vegetal was mentioned.

In 1971, Counselor Adamir, who was at that time the president of the UDV, consulted with an attorney in Rondônia who counseled him to amend the statute, citing the use of the mariri and chacrona in the União do Vegetal, as it reads in the current version.[3] In June of 1971, the name of the institution was changed from Associação Beneficente (Beneficent Association) to Centro Espírita Beneficente (Beneficent Spiritist Center) União do Vegetal.

In November of 1970, Mestre Gabriel needed to travel for health treatments. He went to Fortaleza and afterward he visited his family in Bahia, after being away for 25 years. He then returned to Fortaleza, passed through Manaus and arrived in Porto Velho on March 27, 1971. His disciples went to the airport in their uniforms to welcome him. On this day there was a festive lunch with the members, and in the evening a session took place. This was the first time that the members of the União do Vegetal appeared publically in their uniforms, an act that demonstrated their courage and their trust in Mestre Gabriel, being that this was the height of the military dictatorship, when public manifestations were prohibited. Presently, this date is consecrated in the União do Vegetal as the date of the "Resurrection of the Mestre," with the word

---

[3] Francisco Adamir Lima received his star of Mestre on March 27, 1971, from the hands of Mestre Gabriel.

"resurrection" used in the sense of renewal.

In July of 1971, the Bishop of Porto Velho had made some criticizing remarks about the União do Vegetal in a Sunday sermon. Mestre Gabriel responded by way of an article in the Guaporé newspaper, on July 16, with the title "Keeping Watch While Sleeping." The article assured that a member of the UDV, who had been attending sessions for 60 days, would be free from vices such as alcohol and cigarettes. The Mestre was reaffirming his commitment to good conduct, which is part of the body of teachings of our religious institution.

It is interesting that, before disincarnating, Mestre Gabriel spent a few days in Manaus under medical treatment. There, ailing, he was carried in the arms of some of his disciples to participate in a session. In that session he made the "Rosary of Chamadas" that he had announced for some time, fulfilling his word. From Manaus he traveled to Brasilia, were he was then buried. Some years later, the General Headquarters of the UDV was established there, in the nation's capital. Since then, the União do Vegetal has been expanding throughout Brazil and in other parts of the world, thus, confirming prophesy of the Mestre.

Since the disincarnation of José Gabriel da Costa, in September of 1971, those responsible for the União do Vegetal, the Mestres, Counselors and Disciples, have worked to secure the legal status and the respectability that Mestre Gabriel tirelessly strived for. With the expansion of the UDV to all the states of the Brazilian nation, as well as to the United States and some countries in Europe, we have always provided the clarifications that authorities have requested, working to gain the right to the sincere practice of our religion.

For this purpose, it is important to emphasize the earnest dedication of the leaders of the UDV, along with other Hoasca institutions, notably the historic institutions mentioned above, in establishing directives and ethical principles for the responsible use of the tea, always emphasizing the ritual and religious character that must be preserved on every occasion that we take communion of this mysterious beverage, which we consider to be sacred.

It is worth pointing out here the formal beginning of the partnership that was formed in 1990 and 1991, at a time when the UDV, along with these other entities, composed the Letter of Principles of the Religious Hoasca Tea Entities, signed on November 24, 1991. Since then we have endeavored to strengthen the relationships with those who have the same commitment to religious responsibility, working for the spiritual evolution of humanity.

Bibliography

Alto Madeira Newspaper. "Convicção do Mestre." *Jornal Madeira Newspaper,* October 6, 1967.

Carta De Princípios Das Entidades Religiosas Usuárias Do Chá Hoasca. Rio Branco, November 24, 1991. (Mimeo)

CEBUDV – Centro Espirita Beneficente União Do Vegetal. *Consolidação das Leis.* 4a ed. Brasilia: Sede Geral, 2003.

Costa, José Gabriel da *et al.* "Velando Enquanto Dorme" (Keeping Watch While Sleeping). *Jornal O Guaporé*, Rondonia, July 16, 1971.

The Dialogue between the Government Authorities and the Ayahuasca Religions: the Offering of a Treasure[1]

Antônio Alves

A common aspect among the religions created by Mestre Gabriel, Mestre Irineu and Mestre Daniel is the cultivation of memory. We find this commonality of the cultivation of memory present in numerous moments throughout the development of the Ayahuasca religious institutions, especially within the respect that is given to the elders, whom we consider to be guardians of knowledge.

We say that Mestre Gabriel re-created the União do Vegetal, because, in fact, it is very ancient in the history of humanity. Similarly, we say that Mestre Irineu re-planted a doctrine, 'the holy doctrines,' because he is actually a messenger who came to re-plant the doctrine that other messengers, including he himself, have brought throughout the history of humanity, many centuries before. At the *Centro Casa de Jesus Fonte de Luz* (Home of Jesus Fountain of Light Center), founded by Mestre Daniel, a very ancient Christian mission is also observed. Their patron saint is Saint Francis of Assisi, who walked the Earth almost a thousand years ago.

The cultivation of memory is fundamental to our work. It is the foundation of our legitimacy before the greater society and the world, because we came before the laws and the governments. Before the Supreme Court of the United States was created, Ayahuasca was already on Earth. Before the CONFEN and the CONAD were created in Brazil, Ayahuasca was already on Earth.

When we address the government authorities to assert our legal rights, it is an ancestral history that is coming face to face with the state. This ancestral history needs to be remembered so that contemporary governments may recognize rights that have been developed over many years by generations and generations of our people.

We need to remember, for example, that this history, according to anthropological and archeological records and evidence, began with the indigenous nations that

---

[1] Text based on the verbal presentation at the panel "The UDV and the Historical Hoasca Institutions" at the 2nd International Conference of Hoasca. Brasilia: Centro de Convenções Brasil 21. May 9-11, 2008.

lived on the periphery of the Inca Empire, in the Andes. According to the evidence, the use of Ayahuasca existed in the entire northern portion of the Inca Empire, with the name of *"yagé," "camarãpe"* for the Ashaninka people, and *"runi"* for the natives of the Pano language, etc.[2] The name Ayahuasca was the most widely known because it was a Quechua word, and the Quechua language was central in the vast Inca Empire.

I met an Ashaninka *pajé* (shaman) who told that me his ancestors had learned to make Ayahuasca – *camarãpe,* as they call it – with the Inca people. He told me remarkable things of the time when he was a small boy, accompanying his family on the climb up the mountains of the Andes to gather salt. We thought that salt was brought from the coast to the Amazon, but the Indians in the high Andes had already known salt for a long time. Long ago, three million years ago, that region was an ocean and the salt deposits were created. He told me that they would heat the salt into blocks so as not to hurt their shoulders, and they would descend the mountain carrying blocks of salt.

Ayahuasca is a culture, a living experience, an existential experience which has been part of the paths of the forest for many hundreds of years. This is our history. We claim this history because we are the descendants and the heirs of these people. Thus, we have to challenge the governments to prove that Ayahuasca is not harmful. Is Ayahuasca harmful? Why is it not harmful to the indigenous people who have been drinking it for many generations? The governments will have to prove that it is harmful to the indigenous people in order to say that it is harmful to us.

This institutional challenge appears when Ayahuasca leaves the realm of the indigenous culture and moves to the realm of the rubber tappers, who traveled up the Amazon River, through the Purus, Madeira and Juruá Rivers, up to the headwaters of these rivers, and begin to have contact with the indigenous peoples.[3] Initially this contact caused conflict, but with time it also became a contact of miscegenation. The rubber tappers began to have knowledge of some mysteries of the forest. Amidst these mysteries was a central one: Ayahuasca, cultivated by the shamans of that entire native region. Here begins the part of our history about which we still have memory and

---

[2] Regarding the use of Ayahuasca by indigenous peoples of the Amazon, see Luz (2004), Langdon (2004), Keifenheim (2004), Luna (2004).

[3] The contact of the rubber tappers and the indigenous people is a recurring subject in the oral history of the Ayahuasca religions that are considered in this article: CICLU-Alto Santo, Barquinha and UDV. For the written history of this contact, see Franco and Conceição (2004).

records. This is also when our struggle for the institutionalization, recognition and legalization of the Ayahuasca tea began.

I feel rather at ease in this subject of memory. Though I am not a historian, I have become a storyteller and a collector of histories. One of my greatest pleasures was to drink the Ayahuasca tea and sit with a person three times my age, sipping lemon verbena tea, and talking until dawn, listening to the history told by our silver-haired mestres. I began to hear some stories, some from our elders and some from researchers, historians from Acre and other states.

One of them told me a very interesting story that took place in 1912. That was a great year for rubber. In 1912, rubber was Brazil's second largest export, after coffee. The state of Acre was at the center of rubber production, but the wealth from this extraction did not stay in Acre. The wealth was in Manaus, where the powerful rubber lords lit their cigars with dollar bills. There was so much wealth in Manaus, so much luxury. They built the opulent Amazonas Theater in the city, while deep in the middle of the jungle the rubber tappers worked harvesting rubber. No one suspected that in the following year the trees grown from seeds that an English pirate took to Malaysia would be ready for harvesting, and the price of rubber from the Amazon would drop.

In that year of 1912, a young black man, a descendent from slaves, named Raimundo Irineu Serra, arrived in Acre from the state of Maranhão on the northeastern coast of Brazil. He turned 20 years old that year and came to work as a rubber tapper. After some time he goes to Xapuri, in the Alto Rio Acre and then to Brasiléia, where some of his contemporaries were already organizing what would become the first religious entity in that region. Antônio Costa and André Costa, also black men from Maranhão, started a center called *Círculo de Regeneração e Fé* (Circle of Regeneration and Faith). The abbreviation CRF is still today embroidered on the uniforms of the ladies who are part of the line of Mestre Irineu, as sacred letters: *Centro da Rainha da Floresta* (Queen of the Forest Center).

The interesting thing about the work of the Costa brothers was that their center had a president, bylaws, and it was an organized religious entity. Despite the fact that there was not even a notary in Brasiléia for them to register the entity, they had a structured board of directors and a Center. At that time Acre was a Federal Territory, the first one to be annexed as a federal territory of Brazil. Plácido de Castro had recently been assassinated, and there was conflict at the border with Bolivia. The territory was divided into three sections. The section called Alto Acre was located above the Village of Rio Branco, and the military commanding officer there was named Odilon Pratagy.

Odilon Pratagy was an army colonel, so rigid and angry, that if he went by a corner and saw three young guys talking, he would say, "Listen, I am going over to the church, and when I return I don't want anyone talking here, or you'll be arrested." Because to him, two people talking on a street corner was vagrancy. Three people were already a rebellion. He was the one responsible for maintaining the order in that entire territory.

Colonel Odilon Pratagy received a complaint that the Costa brothers were carrying out "macumba" (sorcery) rituals at the edge of the river, in a place near Vila Brasília, which was the center of that region.[4] So Odilon Pratagy took a few soldiers and went to close down the rituals of the Costa brothers. He went up the river and when he got to their door he said, "Look, I came to close down these rituals because I was told that there is something being served that is making people go mad."

Antonio Costa said to him:

- "Sir, might you want to come up and see what we are doing? We are almost finished with the ritual today, but you can come up and take a look to see if we are doing anything wrong, anything against the law."

Colonel Odilon went up, leaving the troops lined up, and took a seat. He looked for a while at the Ayahuasca drinkers and afterwards he called Antonio Costa and said:
- "I want to try this thing. I want to see how it is."
- "You want some, sir?"
- "Yes, I do."

Antonio brought some *"cipó,"* which at that time was not yet called Daime or Vegetal, and gave it to the colonel. After some time, Antonio said:
- "Well, now we are ending the works for today." To which the colonel replied:
- "No, wait a second. Now it's just getting good for me. You're not going to end it yet."

So Antonio had to extend the session for some time until the colonel gave him the okay to end the works. At the end the colonel stood up and said:
- "While I am the authority in this territory and as long as I am alive and I have the authority, no one will close down your work here. Let me know if you need anything, I will give you protection."

---

[4] Vila Brasilia was the first name of Brasiléa. The name change took place later due to the construction of the capital of the country.

This event is the first in the historical records that an administrative and military authority of the Alto Rios territory came into contact with an organized center of Ayahuasca drinkers. We could call this the first institutional contact.

At that time, the intention of the public agent was to shut down the rituals. That intention was dissolved by the love, beauty and truth contained in the Ayahuasca tea, which he willingly drank. Ever since that time, the challenges have been dealt with in the same spirit.

Around 1914, Mestre Irineu arrived at Vila Brasília and met up with the Costa brothers. He drank Ayahuasca with them and received illumination from the Queen of the Forest, who is known as Our Lady of Conception, the patron saint of his work. Afterwards he built his work and settled in Rio Branco, around 1930. In 1945 he founded the Alto Santo center. At that time there was another encounter between an Ayahuasca community and a public authority.

At the end of the forties, the governor of Acre, army colonel José Guiomar dos Santos, noticed that the riverbank near the capital building seemed very dirty.[5] He decided to have that area cleaned up and told this to some of his officials.

Colonel Fontenele de Castro, who was a well-known authority in Acre, said to him, "I have just the right person for this job."

Mestre Irineu was 1.98 meters, or just under 6 feet, 6 inches tall. Governor Colonel José Guiomar dos Santos looked at this man, who was almost six-and-a-half feet tall, and said:

- "Very well, how much for the job?" To which Mestre Irineu replied:

- "For me it is nothing, but some of my men may want payment." All the men replied:

- "No, none of that! No payment is needed. All we want, Governor Sir, if possible, is that you arrange transportation for us to get to Vila Ivonete, because from there we will go into the forest and walk for another few kilometers to get home to the community where we live."

The Governor provided a truck to take them to Vila Ivonete. From that moment on began a very healthy relationship with the public authorities, through which Mestre

---

[5] José Guiomar dos Santos was governor of Acre between 1946 and 1950. In the seventies he became Acre's state senator in the Federal Congress.

Irineu was able to acquire land to establish his community, and develop an agricultural project with machinery for larger yields, etc.

This is a landmark moment of positive contact between public authorities, through Governor José Guiomar dos Santos, and the Ayahuasca communities in Acre: Alto Santo (Mestre Irineu), and Casa de Jesus Fonte de Luz (Mestre Daniel), which also became known to the governor.

In the challenges with the public authorities there are two extremes: one entangled in conflict where those in lower classes were not understood, but instead were objects of prejudice; and the other extreme marked by friendly relations with those in the highest echelons of public power. Within these polarized interactions, the development of the historic institutionalization of the use of Ayahuasca has taken place.

These are a few of the many historic stories linked to the process of institutionalization and the recognition of the use of Ayahuasca in Brazil. These contacts with the public authorities were unique opportunities for the advancement of this process, even if, at first, these occurrences took place in a climate of prejudice, repression and lack of knowledge of Ayahuasca religions by the authorities and by society at large. We know, however, that nothing happens by chance, and that what may seem to be coincidences are, in truth, signs and hints to show the way. The obstacles in the path many times become the stepping stones. Therefore, where we may encounter a difficulty, an arrest, a repression, in truth this may be an opening for a future accomplishment.

I chose to tell these stories with the objective of illustrating that we are part of an ancient history, a history wrought with suffering, but also with beauty. We must endeavor to merit being part of this history. We must not lower our heads, because we are not asking the government to recognize our legitimacy. We are the ones offering to the government and to the Brazilian people a treasure that may legitimate the people and the Brazilian government as the guardians of the Amazon forest and of the future. Thank you.

Bibliography

Franco, Mariana C. Pantoja e Conceição, Osmildo Silva. "Breves revelações sobre a Ayahuasca. O uso do chá entre os seringueiros do Alto Juruá," *in:* Labate, B. C. e Araújo, W. S. (orgs.). *O uso ritual da Ayahuasca*. Campinas: Mercado de Letras; São Paulo: FAPESP, p. 653-669, 2004.

Langdon, Esther Jean. "A tradição narrative e aprendizagem com yagé (Ayahuasca) entre os índios siona da Colômbia, *in:* Labate, B. C. e Araújo, W. S. (orgs.). *O uso ritual da Ayahuasca*. Campinas: Mercado de Letras; São Paulo: FAPESP, pp. 69-96, 2004.

Luna, Luiz Eduardo. "Xamanismo Amazônico, Ayahyasca, antropomorfismo e mundo natural", *in:* Labate, B. C. e Araújo, W. S. (orgs.). *O uso ritual da Ayahuasca*. Campinas: Mercado de Letras; São Paulo: FAPESP, p. 181-200, 2004.

Luz, Pedro. "O uso ameríndio do caapi", *in:* Labate, B. C. e Araújo, W. S. (orgs.). *O uso ritual da Ayahuasca*. Campinas: Mercado de Letras; São Paulo: FAPESP, p. 37-68, 2004.

The Mission of Mestre Daniel

Francisco Hipólito de Araújo Neto

The *Centro Espírita e Culto de Oração "Casa de Jesus – Fonte de Luz"* (Spiritist Center and Prayer Worship "Home of Jesus – Fountain of Light"), known as *Barquinha* (Little Boat), was founded in 1945 by Daniel Pereira de Mattos, in a rubber-tapping area of rainforest called Seringal Empreza, near what is now the city of Rio Branco, in the state of Acre, Brazil.[1]

Mestre Daniel was one of the pioneers of the use of ayahuasca in urban areas of the Amazon and founded the second of three institutions that use ayahuasca tea in their religious rituals. Mestre Daniel was born in the old village of São Sebastião de Vargem Grande, a slave trading post in the interior of the state of Maranhão, on the northeast coast of Brazil. In 1905, he enlisted in the Brazilian Navy as a cabin boy and went to Acre. In 1907, he settled in the rubber-tapping forests of Acre.

After many years of family and health challenges, he received shelter from his compatriot and friend Raimundo Irineu Serra in 1937, at Vila Ivonete. There, where he was initiated into the works of the Daime, he received a spiritual and physical health treatment that lasted until 1945.

It was during that time that he received the clarifying visions regarding the mission that he was to fulfill on earth, which had appeared in his dreams since childhood. In one of these visions he received a Blue Book, which he opened, and inside it was written the organization of the Mission that he would come to establish on this plane.

The Book contained the 446 doctrinal hymns, psalms, and chants, composed by him and four of his contemporaries, in reverence to God and the Virgin Mary, and general instructions for the spiritual preparation of his followers. In the Book there was also orientation to carry out charitable works in both the visible world and in the invisible world.

---

[1] The rubber tapping area of the rainforest that was known at that time as Seringal Empreza eventually became the village of Rio Branco, which today is the State capital.

Daniel told his vision to Mestre Irineu, who counseled him to carry out what he had been shown. He asked Mestre Irineu for permission to leave his home and requested five liters of ayahuasca to begin his spiritual mission.

When Mestre Irineu went to Alto Santo in 1945, Mestre Daniel remained in Vila Ivonete, where he began his work by building a small chapel with mud walls and a thatched roof, with a table in the shape of a cross, an altar and benches. He consecrated his mission to São Francisco das Chagas (Saint Francis of Open Wounds), of whom Daniel was a devotee, so that the works carried out there would have St. Francis as the Teacher, the Mediator, and the Attorney.

Over almost 13 years he worked structuring his Mission, creating on this plane the revelation of the Blue Book. He prepared the Daime tea and distributed it during the religious rituals held in the chapel, to those who sought his help for various problems, such as alcoholism, physical illnesses, spiritual problems and family issues, among others.

Through the Light he received from the Daime tea, he copied from the Blue Book the hymns, psalms, and chants and with his fiddle he played the melodies. Mestre Daniel developed the Hymnal based on the Christian doctrine, and taught his first followers, 35 men and women, the majority of them simple illiterate rubber tappers and farmers, who memorized the teachings from the Hymns as wisdom for daily living.

He established Charitable Works to benefit those incarnated as well as those already deceased. Initially he began with blessings for children and removing *"panema"* (persistent bad luck or witchcraft) from hunters in the region. Well versed in folk remedies, he taught how to use medicinal plants in teas, baths, and compresses for numerous ailments. As he became known for his work, his home became a place for support, comfort and shelter for those in need of physical and spiritual assistance.

These are the fundamental aspects of Mestre Daniel's work: the *Hymnal,* which reveals the Christian doctrine through chanted poetry, the religious use of the Daime tea, which facilitates the understanding of the teachings, and leads the congregation to carry out Charitable Works, by attending to those in need via the intervention of "good spirits".

This work combines the elements of popular Catholicism, African beliefs and indigenous ayahuasca practices. The Mission was structured with the assistance of the followers who supported Mestre Daniel, by necessity and by their good will to assist him in the fulfillment of a spiritual commitment. They preserved the teachings of Mestre Daniel after his passing to the spiritual plane on September 8, 1959, and persevered in continuing the Mission to benefit those in need.

Among the followers who preserved the teachings and the practices of Mestre Daniel, I would like to mention two: my well-missed father, brother and friend, Manuel Hipólito de Araújo and Mr. Antonio Geraldo da Silva.[2] They preserved the teachings in their hearts and were able to, along with many others, guarantee that our works would continue.

They faced many difficulties in order to practice a doctrine based on the religious use of ayahuasca. It was precisely because of their recognition of the great significance of ayahuasca in their lives that they fought to defend the right to use the tea in their religious rituals.

The history of our Center, since its beginning, is filled with occurrences that demonstrate the struggle that our predecessors endured in order to keep a religious belief alive and that still, to this day, has been denied true freedom of expression.

In the sixties, our followers faced great struggles against prejudice and persecution. They sought legal avenues to guarantee their right to continue using the Daime and carry out the rituals.

The Mission was legally registered in 1959. The charitable outreach work was recognized by the authorities through the granting of the Título de Utilidade Pública Estadual (Federal Public Benefit Organization) in 1966, and the registering of the Center with the National Council for Social Services in 1968.

The children of the followers suffered discrimination in public schools due to their parents being Daime users. Brother Manuel Hipólito de Araújo, concerned with this situation, called on the congregation to take action: together they made bricks and built the St. Francis of Assisi School in 1963. Today it houses 310 children from different neighborhoods near our Center. For 45 years this school has been used by the Acre State Government, at no cost, through an agreement. This school was created to solve a discrimination issue and has served as an example of resistance against religious intolerance.

We suffered several police invasions during the sixties, as well as attacks and several judicial orders demanding that we explain the use of the tea. Once we even had a situation where we had to hide the tea in the Church's ceiling.

---

[2] Manuel Hipólito de Araújo was president and the person responsible for the *Centro Espírita e Culto de Oração "Casa de Jesus – Fonte de Luz"* from 1977 to 2000, when he passed away. Antonio Geraldo da Silva was president and the person responsible for the *Centro Espírita e Culto de Oração "Casa de Jesus – Fonte de Luz"* from 1958, after the disincarnation of Mestre Daniel, until 1977. (See Margarido and Araújo Neto 2005).

Because of these incidents, Brother Manuel Hipólito de Araújo made a request to the Department of Health Secretary, Dr. Carlos Meixeira Afonso, in 1965, to have an analysis done of the Daime tea and the plants used to prepare it, by the National Narcotics Surveillance Service, based in Rio de Janeiro.

The results proved that the Daime tea causes no intoxication and Brother Manuel Hipólito de Araújo asked the secretary to issue a document stating that he had no objection to the use of the tea in the religious rituals. A copy of this document was also sent to the Alto Santo Center (at that time there were only these two Centers in Rio Branco).

We navigated through the decades of the seventies and the eighties being constantly watched and questioned by the Federal Narcotics Council, Federal Police, Catholic Church, evangelicals, newspapers, and other governmental agencies.

From the late eighties through 1991, in order to alleviate this pressure, we sought to unite our forces with other ayahuasca institutions that were having the same issues and were also concerned with the events that threatened the very restricted freedom that we had.

It is with much satisfaction and honor that I recall the names of our brothers Francisco Adamir Lima, Luis Maciel, (both of the UDV) and Manuel Hipólito de Araújo, all now deceased, who bravely armed themselves with their faith and trust to face this challenge. They were joined by dona Peregrina Gomes Serra, João Rodrigues Facundes, Clodomir Monteiro (as spokesperson), Antônio Alves and myself.[3]

We strengthened our bonds of friendship and brotherhood, and along with brothers from other institutions who also preserved the respect for the religious use of ayahuasca, we decided to enter into an ethical agreement which was consolidated in the Letter of Principles. These principles are strongly reaffirmed between us (Barquinha), the UDV and the Alto Santo centers.

This courageous attitude in defense of the good use of ayahuasca in religious rituals turned out to be very positive. Our dialogues became consistent, we got to

---

[3] Francisco Adamir Lima (1932-2001), Mestre Adamir, was one of the Mestres of the Origin in the UDV. Luis Maciel da Costa, a city councilman in Cruzeiro do Sul, Acre, arrived in the Cadre of Mestres of the UDV, and died in an airplane crash in 2002. Peregrina Gomes Serra, known as madrinha Peregrina, widow of Mestre Irineu, director of the Center originally created by Mestre Irineu, the Centro de Iluminação Cristã Luz Universal (CICLU) – Alto Santo. Clodomir Monteiro, retired professor from the Anthropology Department of the Federal University of Acre, author of the first dissertation in the area of Human Sciences regarding the Santo Daime, which he defended in 1983, in the post-graduate Program of the Institute of Human Sciences of the Federal University of Pernambuco. This dissertation is titled: *The Juramidam System, the Santo Daime Sect in Acre: a ritual of Transcendence and de-pollution.*" See the article in this book by CICLU-ALTO SANTO member, Antônio Alves.

know one another better and the respect between us grew. We came to rely on each other when it came to the larger questions and the debates we faced for the legalization of the tea. Those of us who had good principles firmed ourselves, and we still remain firm today.

Throughout these long decades we have lived under the surveillance of society and of the Department of Justice, always watching us, questioning us, and, as they tell us, gravely tolerating us. We have been under the watch of the National Narcotics Surveillance Service, subjected to the scrutiny of the Federal Narcotics Council as well as the National Drug Policy Council.[4] We are also overseen by the Department of Justice, which, despite the Resolutions that favor our cause, does not free us from the constant surveillance of its security agency, in contrast to other religions that freely express their beliefs without the burden of government monitoring.

I believe that the Centers that abide by good principles deserve to be treated differently by the Government, which behaves in a contradictory manner. While these agencies are suspicious of us, they also recognize us for the many social initiatives that we develop.

Regardless of how they judge us, we continue to carry out our activities, firmly abiding to the fundamental teachings that Mestre Daniel left for the Barquinha, Mestre Irineu for Alto Santo, and Mestre Gabriel for the UDV.

I would like to mention some of the activities of the Barquinha center so that you can come to know us better:

- Per orientation of Mestre Daniel, we do not engage in expansionism. This is because our target audience is spirits, our 200 members, plus the approximately 6,000 people we attend to annually at our Center, addressing a wide variety of problems with herbal teas and baths, counseling and prayer.
- Our school has 310 children enrolled from pre-school to 5th grade. Only 5% of these children take communion of the Daime.
- We have a preserve for environmental preservation and a plantation of the plants we use to prepare ayahuasca, the *Jagube* vine (Banisteriopsis caapi) and the Rainha leaf (Psychotria viridis), which is registered with the IBAMA (Instituto Brasileiro do Meio Ambiente e dos Recursos Naturais Renováveis – Brazilian Institute of the Environment and Natural Renewable Resources) and with the Environmental Institute of Acre, with whom we are initiating a

---

[4] See articles on CONFEN and CONAD in this book, section *UDV in Brazil*.

process of reclamation and transformation into a Private Natural Heritage Reserve (RPPN).[5] Our preserve is interconnected with a 100 thousand acre indigenous reservation, located on the Boca do Acre highway in the state of Amazonas.

- We have carried out studies and cultivation of the medicinal plants we use for the healing of those who seek our services, since the time of Mestre Daniel.
- Thirteen years ago we created the Daniel Pereira de Mattos Memorial Home, recognized as a community museum by the National Institute of Historical and Artistic Heritage – IPHAN, with whom we have been registered since 2006 and who requested that we be registered with the National Registry of Museums, a project of IPHAN's Department of Museums and Cultural Centers, in partnership with Spain's Department of Culture. Because of the Memorial Home's preservation work, the Department of Culture, through its Department of Identity and Cultural Diversity, considered us for the Popular Culture Award in 2007.
- In partnership with the Mesa-Brasil-SESC/Acre Program and the Zero Hunger Program, we distribute food items to needy families that come to our Center seeking help.
- We attend to and refer patients to medical services and contribute, as a group, to the blood bank of Acre State. At one time we had to have legal intervention so that we could continue to donate blood to needy individuals, because Hemo-Acre (the blood bank) did not want to receive blood donations from Daime users.

A report on these activities and other information was submitted to the Department of Justice, and on September 8, 2003, we were granted the Título de Utilidade Pública Federal (Federal Public Benefit Organization), by Decree no. 1306.

The challenges that we faced in prior decades were about legalization, discrimination and persecution. These days we have come together once again to deal with some of the old issues, as well as new topics regarding ayahuasca, such as: (1) regulation of the harvesting and transportation of the *Jagube* vine and the *Rainha* leaf by the

---

[5] The Private Reserves have been implemented by Decree 1922 of 5 June 1996 where Article 1 defines Private Reserve of Natural Heritage - RPPN - as areas of private domain to be specially protected, by the owner. To plead to obtain the title of Reserve of Natural Heritage property must meet certain environmental requirements, such as: high biodiversity, scenic look-ecological relevance or by their environmental characteristics that justify actions to recover, as the continuous properties Parks and other units considered priorities for conservation.

environmental agencies of Acre and (2) the petition to the former Minister of Culture Gilberto Gil, with the support of Congresswoman Perpétua Almeida and Acre State Governor Binho Marques, for the recognition of the religious use of ayahuasca to be considered an Intangible Heritage of the Brazilian Culture.[6]

The visit of the Minister of Culture to Acre was widely covered in the local and national media, in the Folha de São Paulo Newspaper and in *Veja* Magazine, causing a new wave of criticism, including claims that the Daime is a drug that causes hallucinations and emotional disturbances.

On the other hand, we are experiencing a beautiful and marvelous time amidst our Centers. This recognition by the Department of Culture, I am sure will become a reality. Let us benefit from this Conference and from the good relations between our Institutions, in order to find strategies for gaining the recognition and respect of the Brazilian society.

I believe it is possible to become free of the monitoring of the Justice Department, the National Drug Policy Council (CONAD), the surveillance of the Federal Police and the Department of Health, which is a new threat that is looming, and most importantly, I believe it is possible to become free of the stigma that has been imposed upon us of being drug users.

I believe that it would be best for us not to be leashed to any Department, but if we must be bound in some way, may it be to the Department of Culture, which assists and accompanies the many cultural and religious manifestations of the Brazilian people. Nevertheless, we do not want to be seen as a folkloric expression, but rather as a religious culture, born from the faith of the people in the heart of the Amazon.

We have, without any doubt, a beautiful history, of struggles and sacrifices, but also of peace and happiness, knowing that we are fulfilling a great commitment to benefit our spirit and the spirit of those in need.

I feel joy for all that we have accomplished, because I am certain that our accomplishments are pure and for the common good. Because of this, our accomplishments deserve the respect and the consideration of the Brazilian people and the public authorities.

In closing, I want to express how beautiful it is to see that, despite our Centers having been created by different individuals, with distinct rituals, we have mutual

---

[6] See in this book the speech by Congresswoman Perpétua Almeida at the opening of the 2nd International Hoasca Conference.

respect and are capable of living with these differences. Because without a doubt we all believe that we are brothers, children of the same benevolent Father, who graced us with two species of plants with great divine power, as Mestre Daniel sings in one of his hymns:

> *From the virgin forests,*
> *From holy love, appeared,*
> *This vine and these leaves,*
> *That show us the glories of God.*
> *The vine, fire, water and leaves,*
> *Together are combined,*
> *To prepare this tea,*
> *That gives us holy visions.*

Once again I invite all of you to reflect together and find ways to open a dialogue with Brazilian society, be it through campaigns to provide clarifications or through the creation of a Council of Historical Centers. Let us find a way for society to recognize who we truly are and the importance of our work, so that we may receive the respect and recognition that we merit.

We certainly will not have an answer by the end of this conference, but I know we will continue to work together, determined to defend the good use of the ayahuasca tea and our religious freedom.

Bibliography

Carta de Principios das Entidades Religiosas Usuarias do Chá Hoasca. Rio Branco, 24 de novembro, 1991. (Mimeo)

Margarido, Silvio Francisco Lima e Araujo Neto, Francisco Hipólito. *Mestre Daniel – histórica com a ayahuasca.* Rio Branco: Fundação Garibaldi Brasil, 2005.

Ayahuasca: from the Sacred to the Mundane
The Conversion of Ayahuasca into a Psychoactive

Jair Araújo Facundes

"'M. (that's what we call her), let's go drink a potent psychoactive? A substance that has a strong impact and will bring you visions, stimulate your senses and your intelligence, enable you to have perceptions that are different from reality, expand your consciousness, plus permit enormous self-knowledge?"
She answered: "God forbid, that is a drug! A thing of the devil! No, I do not want it."
"But you drink the Daime," I replied.[1]
"The Daime is Divinity - it brings me closer to God, to people, to my family. It is not a drug."

In what context does ayahuasca stop being a religious practice and become just a psychoactive substance? Or, as some researchers see it, when does the psychoactive substance become sacred?

The Amazonian "caboclo" (forest dweller), in her simple answer, demonstrates that she knows how to distinguish one from the other, as indicated in the dialogue above, which indeed took place. The simplicity of her answer summarizes this complex question regarding the ritual use of ayahuasca, and reveals how the people who use it differentiate it from other substances and/or from other contexts. At the same time she indicates the important role this beverage plays as a significant element in the creation of her cultural identity.

Ayahuasca, for this simple caboclo people, is not ingested for the purpose of psychedelic sensations or as an attempt to escape, for a few moments, from life and its problems, frustrations and challenges, or for recreation. They ingest ayahuasca with the serene conviction that they are practicing an act of faith, finding in it a communion with the Divine.

---

[1] Term used by some Ayahuasca religions to refer to the tea also known as Hoasca, Vegetal and Ayahuasca

Among the Indians, where this religious practice began, there isn't a single way that it is used. The multiple names (yagé, mariri, natema, etc.) also indicate the diversity in rituals and preparation methods. Despite the differences, there is one common characteristic that stands out: ayahuasca as a sacred element that brings together and integrates man with his environment, his group; ayahuasca as a religion, as a factor of identity, capable of accentuating and stimulating the sense of belonging to a time, a group and a place.

In the urban environment, the first doctrinal use is attributed to Raimundo Irineu Serra, who brought ayahuasca to Rio Branco in 1930, after encountering it in Peru.[2] At the end of the forties, one of his disciples, Daniel Pereira de Matos, who was also in the Brazilian state of Acre, began another doctrinal line known as "Barquinha", with very different characteristics.[3] At the beginning of the sixties, José Gabriel da Costa created the União do Vegetal in Porto Velho, Rondônia, calling the tea by the name of *Vegetal,* with a ritual that has its own very unique characteristics.[4]

These three initial doctrinal lines have managed to maintain, throughout these long decades, the formidable characteristic of the indigenous use. This includes the exclusively ritualistic use of ayahuasca, as well as ayahuasca as an important factor in building community and the development and strengthening of cultural identity and a sense of reality. Ayahuasca, which is beneficial to those who drink it and facilitates a sense of well-being and self-acceptance. Ayahuasca, which makes the person who drinks it feel good about being himself, and for being where he is, at peace with his time and place, connected to the reality of his challenges and place in the world.

The expansion of ayahuasca into large urban centers, and the creation of new doctrines, formats and uses, including the explicitly non-ritual use focused only on its chemical effects and objectives, has finally revealed something that, though it could have been predicted, had not yet been (and continues not to be) perceived. The notable characteristics associated with the religious use of ayahuasca, including the elements that build and strengthen identity, community, and increased individual and collective self-esteem, are not automatic or necessary effects of the ayahuasca tea. Ayahuasca alone is insufficient to produce the beneficial effects, or at least with the degree of intensity and duration desired.

This is because the drink alone is not enough. If it was enough, one could just

---

[2] See article by Alves in this book.

[3] See article by Araújo Neto in this book.

[4] See article by Soares and Moura in this book.

ingest DMT (the active principle found in ayahuasca) in a pill. But beyond the tea is the enchantment, the mystery, the belief, the culture: the physical reality that is constructed by human ingenuity and soul, which is capable of creating meaning that goes far beyond the material. There are those who ingest ayahuasca believing that they will be able to expand their consciousness, develop their creativity and imagination, gain new perspectives on the world and on themselves, but they are forgetting that those effects, if they exist, are a result of the ritual, the belief, and the cultural environment, and not from the ayahuasca tea itself.

Slowly, people from large urban centers around Brazil came into contact with ayahuasca and became fascinated with its effects. Too quickly they began to *'doctrinate the entire world'*, to use a caboclo expression. In their hurry, all they took was the psychoactive substance, the material substrate, the physical, the chemical, and left behind the complex and delicate cultural practice. They left behind the enchantment, the mystery, and the immaterial human aspect that transform the psychoactive substance into a sacrament, a means of communion. In summary: the culture. Indigenous use and the urban use of these initial lines (UDV, Barquinha, Daime) never saw the ayahuasca as a psychoactive substance, a hallucinogen, if we understand this term to mean a substance that causes hallucination, separation, alienation, and that removes a sense of reality, time and place. It is not a hallucinogenic mixture that was created; that wasn't the objective. Furthermore, it is believed that ayahuasca was discovered, not created, and that it is a means of communing with a different, immaterial reality.

The focus, whether intentional or not, on just the chemical aspect, explains why ayahuasca, in certain uses and practices, does not present that special characteristic of being an extraordinary facilitator of integrating people within their surroundings. On the contrary, it presents characteristics with a tendency toward isolation, as if one is fleeing from this "consumerist, violent and unjust society," wanting to return to the forest to be in contact with nature, "far from mundane temptations."

When ayahuasca is diverged from its immaterial, enchanting content, what remains is merchandise, which is subject to being sold, bought or traded. To use an imperfect comparison, the holy host can be reduced to an insignificant wheat cracker, subject to being sold, and yet it can and should be a sacrament of immeasurable value. Faith is what differentiates the cracker from the sacrament.

Faith, the sentiment and the symbolism, is what attributes meaning and significance to something that is pure matter, a chemical compound. The absence of this element explains why some seek to concentrate ayahuasca, boiling its components down more than what is considered correct by the different religious lineages. Pharmacologically speaking, there is the DMT, present in a greater or smaller quantity, according to the proportion of ingredients and boiling time. There is neither right nor wrong: there is only a chemical composition.

The doctrine, faith, and meaning of the religion is what establishes boundaries and rules, clarifies the notion of right and wrong, and provides significance. It is possible for these rules to be altered, and new ritualistic formats formed. Such alterations have been made in fact, but they have been made within the internal logic that preserves the enchantment, the mystery and the faith, precisely in order to not destroy that immaterial element that brings about transformation and contains symbolic value and meaning.

Currently new experiments are being conducted with ayahuasca, including its production by means of the extraction of its chemical elements from other plants, or by the synthesis of DMT, harmine, harmaline, etc. Inevitably, a substance can be obtained that impacts the mind and alters perceptions, stirring the depths of the human psyche, a psychoactive that is almost identical to ayahuasca, chemically speaking. But it will be merely a psychoactive substance, incapable of spawning a doctrinal body of teachings that has a solid set of principles, or providing a consistent vision of the world that brings people together and inspires them to live well with one another.

There are other cultural constructs, equally complex and fragile, that make use of substances that are considered psychoactive, and which in present times have been equally distorted, emptied of their immaterial content and transformed into simple drugs.

Peyote is an example of this phenomenon. Traditionally and ancestrally used by native people in the United States and Mexico, peyote came into contact with the modern marketplace, where religion is just another product. Today it can be obtained over the internet, on its own or combined with a cocktail of other psychoactives.

The same phenomenon happened with this complex and precious sacrament: there were those who, in the complex and rich indigenous ritual, saw only the pharmacology. Again they took the psychoactive and left behind the mystery, the culture and the faith.

The United Nations' Vienna Convention of 1971 anticipated the possibility of excluding substances that are used ritualistically from their schedule of illicit substances. In Brazil, even during the time when Brazilian Law 6368/76 was in effect, which did not consider such a premise, the Brazilian Federal Narcotics Council

(CONFEN), the agency that determined which substances were to be considered drugs and therefore restricted, permitted the ritual use of ayahuasca. The agency that replaced CONFEN, the National Drug Policy Council (CONAD), also permitted the religious use of ayahuasca. Presently, Brazilian Law 11.343/06, Article 2, which is more in alignment with the Vienna Convention, excludes substances used in religious rituals from being considered "drugs", for the purpose of legal restriction.

All codes of law and decisions that recognize the ritual use of ayahuasca represent important victories. They are legal instruments that defend and safeguard the right to plurality, diversity, and freedom of creed. They provide discursive and legal recourses that are instrumental to defending and sustaining this right. There are several studies in the area of Human Sciences, especially in the field of anthropology, upon which these legal determinations are based. Such studies emphasize that the context, more than the pharmacology of a given psychoactive substance, determines the outcome (whether harmful or beneficial).

These studies and legal qualifications highlight the psychoactive properties of the substances that are used ritualistically, recognizing the respective religious practices as deserving of equal constitutional protection, the same as any other religious practice. As a result, a unilateral or partial interpretation that views this religious recognition by the State as a mere act of liberality, tolerance, a concession, or a special consideration for a specific group, is not correct. There are several studies that, based on this reference, study these practices as something exceptional: how it is that a society represses drugs of abuse, and at the same time permits ritual use of a psychoactive substance by a small group, in other words, a "controlled use". This is an implicit affirmation that the substance itself is a "drug", but since the use is "controlled" within a social context, then it is accepted.

A different point of reference, however, is also possible, from the perspective of those who have maintained a tradition since a time when the notion of government was nonexistent. Such people do not feel that they are using, nor would they want to use, any psychoactive substances. It would be compelling to have studies that, instead of focusing on groups that preserve an ancestral indigenous tradition, would invert the focus and study how western market society has transformed an ancient religious sacrament into a hallucinogenic psychoactive substance, one that is just one more product in the virtual and concrete marketplace of psychoactives that can be purchased in pharmacies and on the internet in the form of pills, drops, injections, etc. As a human construct, ayahuasca also touches on that old question of whether or not reality is limited to its exact physical or chemical composition. Ayahuasca, as a religious element, is much more than the leaf Psychotria viridis, the vine Banisteriopsis caapi and water, boiled or not. In addition to those elements, it is enhanced by a constellation of actions, feelings, attitudes, beliefs, practices, and details that lend meaning and value to the symbols, objects, nature, and plants that all together create a human religious experience – an experience that represents the most profound and transcendent experience a religious ritual can make possible.

In relation to ayahuasca, the great challenge of this new century will be the preservation of the sacred nature of ayahuasca in the face of an anxious and voracious expansion that has already begun. The great risk is that people will not accept the slow rhythm of individual learning, the building of the relationship between man and his social, geographical, historical and moral context, as a prerequisite for leadership and personal growth within the doctrine itself. The great risk is that it becomes a *fast track religion,* ayahuasca for the masses, low quality and high quantity, with plenty of DMT, harmaline, harmine, B-carboline and other alkaloids, but *void* of significance, empty of meaning, disconnected from people, from their time and their reality – an effervescent legalized psychoactive, generally harmless, but very distant from its origins and symbolism.

PART III
Hoasca and the Environment

Ecology: Caring for the Mariri and Chacrona and The Preservation and Improvement of the Landscape and the Environment

Paulo Afonso Amato Condé

We are living in the first decades of a new century – a century that we want to be different for humanity. This is a task that demands a long-term significant effort. We believe that this undertaking requires that we begin making changes within ourselves and within the Institution. Respect for nature is a contemporary theme and it is also present in the name and the origin of our União do Vegetal. For this reason, the theme "Environment" was chosen for some of the presentations of the 2nd International Hoasca Conference. This theme will be divided into two parts: "Caring for the Mariri and Chacrona" and "Preservation and Improvement of Landscape and Environment."

The origin of the UDV is connected to the Amazon Forest, where Mestre Gabriel created the UDV with simplicity, together with his family and others who lived in the rubber-tapping regions of the rainforest. The essence of the UDV is directly related to the forest and its sacred plants. We drink a tea, which is the union of two sacred plants: the Mariri and the Chacrona. These plants, which are native to the Amazon forest, give us, through the tea, the opportunity to deeply experience moments of consciousness that facilitate spiritual evolution.

Because of this we have the duty to recognize the value of nature in our lives, revering nature as sacred and recognizing that we are an integral part of it. The search for harmony and equilibrium is one of the principles of our religious society and is also the foundation that sustains nature.

We are aware that we need to care for the cultivation and the conservation of the mariri and the chacrona, upon which our religious society depends. From this awareness we have developed several initiatives that will be presented in the theme "Caring for the Mariri and Chacrona." Data will be presented on cultivation and management, plant sanitation control, forest management, self-sufficiency and the sustainability of our plantations. Permaculture and agro-forestry systems are currently being used on several mariri and chacrona plantations. These principles allow for these species to be cultivated in a sustainable manner, provide the tea for current and future generations.

We are aware of the need to educate our leaders and researchers to develop projects and academic studies in order to identify varieties of the plants we use, and to preserve the original genetic identity of each species through germplasm banks.[1]

The locations where we conduct our religious activities and our plantation areas have some qualities that distinguish them as special areas of land. We may consider the majority of them as areas of environmental preservation, given the biodiversity of plants and trees that are cultivated on site. This leads to another topic that we will address: "Preservation and Improvements of the Landscape and the Environment." Related to this subject is the creation of the "Novo Encanto Association for Ecological Development" that seeks to connect spirituality and ecology. The creation of this organization has facilitated initiatives for the preservation of areas of rainforest and biodiversity, more efficient use of water, and the raising of awareness of the members regarding their daily practices.

The initiatives of the Beneficent Spiritist Center União do Vegetal in partnership with the Novo Encanto Association for Ecological Development are becoming more visible, such as the "Water in the Third Millennium" Festival, which integrates art and ecology in order to raise public awareness to respect and preserve water. This endeavor aims to make each núcleo of the UDV a model of environmental practice, with respect for nature as a key principle.

We take this opportunity to honor one of the mestres of the origin, Mestre Florêncio, who was one of the first mestres to start a plantation of mariri and chacrona in the UDV. In honoring him we also want to honor all the mestres who were trained by Mestre Gabriel, and also all the people who work to benefit the many plantations that are being developed by the UDV.

---

[1] Germplasm is a collection of genetic resources for an organism. It consists of living tissue from which new plants can be grown. It can be a seed or another plant part – a leaf, a piece of stem, pollen or even just a few cells that can be turned into a whole plant. Germplasm contains the information for a species' genetic makeup, a valuable natural resource of plant diversity.

28: Caring for the Mariri and the Chacrona

Distribution, Cultivation, Sustainability and Conservation of the Species Used in the Preparation of the Hoasca Tea

Maria Alice Corrêa

Introduction

Ayahuasca is a traditional decoction from South America. The infusion is made from the caulis of the liana *Banisteriopsis caapi* with the addition of other plants. The leaves of the tree Psychotria viridis are often added, though other species of the genus Psychotria are also used. It is also common among traditional groups of Amazonia, Peru, Colombia, and Ecuador, to add various other plant species.

The use of the vine and the decoctions resulting from combining it with other plant species forms the essential spiritual practices of many of the religious groups in this region of the world. The Quechua term "ayahuasca," used by some of the social groups of South America, is applied not only to the beverage made from these two basic plant combinations, but it can also refer to the *Banisteriopsis caapi* vine itself, or to the tea prepared only with the vine, without any other plant added. Some of these social groups have many names for the different growth phases of the vine, and utilize them in distinct conditions in their rituals.

In the Beneficent Spiritist Center União do Vegetal (CEBUDV) the beverage is called Hoasca or Vegetal. It is considered a sacrament in this religion and is prepared with two plants: *Banisteriopsis caapi* and Psychotria viridis. The beverage has a strong aroma, bitter taste, and a color that varies from brown to reddish brown.

Studies on Hoasca (ayahuasca) have contributed to the elucidation of many questions that involve the beverage and its use in many cultures, under different conditions of preparation and ingestion.

Botanically speaking, very little or almost nothing has been published regarding *Banisteriopsis caapi* and little is known about the plants in their natural habitats, the behavior of the species, dispersion centers, domestication and cultivation processes, genetic variations, crossings, natural hybridization and conservation of germplasm.

The same applies to the other species of these genera that are also used to prepare the ayahuasca tea.

The topics discussed in this article are obviously not conclusive, but they represent observation data over a period of more than 20 years of study and observation of these species, both in their native habitat of the Amazon Forest as well as plants cultivated in bio-geographical regions outside the Amazon.

Taxonomy and Identification of the Species

Starting with the first work conducted for the UDV in Brazil in 1991 (Corrêa 1991a), parameters were established for ethno-pharmacological studies as well as for the observation and data collection of an unlimited amount of information regarding the behavior and taxonomy of these species. Information was gathered about their dispersion centers, natural phyto-geographic distribution range, morphological and physiological characteristics, crossing and hybridization, cultivation aspects, adaptation to the different biomes in Brazil, management in areas with cultivated forests, procedures for the conservation of the germplasm of the plants used, and similar species.

The *Malpighiaceae* family has approximately 63 genera that encompass nearly 800 pantropical species. It was divided into two subfamilies (Niedenzu 1928) based on the shape of the receptacle (torus) and the fruit: *Pyramidotorae* (winged) and *Planitorae* (unwinged). In order to standardize the nomenclature codes, Morton (1968) proposed the names *Gaudichaudioideae* (to substitute *Pyramidotorae*) and *Malpighioideae* (to substitute *Planitorae*). Anderson (1977) removed some of the genera included in *Malpighioideae* and created another subfamily *Byrsonimoideae*. Therefore the family is now composed of three subfamilies: *Gaudichaudioideae, Malpighioideae* and *Byrsonimoideae*. In Brazil there are 32 genera with approximately 300 species distributed throughout several biomes. The genus Banisteriopsis is distributed exclusively in the Neotropics, including several species that are native to Brazil (Gates 1982).

The species *Banisteriopsis caapi* is well represented in Brazil in the Amazon Tropical Forest region. It flowers and produces fruit from December through August, depending on the region. It has been widely cultivated through cuttings and seeds in the southeast, northeast, and central-east regions of Brazil and is in the category of a semi-domesticated plant.

The characteristics that determine that the *Banisteriopsis* be included in this family are:
- opposite leaves with variations in size, sometimes thick and even membranous, with lining (*Malpighioideae* hair), cells with crystals, petiolated leaves, and Malpighia glands at the leaf base.
- racemose or cymose inflorescence, pink or white flowers, floral calix with five sepals, five petals and ten stamens. The sepals each contain two pairs of glands, and sometimes one can be missing. The stamens may be reduced, modified, and unequal in the species. The Banisteriopsis fruit is a samara type and has a curved portion turned toward the center of the fruit (internal side) and the dorsal wings are entirely continuous and membranous (Barroso et al 1986; Gates 1982)

The presence of underground organs, similar to geophytes, is present in the *Banisteriopsis caapi* species. Field observations in both the Amazon forest and in areas of cultivation show that that these organs facilitate the regeneration process of the plant, especially when the part of the plant that is above-ground is harvested for the preparation of the tea.

The table below, presented by Corrêa (1991), shows the comparison between the three *Banisteriopsis* species. For the *Banisteriopsis membranifolia* there are no records indicating its use for the preparation of the tea, but there is a great taxonomical similarity to the *Banisteriopsis caapi*. Future phytochemical analysis may bring new understanding and possibilities for use (See Table 1). The *Rubiaceae* family has varying habits and is divided into three subfamilies: *Rubioideae; Chinchonoideae* and *Guettardioideae*, each one containing a number of tribes, based on habit, shape of calix and lining that are characteristic of the family. The subfamily *Rubioideae* has nine tribes and among them the tribe *Psychotrieae*, which includes, among others, the genera *Psychotria, Palicourea, Cephaelis* and *Rudgea* (Barroso et al. 1986).

Table 1 – Comparison Between Three Species of Banisteriopsis

BANISTERIOPSIS CAAPI	BANISTERIOPSIS MURICATA	BANISTERIOPSIS MEMBRANIFOLIA
Leaf: petiole: 9-25 mm length. blade: (4.8) 8.2 – 15.9 (20.5) mm length X (2.3) 3.5 -7.5 (11.5) mm width, densely ovate, obtuse to truncate at the base, acuminate tip.	petiole: 5-16 mm length blade: (3.5) 5.3 – 12.7 (16.5) cm length X (2.3) 4.8 – 7.5 (9.0) cm wide, oval elliptic or rounded, cuneate or cordate at the base, acuminate or apiculate at the tip.	petiole: 11-20 (27) mm length leaf: 4.7 -12.9 cm length X 2.7 – 6.3 cm wide, elliptic to obovate, obtuse at the base, acuminate tip.
Inflorescence: bracteates and bracteoles: 1.0 – 1.8 mm length, triangular to elliptic, deciduous before or during flowering, rarely after. Peduncles: 7 – 11 mm length.	bracteates and bracteoles: 0.5 – 1.2 mm length, densely triangular, persistent. Peduncles: 3 – 12 mm length.	bracteates and bracteoles: 1.5 – 2.2 mm length, narrowly oblong, deciduous at budding. Peduncles: 11 – 17 mm length.
Flower: elliptic sepals, obtuse at point, 2.0 – 3.5 mm length X 1.5 – 2.0 mm width, petals light pink turning light yellow over time, 5.0 – 8.5 mm length X 4.0 – 6.0 mm width.	Ovate, acute at tip 1.5 – 3.0 mm length X 1.2 – 2.5 mm width, pink turning lighter over time, the posterior petal has a yellow base, 4.0 – 8.5 mm X 3.5 – 8.0 mm width.	Oblong, round at point 3.0 – 3.5 mm length X 1.8 – 2.5 mm width, light pink or white turning light yellow over time, 7.0 – 10.0 mm X 5.5 – 9.0 mm width.
Stamens: filaments 2.0 – 4.0 mm length.	Filaments 1.0 – 3.6 mm length.	Filaments 1.8 – 3.2 mm length.
Ovary: white sericeous 1.0 – 1.2 mm height.	white sericeous 0.8 – 1.4 mm height.	white sericeous 1.0 – 1.2 mm height.
Fruit: winged samara.	winged samara (fruit).	winged samara (fruit).
Flowering: Dec. to Aug. Fruiting: Mar. to Aug.	Collected in all months of the year with flower and/or fruit	Flowering: Feb. to Jun. Fruiting: Mar. and Apr.

The genus *Psychotria* has 954 species (Anderson, 1992) and is characterized by:

- Inferior ovary with one ovule per loculus in the ovary of the flower, with basal insertion;
- Pulpous fruit, drupaceous, indehiscent (does not open);
- Terminal or axillary inflorescence in panicles with spirals of 5 sepals, 5 petals, 4-5 stamens;
- Flowers and fruits during the hottest months of the year;
- The species have leaf domatia (small chambers) found on the underside of the leaf.

The types of chacrona recognized in the UDV by the name of *chacrona* "cabocla", chacrona *"caianinha"* (or *"chacroninha"*) and chacrona *"caneluda"* (also known as *"orelha de onça"* and *"caboclinha"*), identified in the work of Corrêa

(1991) are: *Psychotria viridis* Ruiz & Pavón, Prod. 2:61, pl. 210.1799 – chacrona cabocla; *Psychotria niveobarbata* (Müll. Arg) Britton – chacrona caianinha; *Psychotria carthagenensis* Jac., Enum. Plant. Carib.: 16.1760 – chacrona caneluda.

Table 2 – Comparison Between Three Species of the Genus *Psychotria*

PSYCHOTRIA VIRIDIS	PSYCHOTRIA LEIOCARPA	PSYCHOTRIA CARTHAGENENSIS
Small tree 2-4 m height	Small shrub up to 2 m height	Small shrub (0.5) 1-3(6) m height
Stipules 8-15 mm length, ovate	Stipules 2 mm length, 2 acicular bristles	Stipules 6-8 mm length, with sheath, ovate
Elliptic-obovate leaf, short petiolated (6.5) 9-15 cm length; (3) 4-5 (6) cm width	Elliptic leaf, cuneate base 4-11 cm length; 1.5-3 cm width	Obovate leaf, rarely elliptic, long petiolated (6) 7.5-13 (16) cm length; (2) 2.5-5.5 (6) cm width
White corolla	White corolla	White corolla
Corolla tube 1.5 mm length; 1.0 mm cylindrical	Corolla tube sub-cylindrical	Corolla tube 2.5-3 mm length; 1.5 mm diameter
Stamens 2 mm	Stamens approx. 2 mm	Stamens 3 mm
Fruit: spheroid ripe; ellipsoid dry 4.5-5.0 mm length; 3.0-3.5 mm diameter	Fruit: spheroid ripe 5.0 mm; 7.0 mm diameter	Fruit: spheroid ripe; ellipsoid dry 4.5-5.0 (6) mm length; 3.5-4.5 mm diameter
Flowering: Sep.-Mar. Fruiting: Jan., Jun. & Sep.	Flowering: Nov. to Jan. Fruiting: Apr.- Jun.	Flowering: Oct.-Dec. Fruiting: May. -Jul.

The work presented at the Conference by Corrêa (1991a) contributed to some important clarifications for the UDV, such as the correct taxonomic identification of both plants used in the preparation of the tea by this religious institution. One important clarification is with regard to the names Tucunacá and Caupuri, used by the UDV to denominate the vine. These are actually *chemical forms* of the same species, *Banisteriopsis caapi*, which has wide variation in its morphological characteristics. According to what has been already mentioned by Gates (1982) in the work on the Neotropics with the genera Banisteriopsis and Diplopterys, these variations do not constitute a solid basis to establish a taxonomical segregation of the species.

Other issues were also clarified, such as the identification of three species of the genus *Psychotria*, and the proximity that exists among some species of the genus *Banisteriopsis*, like *Banisteriopsis muricata* (Cav.) Cuatrec. and *Banisteriopsis membranifolia*.

It is important to note that due to the fact that *Banisteriopsis muricata* is used by several Amazonian groups for the preparation of ayahuasca, new studies were made possible related to cultivation research work. This species has received different popular names in the various regions. The word *"bejuco"* translates as "vine." Peru: *"ayahuasca negro," "ayahuasca rosada," "ayahuasca de los brujos," "sarcelo;"* Bolivia: *"bejuco hoja de plata;"* Argentina: *"sombra de tora;"* El Salvador: *"bejuco da casa," "pastora," "ala de zompopo."* The species has a wide distribution, from Mexico to Argentina (Gates 1982). In Brazil it is found in areas of the *"Cerrado"* (savannah) in the central plateau, state of Minas Gerais and state of São Paulo, as well as in areas of Atlantic Rainforest.

Distribution and Preservation of the Species

The delimitation of the center of origin of *Banisteriopsis caapi* is still unknown. According to Gates (1982) it is difficult to know where this plant is native, since it is widely cultivated in the regions of Bolivia, Peru, Ecuador, Colombia and the Brazilian Amazon. This can be probably explained by the very ancient use of ayahuasca by migratory social groups of the Amazon basin, who were able to easily cultivate the plant through cuttings. The challenge of determining its center of origin represents an increasingly urgent need in present times, in order to select centers of germplasm conservation where the species can be cultivated in a way that preserves the genetic identity and variation of the species.[1]

The same could be happening to *Psychotria viridis*, as the species is also distributed throughout different locations of the Amazon region and can also be easily cultivated through its leaves.

In the UDV, the *Banisteriopsis caapi* is called mariri and is recognized in two forms or types: mariri *tucunacá* and *mariri caupuri*. The *Psychotria viridis* is called chacrona caboclo, which is the one most frequently used to prepare the Hoasca tea.

These species that are used for the preparation of the tea are included in the category of semi-domesticated species, as the practice of cultivation, by more than one religious group, has intensified.

Among the religious societies that use the tea, the UDV appears to be the most organized in terms of cultivation and selection of cultivars.[2] The CEBUDV has a

---

[1] Germplasm is a collection of genetic resources for an organism. It consists of living tissue from which new plants can be grown. It can be a seed or another plant part – a leaf, a piece of stem, pollen or even just a few cells that can be turned into a whole plant. Germplasm contains the information for a species' genetic makeup, a valuable natural resource of plant diversity.

[2] A cultivar is a plant or group of plants selected for desirable characteristics that can be maintained by propagation.

Plantation Department within its administrative structure, whose principle function is to provide guidelines for the best practices of cultivation and management throughout all of its núcleos in Brazil. These guidelines are distributed to those members who are responsible for maintaining weekly communication with the national Plantation Department.

The Plantation Department was created in the early 1990's, from a request of a member of the Cadre of Mestres, Luiz Antônio dos Santos Filho, who noticed the need for internal studies related to the plants and the need to adopt uniformity in the cultivation practices within the UDV.[3] At that time the department was established with the decision to practice organic cultivation of the species, along with observations on the acclimatization and adaptation of the species in different regions. This department also provides consulting support to the General Directorate of the UDV and, when necessary, provides expert opinions to the Government.

Presently the UDV has its General Headquarters (in Brasilia) and 165 núcleos and authorized distributions that cultivate the plants. According to a Plantation Department census, in five years the number of cultivated mariri plants increased by 27% and chacrona by 10%. In 2008 the number of plants cultivated by the UDV was 48,939 mariri plants and 16,277 chacrona plants. In 2003 those numbers were 38,579 mariri and 14,868 chacrona. These numbers show that with 14,000 members the UDV is demonstrating self-sufficiency in the cultivation of the plants used in its rituals.

Although criteria have been established for the selection of cultivars to increase the diversity on the plantations throughout the UDV, this process remains empirical. The parameters for choosing these cultivars are widely varied.

One of the existing gaps is in the way that this genetic selection has been carried out over many years by Amazonian populations and over the past 40 years by the UDV in non-Amazonian regions. It is unknown exactly which characteristics are being selected through the seedlings grown from cuttings and those grown from seeds. It is surprising, however, that regardless of the bio-geographical region where the plants are being cultivated, they continue to present their active principles in sufficient quantity for the preparation of the tea, attending to the spiritual objective of the Hoasca tea in the UDV.

[3] Luiz Antonio dos Santos Filho, who belongs to the Cadre of Mestres of Núcleo São João Batista (in São Paulo), began the work of collecting and systematizing the information on mariri and chacrona plants in 1991, according to documentation of the UDV. From 1991 to 1993, there were individuals responsible for the plantation teams at the núcleos, however there was not yet a department or a national coordinator.

Excellent results have been obtained from the practices of cultivation in biogeographical regions outside the Amazon biome, the management and genetic conservation of the variations in the species, and the work of selecting better cultivars that represent ample chemical and genetic variables. Still, there are many questions to be answered, especially those related to the studies that need to be conducted on population and genetic conservation in both Amazonian and non-Amazonian regions.

Genetic variability accounts for a wide spectrum of ecological, physiological and behavioral responses in relationship to the environment. Without genetic variability and its interaction with the environment it would be impossible to obtain superior genotypes, i.e., desired characteristics, through genetic improvement. Therefore, the genetic material of a population is of great importance for the conservation of the species and for use in research, especially for improving the concentration of active principles and adaptation to unfavorable conditions.

Genetic resources consist of the genetic variability organized as a set of materials that are different from one another, called germplasm. This is the element that manages the genetic variability within the species, accounting for the differences that exist in the specific features among the individuals of the same species. Conserving genetic resources requires knowledge of how these resources are distributed in nature. Williams (1991) considers that the genetic resources in the tropical forests are divided into: 1) wild species in natural settings, usually in forests or some populations adapted to wider eco-zones; and 2) cultivated resources, primitively associated with traditional communities. Each population represents a source of genetic variation and diversity in its adaptation to new environments, i.e., material with potential for improvement, use and genetic conservation, as it presents possible economical and other value.

Behavior and Characteristics of the Mariri Vine

Vines, in general, are plants that characteristically have a very peculiar behavior, different from other herbaceous species, shrubs or trees, in terms of their anatomical structure. Vines and lianas present significant differences in the organization of their vascular bundles in comparison to the habits of other plants. Studies in this area are still scarce. One of the reasons for this scarcity is the difficulty of sample collection and the delimitation of populations.

From the point of view of management of vines, very little is yet known; however, it is known that many species develop mechanisms to survive damages to their stems (Fischer and Ewers, 1989). In observations done throughout the years with *Banisteriopsis caapi*, it has demonstrated an incredible capacity for regeneration, observed in the active regrowth of new shoots after partial harvesting for preparing the tea.

The density of vines varies depending on stages of growth and maturity of the forest. Ligneous plants (those with woody bark) such as *Banisteriopsis caapi*, connect the canopy of the tree it is colonizing with the canopies of neighboring trees. Generally, three to nine tree canopies become interconnected, making these plants an important element for the connection and interaction of many species of animals that live in the canopy of the forest.

When a tree falls, either naturally or by cutting, whose canopy is connected to the canopies of other trees by vines, large clearings are created (Fox 1968; Appanah and Putz 1984). This process is directly related to the regeneration of the forest, but if it is caused by intentional deforestation in the natural habitat of the species, it can cause disequilibrium in the colonization process of these areas. Some species of vines have a more aggressive behavior in the production of adventitious (new) shoots and the re-colonization of an area (Pinnard and Putz 1994).

For *Banisteriopsis caapi* there are no published studies on these aspects. The observations carried out in cultivation areas in Amazonian regions show that the species reaches the canopy with great ease. In non-Amazonian regions the same behavior is observed when conditions, such as luminosity, substrate, humidity and temperature, are favorable. This is an elegant plant, with a high capacity for adaption to adverse climatic conditions.

Other aspects can also be considered, such as the fact that vines perform an important function for specific hydraulic conductivity in the forest, due to the type of trunk they have and their anatomical organization, which is superior to trees that are a similar height (Gartner et al. 1990).

Vines may perform much more important functions in the hydrologic cycle of the forest than is presently known, preserving the humidity of the soil for other plants species that also have surface roots. Vines are also important for the survival of mammals, snakes and other animals, establishing pathways throughout the forest canopy that provide access to nourishment and genic flux for these creatures that remain, for their whole existence, in this layer of the forest.

Though we do not yet know the impact that cutting vines could provoke in terms of the alteration of the relative abundance of the species, some studies already show that the cutting of these plants is an important factor in the management of the extraction of wood (Vidal et al. 1998). This represents a threat for many vine species of different families in areas of the Amazon forest, but especially for the *Banisteriopsis caapi* and other species of this genus. It is evident that there is a need to preserve areas where this plant occurs naturally. It is also evident that there is a need for in-depth studies on the biology of regeneration patterns, as well as the elaboration and description of formulas for processes of cutting and regrowth. This can contribute significantly to the development of practices that are based on a better understanding of the beneficial role of this plant for the forest.

Behavior and Characteristics of the Chacrona

The chacrona is a small tree, and the species presents variations in size of the plant, and in the size and shape of leaves, fruits and seeds. *Psychotria viridis* grows to about three meters high (9.8 feet) in some non-Amazonian regions, and up to five meters (16.4 feet) in the Amazon forest. Other species, such as the chacrona *caianinha (Psychotria niveobarbata)* are smaller, usually between 1.5 and 2.0 meters high. These species are also native in semi-deciduous areas of Atlantic Forest. *Psychotria carthagenensis* has a wider distribution, occurring also in semi-deciduous areas of Atlantic forest and in areas of the *"cerrado"* (savannah), generally reaching a height of 3 meters, and rarely as much as 6 meters high. UDV members distinguish the species for use in the preparation of the Hoasca tea by the leaves. The plant is recognized as being chacrona by the presence of what is called the *"guia"* (plant-produced chamber), which is technically called the domatia, a structure present in some botanical families, including the Rubiaceae family. In the chacrona the domatia appears on the under-side of the leaf. The leaf allows for vegetative reproduction through its meristematic tissue, located especially near the domatia, which allows the development of adventitious roots and consequently the forming of a new plant.

Cultivation and Sustainability

The cultivation practices adopted by UDV núcleos, both in Amazonian and non-Amazonian areas, favor interaction with other plant species, through the use of Agroforestry Systems.[4] The species used in the preparation of the Hoasca Tea have been gradually domesticated and acclimated in the different biomes of Brazil. One of the cultivation practices that has been adopted is to obtain cultivars from different

---

[4] Agroforestry Systems combine agricultural and forestry technologies to create diverse, productive, healthy and sustainable land-use systems.

regions of the Amazon Forest, in order to increase genetic variability within cultivation areas. The selection of cultivars is based primarily on the health of the mariri and chacrona plants. From mariri cultivars, cuttings and seeds can be used to produce new seedlings. From chacrona cultivars, leaves, cuttings and seeds can be used.

Most of the time, the properties where núcleos of the UDV are located are close to rural areas. Often the land acquired has no plantings, or the original vegetation has been altered or partially removed. Therefore, the first task is to restore the vegetation, and afterwards to gradually introduce the species to be cultivated for use in the preparation of the tea. In these areas, soil analysis and correction is done in order to encourage soil characteristics similar to the areas of the forest where the plants originated. The soil amendments used are exclusively organic.

In terms of mineral nutrition, nitrogen is one of the most important elements in the life cycle of plants. An absence or excess of nitrogen may significantly compromise the development of a plant. When nitrogen is lacking, growth is stunted. When necessary, nitrogen is mobilized from older leaves to areas of new growth. One of the typical symptoms of this condition is the characteristic chlorosis (yellowing of normally green leaves) and precocious leaf fall, as well as changes in the morphology of the plant, such as a reduction in the aerial/root ratio and reduction in length, width and thickness of the leaves. Excess of nitrogen is also unfavorable, causing excessive growth of the aerial part of the plant to the detriment of the roots, impeding absorption mechanisms and altering the balance of phytohormones.

For this reason, cultivation techniques include the use of mycorrhizal fungi, liquid organic compost and leguminous cover crops with plants, for biological nitrogen fixation in cultivation areas of *Banisteriopsis caapi* and *Psychotria viridis*.

The cultivation of both species is conducted in two manners: through seeds obtained via sexual reproduction and asexual reproduction (or vegetative) through the vegetative parts of the plant. In the cultivation of *Banisteriopsis* and *Psychotria*, the seeds are obtained after the flowering of the adult species. For the cultivation of vegetative parts of the Banisteriopsis, a cutting is used that includes the "knot", as it is called in the UDV. Preferably a young branch, with very active meristematic tissues, is selected. For the Psychotria, mature leaves are used, as well as cuttings.

Field observations of the species' behavioral physiology have been important in the understanding of the species' nutritional needs, limiting growth factors and production of sufficient quantities of alkaloids.

The seedlings, in the initial phase of development, are kept in soft plastic pots (pictures 10 & 11) in nurseries (picture 13), or in small plant beds, directly on the forest floor (picture 12). In both instances, they are kept close to the areas they will be transferred to permanently along with a tree for support.

In many locations a wooden arbor is used to support the vine where the vegetation has not yet developed sufficiently or there are no trees for support. (Picture 14)

In the procedures for harvesting the *Psychotria viridis* to prepare the tea, timing is taken into consideration since differences in the concentration of the alkaloids have been observed, according to Callaway (2002). The leaves are harvested in the morning or at dusk, when a higher concentration of alkaloids is observed. The leaves are harvested one at a time preserving the two leaves next to the leaf primordium. Successive harvests are not done on the same chacrona tree, allowing for leaf regeneration.

The harvesting of the mariri, both in the forest and in cultivation areas, is done starting from the top, down to the base, untangling the mariri branches from the canopy to avoid harming the supporting tree. In some locations a type of harvest management is done that considers the regeneration process, maintaining some developing branches or a small shoot near the root so that the plant can develop again. This practice saves time in the process of cultivation. One of the plant monitoring records showed the possibility of harvesting 3,100 pounds during a period of 25 years, beginning the harvest 12 years after planting. For the harvesting of the mariri the vine needs to have flowered at least two times in order for the plant to reach maturity. (Picture 15)

Companion Plants

Issues related to the interaction of the species *Banisteriopsis* and *Psychotria* with other species – called "companion plants" - show the relevance of phytosociology (relationships between plant species), floristic studies (relationships of plant species over geographic areas) and ecological biochemistry studies. These studies allow us to understand more about the distribution of species, biochemical communication and the behavior of species in occupation processes in niches of the Amazon forest, and in the biomes where they have been cultivated and integrated with species different from the ones in their natural habitat.

Allelopathy (a biological phenomenon by which an organism produces one or more biochemicals that influence the growth, survival and reproduction of other organisms) is a promising field of study in the area of ecological biochemistry, though there are many variables. Laboratory experiments and open field experiments many times take years to arrive at conclusions. Some people in the UDV have described their field observations associated with the preparation of the tea over many years. These individuals have brought up questions regarding the biochemical communication among the plants. There are also some shamans from Amazonian traditional groups who describe that, during the effect of the tea, there is a "memory of the plant" which causes images of insects to appear; tastes of elements directly related to the place where the plant grew also are evident, as well the interaction of plants and animals in the surrounding area.

In the UDV, companion plants are also considered indicative of the presence of the mariri and the chacrona in their natural habitats. The locations where the mariri and chacrona occur in large numbers are called *"reinados"*, or "kingdoms." In areas of native forest the plants considered to be companion plants are: *sororoca, palmeiral, samaúma, apuí, castanheira, pau d'arco, mulateiro, imburana de cheiro, maçaranduba, carapanaúba, breuzim* and *joão brandim*.[5] These are plants that may appear as indicators of the presence of kingdoms of mariri and chacrona and thus are considered companion plants. In addition to those cited, other plants may grow near the kingdoms and may also be considered companion plants.

Perceptions of flavor and characteristic effects of plants that grow naturally or are cultivated intentionally near the *Banisteriopsis caapi* and the *Psychotria viridis* appear to interact and contribute to this biochemical communication. Whether this influence takes place through metabolic routes, directly through the soil, or through the air by means of substances released by aerial parts of the plants is a subject that

---

[5] Some of the plants considered to be companion plants in the UDV, are listed here with their common and scientific names: *sororoca* includes various species of the *Maranta* genus of the *Marantaceae* family; *palmeiral* is a designation given to many species of palm trees such as *Buriti*, which is the common name for species of the genus *Mauritia, Mauritiella, Trithrinax* and *Astrocarym* of the *Arecaceae* (or *Palmae*); *samaúma* is the common name for some species of *Ceiba pentrandra, Ceiba speciosa* and *Ceiba insignis* (Kunth) P.E. Gibbs & Semir, *Malvaceae* family; *apuí* is the common name for *Ficus insipid* Wild; *Ficus fagifolia* (Miq.) Miq., *Moraceae, Clusia grandiflora* Splitg; *Clusia insignis* Mart, *Clusiaceaae* family; *castanheira* is the common name for *Bertholletia excels* Hum & Bonpl, *Lecythidaceae* family; *pau d'arco* is the common name for *Tabebuia impetiginosa* (Mart) Standl; *Tabebuia avellanedae, Tabebuia heptaphyla, Tabebuia serratofilia* (G. Don) Nichols.; *Tabebuia chrysotricha* and others also known as *Ipe Roxo, Bignoniaceae* family; *mulateiro* is the common name for *Calycophyllum spruceanum* (Benth) K. Sch., Rubiaceae family; *maçaranduba* is the common name for *Manikara huberi* (Ducke) Cheval.; *Manikara cavalcantei* Pires & W.A. Rodrigues; *Manikara bidentata* (A.DC.) Cheval., Sapotaceae family; *carapanaúba* is the common name for *Aspidosperma carapanauba* Pichon; *Aspidosperma nitidum* Banth., *Apocynaceae* family; breuzim is the common name for *Protium aracouchini* (Aubl.) March., *Protum icicariba* (DC) March., *Protium heptaphyllum* (Aubl.) March.; *Protium opacum* Sawr., Burseraceae family.

requires study, in addition to studies related to the physiology of the species *Banisteriopsis caapi* and *Psychotria viridis*. Many people who grow these plants know empirically that Banisteriopsis caapi, because it develops supported by another plant, causes a biochemical communication of the secondary metabolites of the supporting plant. In this interaction there is a differentiated behavior in the production of alkaloids and other substances, for instance, tannins. This means that the support plant has an influence on the synthesizing biochemical behavior of the *Banisteriopsis caapi* in relation to support species and to surrounding species, i.e., companion species.

Evidently, several studies and analyses of many variables with plants and controlled environments will be necessary before conclusions are made in this area of scientific knowledge. This is an area of knowledge which is interesting and promising for the elucidation of questions related to the mariri and chacrona, plants that are considered sacred and mysterious by the religious institution União do Vegetal.

Bibliography

Anderson, L. "A Provisional Checklist of Neotropical Rubiaceae Scripta Botanica Belgica." Meise Nat. Bot. Gard. of Belgium, 1:1-199, 1992.

Anderson, W. R. "Byrsonimoideae, a new subfamily of the Malpighiacee." Leandra 7:5-18, 1977.

Anderson, W.R and Gates, B. "Notes on Banisteriopsis (Malpighiaceae) from south central Brazil." Contributions from University of Michigan Herbarium, 11(2), pp. 51-55, 1975.

Anderson, L. "A Provisional Checklist of Neotropical Rubiaceae." Scripta Botanica. Belgica 1. Muller, J. 1881-1888. Rubiaceae, in: Martius, C.F.P. von (ed.). Fl. bras. 6(5): 1-486. Leipzig: Fleischer, 1992.

Appanah, S. e Putz, F. E. "Climber abundance in virgin dipterocarp forest and the effect of pre-felling cutting on logging damage." Malasian Forester, 47, pp. 335-342, 1984.

Barroso, G. M.; Peixoto, A. L.; Cost A, C. G.; Ichaso, C. L. F.; Guimarães, E. F. E Lima, H. C. Sistemática de Angiospermas do Brasil. Viçosa: Editora da Universidade Federal de Viçosa, 1991.

Callaway,J. C; Brito, G. S. E Neves, E. S. "Phytochemical Analyses of Banisteriopsis Caapi and Psychotria Viridis." Journal of Psychoactive Drugs; Jun 2005; 37, 2; ProQuest Medical Library, p. 145, 2005.

Callaway, J. C. "Fitoquímica e Neurofarmacologia da Ayahuasca", in: Metzner, R. "Ayahuasca- Alucinógenos, conciência e o espírito da Natureza." Rio de Janeiro: Ed. Gryphus, p. 116-150, 2002.

Corrêa, M. A. "Aspectos botanicos e taxonomicos das plantas Banisteriopsis sp. e Psychotria sp." Symposium paper presented at 1st Health Congress, Centro de Estudos Médicos- União do Vegetal. São Paulo, Brasil, 30 maio a 02 junho, 1991a.

Corrêa, M.A. "Etnobotânica Aspectos taxonomicos de Banisteriopsis sp e Psychotria sp." Anais. 1st Health Congress, Centro de Estudos Médicos- União do Vegetal. São Paulo, 1: 55-58, 1991b.

De Candolle, A. P. "Malpighuiaceae", in: De Candolle, A.P. (ed.) Prodomus Systematis Naturalis Regnis Vegetabilis. Paris: Treutel et Wi.irtz, vl., p. 577-592, 1824.

Dillenburg, C. R. E Porto, M. L. "Rubiaceae Tribo Psychotrieae", in: Flora Ilustrada do Rio Grande do Sul. Rio Grande do Sul: Boletim do Instituto de Biociências da Universidade Federal do Rio Grande do Sul, 39, p. 1-76, 1985.

Fisher, J.B. E Ewers, F.W. "Wound healing in stems of lianas after twisting and girdling injuries." Botanical Gazzete 150, p. 251-265, 1989.

Fox, J. E. D. "Logging damage and the influence of climber cutting prior to logging in the lowland dipterocarp forest of Sabah." Malaysian Forester, 31, p. 326-347, 1968.

Gartner, B. R.; Bullock, S. H.; Mooney, S. H.; Brown, V. B. E Whitebeck, J. L. "Water transport properties of vine and tree stems in a tropical deciduous forest." American Journal of Botany, 77, p. 742-749, 1990.

Gates, B. "Banisteriopsis, Diplopterys (Malpigiaceae)." Flora Neotropica, Monograph 30, p. 1-126, 1982.

Grisebach, A H. R. "Malpighiaceae." In Flora Brasiliensis (Martius, C.P.F. ed), 12(1): 1-123, 1858.

Lima, H. A. "Contribuição ao Estudo da Biologia Floral, da Fenologia e do Sistema de reprodução de Psychotria leiocarpa Cham. et. Schl." (Rubiaceae). (Tese de Mestrado em Botânica) Rio de Janeiro: Universidade Federal do Rio de Janeiro, 1986.

Mamede, M. C. H. "Revisão da lista de Malpighiaceae e Checklist das plantas do Nordeste." 2005.

Niedenzu, F. "Malpiguiaceae." In: Engler, A. (ed.) Das Pflanzeireich, IV 14, pp. 1-810, 1928.

Morton, C. V. "A typification of some subfamily, sectional and names in the family Malpighiaceae." Taxon 17, p. 314-324, 1968.

Müller, J. "Rubiaceae", in: Martius, C. P. F. (ed.) Flora Brasiliensis, 6 (5), pp. 1-60, 1881.

Pinard, M.A. and Putz, F. E. "Vines infestation of larges remnant trees in logged forests Sabah. Malaysia: biomechanical facilitation in vine succession" Journal of Tropical Forest Science 6, p. 302-309, 1994.

Taylor, C. M.; Sieyermark, J. A.; Delprete, P. G.; Vicentini, A; Cortés, R.; Zappi, D.; Persson, C.; Costa C. B. and Anunciação, E. "Rubiaceae." In: Steyermark, J. A., Berry, P. E., Yatskievych, K., E Holst, B.K. (eds). Flora of the Venezuelan Guayana 8, p. 497-847, 2004.

Vidal E.; Johns, J.; Gerwing, J.; Barreto, P. E Uhl, C. "Manejo de Cipós para a redução do impacto da exploração madeireira na Amazónia Oriental." Série Amazonia n° 13, Belém, 1998.

Williams, J. T. "Scientific issues affecting gene conservation and exploitation of some tropical perennials." In: Gustafson, P.; Appels, R. and Raven, P. (eds). Gene conservation and exploitation. New York: Plenum Press, p. 15-28, 1991.

Genetic Conservation of the Mariri (Banisteriopsis sp) and Chacrona (Psychotria sp) – Germplasm Bank

José Henrique Cattânio
José Beethoven Figueiredo Barbosa
Maria Alice Corrêa

Ayahuasca, the vine of the soul, is considered by many to serve as a holistic purge for the body, the mind and the spirit, cleaning and healing those who seek its benefits in good faith, with open heart and mind (Blanco 2002).

Natural resources, which are essential for the survival of the planet and for sustainable development, are being increasingly destroyed and exhausted. The action that is required in order to address the more serious conservation issues, and to prevent situations that are far worse, demands a lot of time in terms of planning, education and training. Better organization and the conducting of studies are also necessary in order to address these problems (Ferreira and Varela 1987). In addition, it is important to understand that the response of the ecosystems is not immediate; the regeneration of degraded lands, reforestation, and natural processes in general require time to be implemented and often involve high costs.

Until the present time, few investments have been made towards the conservation of the genetic resources of natural populations in tropical areas, due to an obvious reason: these resources renew themselves naturally in their native environments. Nonetheless, given the changes in land use, these plant communities tend to disappear at an alarming rate. This loss of genetic diversity can be divided into three hierarchical levels: ecosystems, species and genes.

Unfortunately, the majority of studies on biodiversity do not take into account the importance of the forest's genetic resources, nor the potential impact that the loss of these resources may have on raw material sectors such as forest and pharmacological goods. Paradoxically, despite the increasing losses already taking place, forest

[1] Term used by some Ayahuasca religions to refer to the tea also known as Hoasca, Vegetal and Ayahuasca

materials continue to be in high demand, both for providing genetic materials for use in rapid growth forests, as well as for supplying numerous direct and indirect products, especially from native forests.

The Brazilian Department of Science and Technology, considering the different hierarchical levels of biodiversity and the great diversity of the Brazilian forest ecosystems, has indicated that it is extremely important to establish strategies to prioritize actions (especially in Research and Development) on both national and regional scales (IPEF 2008). These strategies must include long-term programs related to the conservation and use of genetic forest resources. They must also consider regional variations, as well as present and future demands from the raw materials sector, including for the production of different products, such as cellulose, paper, particle board, lumber, and non-wood products such as rubber, resins, oils and pharmacological products.

Genetic variability is understood to be the diversity within a species caused by differences in phenotype or in genetic material. In all species, though there are common characteristics present, there is diversity among the individuals of that species, such as leaf format, time of flowering, concentration of constituents, growth behavior, presence of hair and resistance to adverse factors (pests, flood, and drought), among others. The reason for this diversity is the existence of differences in the genetic information brought by each individual within a population. The loss of genetic variability results in the population's decreased ability to adapt to environmental changes, causing many species to reach an evolutionary limit.

Preservation of genetic resources requires knowledge of how these resources are distributed in nature. Williams (1991) divided tropical forests' genetic resources as: 1) wild populations in natural surroundings, usually in the forests or populations adapted to greater biomes; and 2) cultivated materials, primarily associated with original communities. Each population represents a source of genetic variation and diversity with adaptation to new surroundings, i.e., material with potential for improvement, use and genetic conservation, because it has possible economic or other value.

Diversity of the Mariri

The tea known as ayahuasca (or Hoasca for the UDV), which exists in the Amazon, is the union of the mariri *(Banisteriopsis sp)* with the chacrona *(Psychotria sp)*. There are 42 known indigenous names for this union. It is notable and significant that at least 72 different indigenous tribes in the Amazon, though separated by extensive territory, language and cultural differences, manifest total and detailed common knowledge of ayahuasca and its use. Some of the 42 different names include: *ayahuasca amarillo* (yellow ayahuasca), *ayahuasca negro* (black ayahuasca), *ayahuasca blanco* (white ayahuasca), *ayahuasca trueno* (thunder ayahuasca), *amarrón huasca* (untamed ayahuasca), *ayahuasca colorada* (red ayahuasca).[1] Through the analysis of the varied names we are able to identify the existence of variations in color and effect coming from the use of the same tea.

The scientific literature recognizes approximately 100 species of the genus *Banisteriopsis,* making this the largest genus of the *Malpighiacea* family (Anderson and Gates 1975). Among them, besides the *Banisteripsis caapi* (Schultes 1970), the species *Banisteriopsis muricata* and *Banisteriopsis inebrians* (Schultes 1970) are utilized in the preparation of ayahuasca within different groups of traditional populations in Brazil, Peru, Argentina, Colombia, Bolivia, Ecuador, El Salvador and Mexico.

There are at least two varieties of *Banisteriopsis caapi* that are chemically and morphologically distinct, and the UDV refers to them as *tucunacá* and *caupuri*. Indeed, superficial analyses of transverse cuts of samples of these varieties of mariri do reveal a variation in the sap transporting structures. In addition, some people of the UDV recognize variations within these two varieties, such as mariri caupuri without knots, pajézinho, mariri tucunacá amarelo, etc.

Diversity of the Chacrona

Among the genera of the Rubiaceae family, the genus Psychotria is the largest with a pantropical distribution, encompassing about 1,500 different species, of which approximately 700 are Neotropical. There are several varieties of chacrona recognized in the UDV. Among them, three were identified in 1992 and confirmed at the Instituto de Botanica de São Paulo (São Paulo Botanical Institute). The varieties of chacrona most known in the UDV are: Chacrona "Cabocla" – *Psychotria viridis*, Chacrona "Caneluda" – *Psychotria carthagenensis,* and Chacrona "Caianinha" – *Psychotria niveobarbata.* There are also "Lingua de Vaca" (also known as "Orelha de Onça"), "Olho Róseo", "Chacroninha" and likely some hybrids derived from crossings between the species.

Genetic Variability

Genetic resources are constituted by genetic variability organized in a set of distinct materials called germplasm. The germplasm is the element in the genetic resources that manages the genetic variability within the species, providing the differences existing among individuals of the same species related to specific characteristics, such as eye color, type of hair, etc.

Genetic variability provides for a wide spectrum of ecological, physiological and behavioral responses to the environment. Without genetic variability – and its interaction with the environment – it is impossible to obtain superior genotypes, i.e., individuals with desirable characteristics by way of genetic improvement. Therefore the genetic material of a population is of great importance for the conservation of the species and for use in research, especially in order to improve the concentration of the active principles and for the purpose of adaptation to unfavorable conditions.

The pressure on natural resources caused by shifts in land use, the growth of large cities and the need for energy and mineral production, is threatening these genetic resources, often before their economic or functional potential is even known. In order to preserve such genetic information, a Germplasm Bank is used, which is a place where the genetic resources of a species are stored for the purposes of:

- Preservation of the species for future populations
- Knowledge of the "size" of the genic variability through phenotype and genetic comparisons
- Experiments with genetic improvement such as adaptation to adverse locations, increase in productivity, resistance to diseases, and increase in the production of active principles (in the case of medicinal and aromatic plants).

There are several ways that genetic material can be stored:
- Through seeds
- Through dead plants in a herbarium
- Through live plants:
    - at the place of origin *(in situ)*
    - outside the place of origin *(ex situ)*.

The classic strategies of genetic conservation – *in situ* and *ex situ* – are widely used in Brazil, however, there is an increasing necessity for complementary strategies that definitively advance the conservation of the genetic resources of the Brazilian forests.

Seed Storage

The objective of storing seeds is to safeguard the seeds, preserving their physical, physiological and sanitary qualities for later cultivation of healthy plants. There may be several different purposes for the stored seeds, ranging from cultivation of new plantations to gene banks for native forests. The main storage methods utilized are cold storage, dry storage, and dry-cold storage. Dry-cold storage is the method that is most adaptive to the majority of seed storage needs.

The embryo is the essential part of the seed and in this type of germplasm bank the main concern is to maintain the embryo alive and ready for resuming growth when it is planted. Nonetheless, any stored seed suffers from deterioration, which can be faster or slower, depending on the environmental conditions of the storage site and the characteristics of the seeds themselves. Depending on the species, seeds of trees may remain alive for periods that range from a few days to a few decades. The main factors that may impact the seed's longevity or cause deterioration are:

- Deterioration of the embryonic DNA
- Humidity
- Temperature
- Amount of the seed's reserve substances
- Oil content in the seed
- Luminosity
- Length of storage
- Oxygen

Conservation at the Place of Origin *(In Situ)*

In Situ conservation considers the conservation of the ecosystem and of the natural habit as a whole, or the maintenance and rescuing of species populations in the location where they originate (origin center).[2]

The preserved area is demarcated and protected, and the adult individuals are identified for periodic follow-up. The original environmental conditions of the area are maintained to carry out seed collection, production of seedlings and the measurement of growth.

This method of conservation has the following advantages:

- Preservation of the greatest amount of variability possible within the species (center of origin)
- No need for the species to adapt
- No need for seedling production and cultural treatment
- Lower cost of manual labor for silviculture and maintenance.

---

[2] The origin center is the region where a species exhibits the greatest genetic diversity for a selected number of characteristics.

There are also some important disadvantages to this method in comparison to other types of genetic material conservation:
- Establishing in situ conservation areas in tropical forests is very difficult due to the wide diversity within species and between species, and lack of knowledge needed for establishing solid bases
- Degradation of the environment caused by changes in land use and consequent loss of genetic material
- High cost of maintenance and protection of large areas since small areas may not represent an entire population
- Risk of "genic contamination" by another variety or species.

Ex Situ Conservation

Ex Situ conservation is the conservation of genetic material outside of the natural habitat (center of origin). This practice is common in agricultural activities in the collection of germplasm, especially those being researched. The area designated to be the "Germplasm Bank" is controlled, starting with the collection of seeds, and including the production of seedlings, planting, and observation of growth.

This type of conservation has the following advantages:
- Preservation of the greatest amount of inter-specific variability (between the different species)
- Collection of information in all phases and total control over the genetic material
- Research and/or comparison between different varieties
- Greater control of the area with greater inter-specific diversity within the same location.

There are also important disadvantages in comparison to other types of genetic material conservation:
- Difficulty in obtaining the whole genetic potential of the species
- Cost of maintenance and protection, depending on the size of the area
- Need for adaptation of the species
- Cost of seedling production, planting and cultural treatment.

Priorities for the UDV

1. Develop knowledge of the genetic heritage of our plants (how our plants are different)

a. There is general agreement that reserves and tropical forest national parks should be established and managed in a way that preserves the maximum genetic variability within the species (Whitmore 1980). However, without data on the distribution of this variability within or between populations, reasonable decisions regarding the most effective preservation methods cannot be accurately made (Ashton 1981). The importance of genetic structure for advancement and direct evolutionary modification is clearly evident within current efforts that are focused on genetic conservation
b. Surveys must be conducted of locations where native mariri tucunacá and caupuri grow, and projects of genetic material collection must be done for the quantification of genetic diversity of the natural population.
c. Evaluate the genetic diversity between and within the natural and cultivated populations of Banisteriopsis sp, considering materials originating from both natural and cultivated populations in Brazil
d. All the genetic material must be collected using scientific methodology so that all information is preserved.

2. Demarcate this resource for preservation of genetic material
   a. It is necessary to preserve original material that has already been researched to serve for future research
   b. Collected material should be demarcated at the place of origin or be reproduced by vegetative method in a secure place
   c. Evaluate the genetic diversity between and within the natural and cultivated populations of *Banisteriopsis sp,* considering materials originating from both natural and cultivated populations in Brazil.

3. Decision on in situ or ex situ preservation
   a. The analysis of allele frequency may indicate the degree of variability both within and between populations and their progenies; the presence of alleles that are exclusive to progenies indicates that there is a genic flux between the populations of the fragments studied and other fragments.
   b. The detected rates of genetic diversity will indicate the type of genetic conservation needed: *in situ* conservation if the rates are high, or *ex situ* conservation may be possible if rates are lower.

Bibliography

Anderson, W. R.; Gates, B. "Notes on Banisteriopsis from South Central Brazil." Contributions from University of Michigan Herbarium, 11, p. 51-55, 1975.

Ashton, P. S. "Techniques for the identification and conservation of species in tropical forests", in: Synge, H (ed). "The biological aspects of rare plant conservation." New York: John Wiley & Sons, p. 155-164, 1981.

Blanco, O. "Teacher Healer Plants of the Peruvian Amazon." 2002. http://www.biopark.org/peru/four.html. (last visited 9/2013)

Ferreira, M. E Valera, F. P. IPEF, 35, p. 92-100, 1987.

IPEF - Instituto De Pesquisa E Estudos Florestais, 2008. http://www.ipef.br/, last visited 9/2013.

Whitmore, T. C. "The conservation of tropical rain forest", in: Soule, M E. and Wilcox, B. A. (eds.), Conservation biology: an evolutionary-ecological perspective. Sunderland: Sinauer Associates, p. 303-318, 1980.

Wlliams, J. T. "Scientific issues affecting gene conservation and exploitation of some tropical perennials", in: Gustafson, P.; Appels, R. and Raven, P. (eds.), Gene conservation and exploitation. New York: Plenum Press, p. 15-28, 1991.

Agroforestry Systems in Plantation Areas

Maurício Hoffman

The cultivation system and the techniques used in the plantation departments of the Centro Espírita Beneficente União do Vegetal (UDV) are changing. With the exception of a few experiments based on organic agriculture, the cultivation methods used by this institution, until the end of the last century, were mostly based on knowledge of conventional agricultural methods. Production in monoculture systems caused loss of soil fertility and environmental imbalance. Consequently, problems appeared related to pests, fungi, and bacteria. However, through reflection and by necessity, current thinking is being redirected towards cultivation practices of the mariri *(Banisteriopsis caapi)* and chacrona *(Psychotria viridis)* that are in alignment and in harmony with nature.

In this new millennium the CEBUDV has adopted organic agriculture and Agroforestry methods for the production of the Vegetal, which have produced significant results in some of the Núcleos and Authorized Distributions, and have met the demands of the Plantation Department.[1] Among the main demands are increased soil fertility, phytosanitary control, decreased water use for irrigation and adaptation to new environments of the species, which are native to tropical forests (Penereiro 1999).

Ecological Principles

Among the various types of Agroforestry Systems, the primary model used for reforestation is based on natural succession and the biodiversity found in native forests. The formation of forests is a continuous process that occurs in the following way: a clearing naturally becomes an area of climax vegetation. In this process, based on the movement of plant growth, plants with shorter life cycles grow first, and above

---

[1] Agroforestry incorporates at least several plant species into a given land area and creates a more complex habitat that can support a wider variety of birds, insects, and other animals. Biodiversity in Agroforestry systems is typically higher than in conventional agricultural systems. Agroforestry also has the potential to help reduce climate change since trees take up and store carbon at a faster rate than crops. Agroforestry Systems are currently being taught and used in Brazil for food production (Armando 2003).

them grow trees that have a longer life and will be part of the climax vegetation. This is called natural plants succession. It is a process that is always repeating itself, at the rate that the climax species fall and open new clearings.

All living organisms participate in this natural movement of life: insects, fungi, bacteria, each with their own eco-physiological function (Götsch 1996, 1997). The results of this process are fertile soils, a high humidity microclimate, ecological balance between species, as well as other agronomic advantages that are important for the cultivation of numerous plant species.

Succession Agroforestry System Model

The succession Agroforestry cultivation system has been studied and taught for three decades by the agriculturalist Ernest Götsch in the south of the state of Bahia. He calls this system of production "forest gardening" and the objective is to recreate an ecosystem that is similar to the natural habitat. When he acquired his rural property in 1985, it was a deforested area, with erosion collapses caused by heavy rains. This same location in 2008 is now a forest.

Another important result obtained in the reforestation of that property using the Agroforestry system is related to water: the springs reappeared and a crystal clear creek, about three feet wide and one foot deep, began running through the trees. The forest brought back the water that used to run on that very spot. In his own words, Ernst said: "It is not water that brings life to a place, but life that brings water."

In an endeavor such as this, economic feasibility is just as important as the environmental and ecological aspects. There is less of a demand for financial resources for both implementation and maintenance. Comparing the Agroforestry system to other similar conventional reforestation systems (Hoffman 2005), the possibility of short-term return on investment, in conjunction with long-term production, generates greater financial stability. The clusters of *pupunha* and cacao fruits are examples of how the forest can be productive.[2] In another area at the same location, *cupuaçu* trees (a relative of cacao), Brazil nut trees, orange trees, and other species are also cultivated, in partnerships with other planters.

Essentially, this system of production is based on observing nature and considering nature's dynamics of transformation in the forming of a forest. On our plantations, we seek to reproduce the biodiversity and the density of plantings found in the natural clearings. Through pruning we are able to accelerate the process of natural

---

[2] In English the *pupunha* tree is referred to as peach-palm and the fruit is sometimes called a peach-nut. The cacao tree produces pods also known as cocoa, used in the production of chocolate.

succession, encouraging the cycling of nutrients and the processes of transformation of the environment, recreating a forest more quickly.

Experiences with Agroforestry within the UDV

Among the UDV Núcleos and Authorized Distributions of Vegetal that use agroforestry systems in their plantation work we will mention only two.

In 2004, at Núcleo Luz do Oriente in Brasília, Agroforestry plantation activities began in a deforested area of about 7.5 acres containing only the grass *Brachiaria decumbens*.

Within the existing soil and vegetation conditions the Agroforestry system was implemented. More than 80 different species were planted, resulting in over 20,000 established trees. By 2008, some of these trees were already taller than a human being . With this technique, the objective is to reproduce an environment that is as close as possible to the natural habitat of the mariri and the chacrona so that these plants can develop in a healthy way, allowing them to preserve their original characteristics.

Another location is at Núcleo Florestal in Alta Floresta, state of Mato Grosso. The work there began with agroforestry gardening inspired by lectures and courses on the subject. Because this system of cultivation differed so much from conventional methods, it provoked deep reflection within that group and led to changes in ways of perceiving the natural environment, and later changes in methods of soil and vegetation management.

Initially there was a process of experimentation by one person who accepted the new challenge. Only after experimenting with the system and evaluating the results obtained was this person able to convince and mobilize the rest of the group to implement the Agroforestry methods in their plantation area.

The plantation team, supported by the members of Núcleo Florestal, is currently conducting experiments where changes can be observed within the same location. One year prior, in a monoculture system in an open environment, the chacrona was growing slowly, with small and yellowish leaves. After the implementation of the agroforestry system, the chacrona plants are growing and producing large, dark green leaves, alongside other plants including *mamonas* (castor shrubs), *mandioca* (manioc), *amora* (mulberry heliopsis), and *guandu* beans (*Cajanus bicolor* DC), *paricá (Schizolobium amazonicum)* among others. As of 2008 the system was over six feet tall, forming a forest similar to the natural habitat of the chacrona. After only one year the Agroforestry plantation showed significant results in the development of the chacrona as can be observed in the large and shiny dark green leaves.

Another important experiment was conducted with the mariri: pruning the canopy of the trees instead of pruning the undergrowth. Afterwards, the pruned branches were placed in an organized manner over the soil, avoiding covering the plantules. With the use of this technique, there was a higher rate of sprouting and greater growth of the mariri and plantules of other trees, which were just waiting for the moment to grow.

Prior experiments, before the adoption of the Agroforestry method, were based only on the clearing of undergrowth; this caused a delay in natural succession and the surroundings became stagnated by the canopies of old trees.

It is observed that after the pruning, using the agroforestry system, the tree reestablishes itself within one to two years, depending on the species. The most important factor is that the reestablishment of the pruned tree is accompanied by the simultaneous growth of a new forest.

The recycling of plant biomass, derived mainly from pruning, allows this system of cultivation to transform deforested areas into productive forests with high fertility soils. The synchronization of the species involved in the natural succession guarantees that plants develop well. This is possible without the use of expensive, polluting chemicals and even without irrigation.

These experiments indicate the potential that this cultivation system has to meet the need for production of Vegetal for this beneficent institution.

Bibliography

Armando, M. S. "Agrodiversidade: ferramenta para uma agricultura sustentavel." Brasília: Embrapa Recursos Genéticos e Biotecnologia, 2003.

Götsch, E. "O renascer da agricultura." Trad. de Patricia Vaz. 2nd ed. Rio de Janeiro: AS-PTA, 1996.

Götsch, E. "Homem e natureza, cultura na agricultura." 2a ed. Rio de Janeiro: AS-PTA, 1997.

Penereiro, F. M. "Sistemas agroflorestais dirigidos pela sucessão natural: um estudo de caso." Dissertação de Mestrado. Piracicaba: Escola Superior de Agricultura "Luiz de Queiroz", Universidade de Sao Paulo, 1999.

Hoffmann, M R. "Sistema Agroflorestal Sucessional - Implantação mecanizada." Um estudo de caso. (Monografia) Brasília: Universidade de Brasília, 2005.

Environmental Work in the UDV

Flavio Gordon[1]
Iára Reinke Soares Castro[2]
Sara da Silva Abes[3]

The purpose of this article is to present the environmental vision of the Centro Espírita Beneficente União do Vegetal - CEBUDV. This vision is related to our sacrament, to the sacred communion with the Hoasca tea, and to the teachings we receive from the União do Vegetal (UDV) with which we orient our lives. These experiences have provided us with a new understanding and a new attitude with respect to Nature. This new attitude of reverence, gratitude and practice has been cultivated since the establishment of the UDV by Mestre José Gabriel da Costa.

Our dependence on Nature is clear from the very beginning, since the preparation of the Hoasca tea requires the Mariri and the Chacrona, as well as the entire forest ecosystem that sustains these plants. We need water, which represents the Mineral Kingdom, and we need the Plant Kingdom from whence come our sacred plants. In the spiritual vision of the UDV the Mineral and Plant Kingdoms serve the Animal Kingdom because they are superior, they manifest Divine Love. Nature is not something to be carelessly and disrespectfully manipulated. It is a totality emanating from the Force of Creation which humanity generally represents through the word "God." This vision orients us toward a reverential and respectful use of the material expressions of Nature. We need this Planet Earth in good condition in order to have a healthy place to conduct our spiritual development.

Over the years this new attitude has facilitated an increasing number of initiatives aimed at preserving and regenerating forests, water and biodiversity. These

---

[1] President of the Novo Encanto Association for Ecological Development (triennium 2006-2008)

[2] Agronomy Engineer and Environmental Educator. Coordinator of the Novo Encanto Association for Ecological Development – Southern Region (Paraná, Santa Catarina e Rio Grande do Sul - triennium 2006-2008)

[3] Biologist. Doctor in Environmental Sciences by the Maringá University- Paraná State. University professor and Environmental Analist in São Paulo. Regional Novo Encanto Coordinator for the 3rd Region – São Paulo (triennium 2006-2008.)

initiatives have generated opportunities for transformation in our daily practices as well. We have the opportunity to gradually transform our practices at home, at work, and at the Núcleos of the UDV, aligning our practices with a more realistic and responsible respect for the environment and for the sacredness of Life and Nature, of which we are a part.

The consciousness acquired through this rich and transcendent experience has encouraged us to be more proactive, as is evident in our initiatives that are aimed at environmental balance and the development of true Human Fraternity.

This proactive stance resulted in the creation of the Associação Novo Encanto de Desenvolvimento Ecológico (New Enchantment Association for Ecological Development) in 1990, in Rio de Janeiro. Mr. Raimundo Monteiro de Souza proposed that the Novo Encanto Association be created, with the primary goal of preserving an area of Amazon Forest with high biodiversity, located in the state of Amazonas near Rio Branco, Acre.[4] The 20,000+ acre property, called Seringal Novo Encanto, was donated to us for this purpose. The establishing of the Novo Encanto Association was also a response to the growing need for structuring and developing UDV environmental initiatives that were already taking place. In September of that year the 1st Gathering of Environmentalists of the UDV took place at Núcleo Lupunamanta, in Campinas, São Paulo. This gathering marked the founding of the Novo Encanto Association within the UDV and the first project area groups were formed: Pro-Amazonia, Environmental Education, Ecology and Spirituality, as well as the Communications, Legal and Cultural departments. The first local branches, called monitorias, were also established at this time at the núcleos of the UDV. Today there are numerous branches of this entity throughout Brazil and overseas (Spain and US).

The relationship between the UDV and the Novo Encanto Association is significant, as the entire Board of Directors of the Association, since its beginning, has been composed of members of the UDV, and the position of President has always been held by a member of the Cadre of Mestres (Gordon, Stefanuto and Hacker, 2008).

The Novo Encanto Association has a management structure linked to approximately 150 UDV núcleos and authorized distributions of the Vegetal, the majority of which have established local branches of the Association. In addition to the local branches, Novo Encanto Association also manages several ongoing projects: the Gerência Serra da Estrela, which administrates a forest preservation area in Magé, in the state of Rio de Janeiro; the Gerência de Caldas, in the state of Minas Gerais, that promotes the annual "Festival Água no Terceiro Milênio" (Water in the Third

---

[4] Raimundo Monteiro de Souza is a mestre of the Council of the Recordation of the Teachings of Mestre Gabriel.

Millenium Festival); and the Gerência Mairiporã, in the state of São Paulo, which manages seedling nurseries and promotes environmental education through cultivation.[5]

The Novo Encanto Association has also eight regional coordinating centers encompassing the states of: São Paulo, Acre, Regional South (Parana, Santa Catarina, Rio Grande do Sul), Mato Grosso and Mato Grosso do Sul, Bahia, Alagoas, Amazonas and Roraima (eastern Amazonia), and one in the city of Brasilia, Federal District.

The structure of the Novo Encanto Association has a National Board of Directors, which includes a a President, four vice-presidents, and the Departments of Forest Area Management and Certification of Organic Products. It also has a Board of Advisors that defines the program goals of the entity, and a Fiscal Council which supervises the financial transactions and fiscal reports of this Association. An acknowledgment is due here to the late Mr. Luiz Maciel da Costa, who in 1989 informed us that the Seringal Novo Encanto was for sale, and mobilized to find support for this this initiative both in Brazil and in the United States.[6] The Seringal Novo Encanto property was purchased by Mr. Jeffrey Bronfman and subsequently donated to the Novo Encanto Association for Ecological Development.[7]

We also acknowledge the many friends of our Association, the local branch monitors, our managers and coordinators, all of whom contribute their work voluntarily, almost anonymously, in many locations throughout the country and overseas, teaching children and adults to separate trash at the Núcleos, cultivating native species and organic gardens, and carrying out many other initiatives that engage our members in the practice of Goodness. This practice of Goodness benefits each person, each community, and the places where we live, as well as humanity as a whole and our planet, putting into practice the premise of environmental preservation, which is to think globally and act locally.

We acknowledge all those who, like worker ants, conduct this work slowly and gradually. This work has the same gradual pace as our learning in the UDV, as we become more conscious and sensitized to the reality in which we live. Novo Encanto has approximately a thousand members and its initiatives are conducted by volunteers

---

[5] For more information see http://www.novoencanto.org.br/00/

[6] Luís Maciel da Costa arrived in the Cadre of Mestres of the UDV and was a Councilman in the city of Cruzeiro do Sul, state of Acre. He disincarnated in a plane crash in 2002.

[7] Jeffrey Bronfman is a member of the Cadre of Mestres of the UDV. He drank Vegetal for the first time in 1990 and participated actively in the founding of the Novo Encanto Association. He is a key figure in the defense of religious freedom for the UDV in the United States. See articles by Bronfman and Boyd in this book.

who are doing this work with commitment and dedication, in the same manner as our spiritual work is done in the União do Vegetal.

Main Initiatives

- Seringal Novo Encanto Expedition, an important eco-tourism and environmental education initiative connected to our preservation efforts
- Water in the Third Millennium Festival, a cultural initiative that takes place annually in Caxambu, Caldas, Brasilia, Campo Grande and Madrid, Spain
- Ecology and Spirituality event in Fortaleza
- Week of Phyto-Therapy in Campinas and Manaus, in partnership with local public administrations
- Agro-Forestry and Permaculture training courses

Regional Projects

The following projects take place in specific regions of Brazil:
- Encantos do Artesanato (Arts and Crafts Fair) in Maceio
- Estação Florescer, an environmental education initiative that trains youth in the areas of agro-ecology and gardening in Brasilia
- Permaculture in the Cerrado (Permaculture project in the savannah region) in Brasilia
- Preservation of the Cattleya Warneri Orchid, in Espirito Santo

In addition to these regional projects, Novo Encanto Association also participates in the following campaigns:

Samaúma Viva Para Sempre (Samaúma Alive forever), which petitioned the federal government to provide "immunity from cutting" for the Samaúma tree (Eriodendron Samaúma), which has vital importance in the preservation of the Amazon Forest and consequently the people of the forest.

Plante Essa Idéia (Plant this Idea), an initiative whose goal is to plant trees to compensate for the carbon dioxide emitted by buses, airplanes and automobiles for participants to travel to attend the 2nd International Hoasca Conference. We calculated that we would have to plant 3,200 trees to compensate Nature for the resources used to realize this event. This campaign began before the Conference and engaged more than 30 Núcleos of the UDV. Overall we have already planted 13,000 trees in Brazil and 350 in the US. This commitment includes the caring for each one of these plantings so that the carbon is indeed replaced.

Publishing of materials:

- Manual for the Monitors of the Local Branches
- Energy Use Manual
- Water Manual: Conservation, Rational Use, and Water Re-use, published in partnership with the Department of the Environment, which is being used by the UDV and by rural and urban landowners who are involved in water catchment, treatment and conservation efforts.[8]
- Ecological Calendar, which describes activities that can be carried out at the Núcleos and Authorized Distributions of the Vegetal of the UDV, emphasizing activities that encourage the celebration of commemorative ecological dates such as the International Day of the Environment, The Day of Water, and The Day of the Forest.

Preservation of Areas:

The acquisition of areas for the purpose of forest preservation is one of the goals of our Association. As mentioned, the major one is the Seringal Novo Encanto. We also preserve other smaller areas in the following locations:

- Serra da Estrela, Magé, Rio de Janeiro state, which preserves an area where there are important headwaters for that region
- Ubaiataba, in the state of Bahia
- Jangada, in the state of Mato Grosso
- Palmas in the state of Tocantins
- Antonina, in the state of Paraná, an area held in partnership with the CEBUDV

In addition to these initiatives, the Novo Encanto Association participates on several councils including Environment and Urbanism, and Environmental Protection Areas in Brazil. We also have a natural and organic products certification project in the states of Bahia and Ceará. Our monitors coordinate cultivation of native species, organic gardens, development of nurseries and cultivation of ornamental plants throughout UDV Núcleos and Authorized Distributions.

In 2001 we began to systematically track the activities of the local branches. From 2001 to 2007 there were 321 activities. In 2007 we developed 124 educational activities on environmental education and 72 activities on general cultivation and the cultivation of medicinal and native plants.

---

[8] This manual was published in partnership with the Brazilian Federal Environment Department and the Associação Novo Encanto de Desenvolvimento Ecológico, in 2009.

A phrase from the Letter of Principles of Novo Encanto, written by Nancy Mangabeira, philosophy professor at the Federal University of Bahia, sums up well our work in defense of life and peace:

> Thus we align ourselves with all those, all over the Planet, who work with this same goal to once again weave together the threads that bonds us to Nature, to our fellow human beings, and to ourselves.

Environmental Education

In the Thanksgiving Address – Greetings to the Natural World, of the Iroquois native people of North America, there is a greeting to nature, that begins:

> "Today we have gathered and we see that the cycles of life continue. We have been given the mission of living in balance and harmony with each other and with all living things…"[9]

These words mention the cycles of Nature that humanity lived with for thousands of years, in a completely sustainable manner. Our ancestors provided us with clean water, clean air and wholesome foods. Over the course of a few decades, humanity has engaged in a process of economic development and in lifestyles that significantly impact the planet and compromise resources that are essential to life: water and air. According to Derivi (2007), the International Panel on Climate Change – IPCC, conclusively stated that human activity is 90% responsible for the current impacts on the environment and for global warming. This report establishes that in the history of mankind, in at least the last 10 thousand years, this degree of impact has never before occurred.

A long historical process placed society and culture in opposition to Nature as result of a movement known as anthropocentrism, which LAYARGUES (2002) refers to, stating "it is in society that real disequilibrium exists, not in nature, as is often inferred by the reductionist perspective."[10] This understanding is the basis for the environmental education initiatives at the present moment and Novo Encanto places a priority on this line of action.

---

[9] Thanksgiving Address – Greetings to the Natural World, also known as The Iroquois Thanksgiving Address. The Iroquois is also known as the Six Nations.

[10] Anthropocentrism is a major concept in the field of environmental ethics and environmental philosophy, where it is often considered to be the root cause of problems created by human interaction with the environment, and something that is profoundly embedded in our culture and conscious acts.

Considering these factors, we return to the "Thanksgiving Address" which speaks of our mission to "live in balance and harmony with one another", which is the essence of spirituality, "and with all living things," which is the core concept of ecology. The necessity to reestablish the connection with nature as sacred, as a work of the Creator, and to reestablish the place of man as sacred as well, explains the significance of Novo Encanto's environmental work having its focus be "Ecology and Spirituality". When the human being comprehends that he is an integral part of Nature and becomes aware that Nature is sacred, it becomes easier for him to understand the necessity to preserve it.

The Report of the World Commission on the Environment considers sustainable development as "…that which attends to the needs of the present without compromising the ability of future generations to attend to their needs" (CMMAD, 1991). This statement leads us to the following considerations: What environment will we leave for future generations? What planet are we leaving for our children? Or even, what children are we leaving for this planet?

The answers to these questions are the primary reasons that lead Novo Encanto Association to develop initiatives and projects with an environmental education focus. We are still learning how to go about implementing these practices and we acknowledge the many non-governmental-organizations that have been competently working to address these same concerns in their projects.

Novo Encanto Association's Environmental Education Initiatives at the Núcleos of the UDV[11]

The majority of the environmental education initiatives of the Novo Encanto Association are conducted at the Núcleos and Authorized Distributions of the UDV. We have approximately 40 waste separation and collection projects, which include activities that utilize the arts, such as music and theater, as a means of raising awareness about the importance of developing this habit. There is still a long way to go on this endeavor, because more important than separating waste for recycling is the awareness of how to reduce waste in the first place, consuming less and causing less impact on the environment. Waste reduction begins with replacing industrialized food products with natural foods that produce waste that is easily degradable through composting practices that result in fertilizers to be used in the cultivation of gardens and landscaping.

---

[11] This data was collected from the Novo Encanto 2007 National Annual Activity Report at UDV Núcleos.

There are 32 programs focused on the cultivation of native tree species at the Núcleos of the UDV. This is an example of how Novo Encanto is developing, through this practice within its membership, a consciousness focused on the preservation of the natural environment. The campaign called "Plante Essa Idéia" (Plant this Idea) mentioned above, showed a positive response to the planting of trees that today demonstrates a significant contribution to the remediation process of damaged areas and for carbon compensation.

This environmental education initiative utilizes themed day trips that provide adults and children with the opportunity to come into contact with local fauna and flora. These outings also encourage and expand the contact between children and their parents. Through this campaign, the planting of native tree species took place in all five biomes of Brazil: the Amazon, the semi-arid region, the Pantanal (wetlands), the savannah and in the Atlantic Forest. These plantings also took place in some areas of the U.S.

Novo Encanto follows an environmental calendar commemorating dates such as World Water Day, Environment Day and Day of Trees. In the Novo Encanto 2007 National Annual Activity Report there appear more than 30 activities designed to increase awareness of these dates. The activities have the objective of captivating the participants by demonstrating how important these elements are in creating quality of life.

Newsletters and email lists are used to increase awareness of environmental issues. These communications facilitate the networking of various Núcleos when a campaign or activity is taking place, or to distribute technical information. The Novo Encanto email network and the Plantation email network serve as discussion forums, promote education, facilitate the speedy exchange of ideas and the sharing of experiences.

A growing number of workshops are being offered throughout the regions. Workshops on natural foods teach people that it is possible to prepare healthy and flavorful foods, different from the processed foods prevalent in the mainstream. Natural foods are not only healthy for the body; they also reduce waste, mainly due to less packaging.

Paper making workshops are very popular among the children and help to create awareness regarding reduction of waste as well as the importance of recycling.

Soap making workshops increase awareness about the toxicity of commercial cleaning products and demonstrate that cleaning can be done with homemade products that are biodegradable. The products contribute to reducing water pollution through recycling cooking oils, which are used as ingredients in the homemade cleaning product recipes.

Other areas of education at Núcleos of the UDV include permaculture, Agroforestry and bio-construction. These are sustainability practices using creative and advanced methodologies to remediate degraded areas.

The campaign "Samaúma Alive Forever" continues and has already gathered 20 thousand signatures throughout the country, which were submitted to the National Congress, seeking the preservation of this endangered species. Núcleo Samaúma, in São Paulo, is developing a proposal to multiply this species and distribute seedlings locally, with the participation of children.

Lectures are offered to inform, raise awareness, captivate and propose changes in attitudes and habits. They are fundamental for raising environmental awareness that leads to transformation of our daily practices.

Regional gatherings are held in order to facilitate this process of re-education and primarily to train the regional monitors. The regional gatherings provide opportunities for sharing experiences, training teams that carry out cultivation activities at the Núcleo level, as well as promoting the pollination of ideas and the socialization of methodologies. At the gatherings the monitors have an opportunity to learn, teach, implement and perfect their approach. Despite the importance of these gatherings they are still sporadic.

Regional Gathering in São Paulo – A Proposal from Novo Encanto's Regional Sul (South Region)[12]

The regional branches of Novo Encanto in Brazil are mobilizing, through gatherings and focused planning, in order to develop more holistic and ongoing action plans for improving the environment and increasing environmental awareness.[13] As an example the Novo Encanto-South Region initiated a dialogue among the Núcleos of the UDV in that region and proposed to not generate new work demands since the Núcleos already have numerous initiatives to maintain for their own operations.[14] They proposed to work together with the Núcleos to provide services in the area of environmental support as it is a theme that broadly impacts all the activities of the

---

[12] Thanksgiving Address – Greetings to the Natural World, also known as The Iroquois Thanksgiving Address. The Iroquois is also known as the Six Nations.

[13] There are 8 regional branches of Novo Encanto: 1) São Paulo, 2) Acre, 3)Sul (Paraná, Santa Catarina and Rio Grande do Sul), 4) Mato Grosso and Mato Grosso do Sul, 5) Bahia, 6) Alagoas, 7) Amazonas and Roraima, 8) Federal District.

[14] All Núcleos of the UDV have in their organizational structure the presidency, secretariat, treasury and monitors for three departments: Memory, Beneficence and Plantation, as well as a monitor of Novo Encanto.

Núcleo: building, cultivation, food preparation, education and gardening.

Through the regional gatherings the Novo Encanto Association – South Region branch, along with the Plantation Department and the Educational Support Group, a process of department integration was initiated, aiming to create more collaboration within the operations of the Núcleos. The partnerships brought positive results, facilitating unified action among the different operational sectors. This allowed for a regional gathering to take place in 2008 that brought together the presidents of the Núcleos and those responsible for youth education. At this gathering an action plan was developed of integrated efforts in which Novo Encanto supports the presidency by researching ecological building materials and products. Support is provided in all aspects that make it possible to develop a Núcleo focused on sustainability, such as methods for the remediation of damaged area and rain water catchment systems. Within the Núcleos, Novo Encanto monitors work alongside those responsible for the kitchen organization, supporting the purchasing of food products, cleaning products and the set up of the kitchen space. This way there can be a focus on the consumption of natural foods and the promotion of alternative cleaning products and practices that conserve water. This same proposal allows for educators to train the children and the youth through processes of environmental education, as well as facilitating the implementation of environmentally minded practices for the entire membership of the UDV.

It is believed that through these integrated efforts we will be able to create a more environmentally focused approach to the operation of all the Núcleos of the UDV. Presently, despite the slow pace of this movement, small steps towards this goal are starting to be visible, as this endeavor depends on the ability to captivate and motivate individuals through organized activities and initiatives. The most important factor for the achievement of this goal is that the initiative becomes a part of the training of the leaders of the UDV, beyond just the training of Novo Encanto monitors and their teams who are working on the local level.

Environmental Projects of the Novo Encanto Association

The significant initiatives implemented by Novo Encanto, along with the ones implemented by the Department of Beneficence of the UDV, provide the basis for the UDV to continue to be awarded the Certificate of Federal Public Services (Utilidade Publica).

In November of 2006, the 2nd Gathering of UDV's Environmentalists was held in Campinas, in the state of São Paulo. Strategic actions were planned for Novo Encanto's role within the Núcleos and Authorized Distributions of the UDV. At that time a document was created called Diretrizes Ambientais para o CEBUDV (Environmental Directives for the UDV), which demonstrates a commitment towards environmental quality (Gordon & Stefanuto, 2006).

The working group that created these directives identified sectors of immediate need for intervention within the Núcleos, called "ABC": *Agua, Biodiversidade, e Cultura* (Water, Biodiversity and Culture). These directives are currently in the implementation phase.

Novo Encanto's projects are usually implemented informally at the Núcleos of the UDV. Generally, these informal initiatives were forerunners of projects that aimed to respond to Requests for Proposals issued by corporations and non-governmental organizations that provide incentives to environmental and sustainability projects. Many of these projects eventually became recipients of development grants.

Among the projects carried out by Novo Encanto, the main environmentally focused projects that received external grant support are: *Festival Agua no 3o. Milenio* (Water in the 3rd Millenium Festival), *Estação Florescer* (Flowering Season), *Encantos do Artesanato* (Enchanting Crafts), and *Permacultura no Cerrado* (Permaculture in the Savannah). We will summarize in this article some of the accomplishments of these projects, and note that there are many other projects being developed in the many locations where Novo Encanto is active.

Water in the 3rd Millennium Festival is a project conceived by Marisa Machado.[15] She observed, in her visits to thermal mineral springs, that some of them were in a state of environmental deterioration. She then conceptualized the project Water in the 3rd Millennium with the objective of bringing awareness to water preservation, under the theme "Water for Peace." The Festival was created in 2000 in Caxambu, in the state of Minas Gerais, as a way to alert the population to the inappropriate use of springs, especially mineral springs. This Festival incorporates fine arts, crafts, theater, poetry and music alongside ecological lectures, presentations and workshops in Nature and is now taking place in many locations throughout Brazil. Presently, the coordinator of these national events is Flávio Mesquita.[16]

The Water in the 3rd Millenium Festival is part of UNESCO's Peace Network within the United Nations' Global Educational Program for Peace and the Organization

---

[15] Marisa Mendes Machado, attorney, General Coordinator of the Legal Department of the CEBUDV from 1982-1998, and a Counselor in the UDV.

[16] Flavio Mesquita De Silva, a researcher from Brazil, is a doctorate candidate at Fielding Graduate University studying the impact of cultural dialogue, cultural design, and creating a culture of peace in a multi-generational context. He is former President of the UDV's General Directorate (2009-2012).

of American States (OAS). The Brazilian Federal Environment Department and the Aurora Foundation (private foundation based in the US) provide institutional support towards this effort.

Members of the local community that participate in this event have free access to the artistic, cultural and environmental activities, such as lectures, workshops, seminars, hands-on practicum, music and poetry events, painting exhibits, crafts fairs, ecological hikes, and other activities that promote contact with Nature. In 2007 the following Water Festivals took place:

- 7th Annual Water in the 3rd Millennium Festival in Caxambú, Minas Gerais, May 17 to 20.
- 1st Annual Water in the 3rd Millennium Festival in Campo Grande, Mato Grosso do Sul, June 7.
- 3rd Annual Water in the 3rd Millennium Festival in Brasilia, August 9 to 12.
- 4th Annual Water in the 3rd Millennium Festival in Caldas-Pocinhos do Rio Verde, Minas Gerais, on November 23 to 24.

The festivals have brought positive results as partnerships with public and private organizations have increased. The local community has felt encouraged and has increasingly participated in the elaboration of public policies and UN's Environmental initiative Agenda 21. Environmental education has broadened its spectrum from UDV Núcleos to public schools and communities through social-environmentally focused activities. The environmental education activities at the festivals provided a way for public school students to have contact with art and ecology.

Environmental education has been emphasized in Brazil and globally since the seventies as a basic strategy to combat the environmental crisis. This strategy is affirmed in Brazil's Constitution of 1988, and also incorporated in state constitutions (Antunes 1999). In the perspective of this author, Environmental Education is an effective instrument for the practice of an important principle of Environmental Rights, which is the principle of prevention.

For this purpose, Jacobi (2003) emphasizes that Environmental Education must embody, more and more, a transformative function in which the collaborative responsibility of individuals becomes the essential objective in promoting sustainable development. And yet, though environmental education is the necessary condition to modify a growing spectrum of socio-environmental degradation, it is not sufficient. The educator is also a mediator in the building of environmental references and must know how to use them as instruments to encourage the development of social practices focused on the concept of nature. As environmental risks intensify, the relationship between environment and education for citizenship takes on an ever more challenging role, demanding the emergence of new knowledge and the learning of socially complex processes. The challenge is to formulate environmental education initiatives which are significant and innovative, on both the formal and informal levels.

The Projeto Estação Florescer (Flowering Season Project) was approved in 2005, sponsored by the Water and Sewer Works Company of Brasilia (CAESB). This financial backing allowed the Project to provide trainings for the local community, and the UDV community on the use of Agroforestry Systems.

Flowering Season is a social inclusion program, training youth then seeking to facilitate placing them in available jobs. Youth who participated in this program were able to find job positions on agro-ecological farms and in the field of organic food production.

This project has provided courses in Landscaping, Agroforestry and Permaculture. The courses were designed with integrated activities and the goal of training participants to acquire skills desired by the local job market. The main training activities provided opportunities for the youth of the UDV and of the large rural communities of Rodeador and Brazlandia. Some of these activities were:

- Courses in Agroforestry, Landscaping and Permaculture taught by Professor José Augusto from the Rodeador Fundamental Education Center (CEFR), who is responsible for the Coordination of a plantation of medicinal plants called the Green Pharmacy Project and for the maintenance activities of the Forest Gardening Course.
- Workshops in Succession Agroforestry Systems with Ernest Götsch, in collaboration with Núcleo Luz do Oriente[17]
- Construction of a multi-use space for the Flowering Season Project at Núcleo Luz do Oriente
- Technical learning visits to nurseries and gardens at EMBRAPA (Empresa Brasileira de Pesquisa Agropecuária: Brazilian Agricultural Research Corporation)
- Four lectures and workshops titled "Water Forest" at the Water in the 3rd Millennium Festival

---

[17] Ernest Götsch is a Swiss expatriate who has lived in Bahia, Brazil for more than 20 years and he is an international reference on the development of Agroforestry Systems.

- Two workshops on Agroforestry in Florianopolis, state of Santa Catarina
- A 32-hour Training Course in Bio-Architecture at Flowering Season for participants from CEFR and the UDV
- Activities and lectures on Environmental Education at CEFR
- Workshop titled "The Art of Reforestation" for UDV members from the Central-West region in Planaltina and at Flowering Season in Brasilia.
- Implementation of new Agroforestry System areas, evaluation of participants and placement in the job market.

Agroforestry Systems are sequential arrangements of species or combinations of species, including woody perennials, herbaceous plants, shrubs, trees, agricultural crops, forage crops and sometimes livestock. The objective is to create long-term sustainability through recreating the structure and the succession dynamics of the original vegetation, to attend to human demands (Götsch, 1992 and 1995; Peneireiro, 1999; Silva, 2002).

In Agroforestry Systems sustainability is based on fundamental concepts that take into consideration local variables and designing the productive systems adapted to natural potential. In effect, Agroforestry Systems were, and still are, developed by indigenous people or traditional populations throughout the world, whose principles are intrinsically related to millenary cultures which have been, through the ages, adapting to environmental changes and human activities (Penereiro, 1999).

Within this agro-ecological context, the Flowering Season Project has also done trainings with members of the UDV in Florianopolis and Porto Velho, focused on developing sustainable Agroforestry Systems for the cultivation of Mariri and Chacrona.

Flowering Season's multi-use space located at Núcleo Luz do Oriente in Brasilia, was built with the objective of training young members of the UDV through lessons, lectures, courses, experiential activities, workshops, and other modalities. The most significant results achieved are mostly related to the inclusion of youth through training opportunities that evaluate and certify them for eventual job market placement.

Approximately 70% of participants trained demonstrated satisfactory levels of knowledge and basic concepts within the implementation and management of Agroforestry Systems and maintenance of gardens. In general, it can be said that the young apprentices showed significant understanding of the importance of work and the need for professional training in their lives.

At this time there are future possibilities for the Flowering Season Project to expand its activities and goals of creating a training center for Agroforestry, Gardening and Permaculture, dependent on financial support from new sponsoring entities and new partnerships.

Encantos do Artesanato – **Enchanting Crafts** – is a 'solidarity economy' project aiming to train approximately 400 new artisans in the state of Alagoas in the renowned traditional art of woven lace embroidery, as well as marketing their crafts within a sustainable development model. (Melo, 2007).

In general terms, solidarity economy is defined as a means of production in which workers collectively share rights and the ownership of production methods (Singer 2008). Initially it may seem that this approach to collective production and distribution may be a hybrid between capitalism and a cottage industry system, however, it is a combination that surpasses both. The typical common denominator of solidarity economy is a cooperative production system in which the principles of organization is the collective ownership of production methods and a democratic business management system.

The Enchanting Crafts Project was sponsored by Petrobrás (the nationally owned Brazilian petroleum company) and supported by the City Hall of Marechal Deodoro, the town in Alagoas state where two phases of this project took place in 2005 and 2006.

A third phase of this project is currently taking place in the settlement of Massagueira, in the township of Marechal Deodoro. New artisans are being trained to develop skills to develop the craft of woven lace embroidery.

At first, artisans are identified and trained to lead the formation of production associations to market their crafts in local and national fairs. The trainings consist of lectures, workshops and courses on design, networking, marketing, quality control, customer care, cooperativism, bookkeeping, women's health, painting, citizenship, environment, among others. The training also includes travel to related crafts production locations, cultural activities, and networking events with the participants.

The main results of Enchanting Crafts Project include the social inclusion of artisans through training opportunities and the organization of production groups, the opportunity for artisans to improve their craft, and market opportunities. Future opportunities are possible for expanded partnerships, training of future leaders and project sponsorship.

The Projeto de Permaculture no Cerrado – **Permaculture in the Savannah Project** aims to train UDV members in several regions of Brazil in the area of Permaculture (Marin, 2008).

Renowned Australian author Bill Mollison is considered the "father of Permaculture". A scientist and tenured university professor, who had been a fisherman, lumberjack, and hunter in his youth, Mollison retired from academic life to live in a remote area of Tasmania. He came to create "Permaculture", or "permanent culture", by integrating his scientific knowledge with observations from the patterns of nature and indigenous traditions, which he consider to be the foundation of society (Soares, 1998).

The Ethical Principles of Permaculture are care for the earth, care for people (and other living species), distribution of surplus, and consumption limits that are based on sustainability. Permaculture develops sustainable models of human occupation in harmony with the environment.

In April of 2007, an Introduction to Permaculture and Bio-Construction (building with environmentally low-impact materials) Course took place at the Institute of Permaculture and Eco-Villas in the Savannah (Ecocentro IPEC). There were also workshops on building rain water-catchment cisterns at several UDV locations in Brasilia.

The cisterns were built using low-impact materials (ferrocement: mixture of Portland cement and sand applied over layers of woven or expanded steel mesh and closely spaced small-diameter steel rebar). Structures of rebar shaped like a basket were filled with the mixture of cement and sand in the proportion of two to one.

During these workshops an adobe bench was built at Núcleo Gaspar, using clay from the property and at Núcleo Canário Verde a composting structure to deposit organic refuse was built.

A course on Permaculture Design, with a certification by the Brazilian Permaculture Network in partnership with the Permaculture Institute: Organization, Eco-Vilas and Environment (IPOEMA), was provided to UDV members including 30-hour training on Agroforestry.

The environmental projects of the Novo Encanto Association have also provided benefits to the general public, including trainings in Environmental Education, Permaculture, Agroforestry, Organic Gardening, and Solidarity Economy, among others.

The growing participation of the community at large in these projects has produced positive impact on the local level, such as the Water in the 3rd Millennium Festival, which creates a stimulus for the community to participate in the elaboration of public policy and Agenda 21 on the local level.

The environmental projects presented here can be considered representative of the work of Novo Encanto. Future projects will seek to increase partnerships with both public agencies and private entities.

Bibliography

Antunes, P. B. "Educação Ambiental." Revista de Direito, Rio de Janeiro, v.3, n. 6, jul./dez., p. 73-80, 1999.

Barbosa, A. L.; Barbosa Neto, M. L. "Projeto Encantos do Artenasato." Alagoas: Manuscrito da Associação Novo Encanto de Desenvolvimento Ecológico. 17p., março, 2007.

CMMAD. "Nosso Futuro Comum." RJ: Fundação Getulio Vargas, 1991.

Derivi, Carolina (2007). "IPCC confirma responsabilidade humana para o aquecimento global." See at: http://www.amazonia.org.br/noticias/ (last visited 9/2013).

Gordon, F.; Stefanuto, G. "Relatório do 2° Encontro de Ambientalistas do CEBUDV." Campinas: Manuscrito da Associação Novo Encanto de Desenvolvimento Ecológico. 9p., dezembro, 2006.

Gordon, F.; Stefanuto, G.; Hacker, C. V. B. "Manual do Monitor." Campinas: Manuscript of the Associação Novo Encanto de Desenvolvimento Ecológico. 71 p., 2008.

Götsch, E. "Natural succession of species in agroforestry and in soil recovery." Manuscript, Bahia, p. 1-19, agosto, 1992.

Götsch, E. "Break-through in agriculture." Rio de Janeiro: AS-PTA. 22p., 1995.

Jacobi, P. "Educação Ambiental, Cidadania e Sustentabilidade." Cadernos de Pesquisa, n. 118, março, p. 189-205, 2003.

Layargues, Philippe P. "Por uma educação ambiental crítica." Senac e Educação Ambiental, Rio de Janeiro, ano 11, n. 1, p8-11, jan./março, 2002.

Marin, J. V. "Relatório de Atividades." Brasília: Manuscript of the Associação Novo Encanto de Desenvolvimento Ecológico. 75p., março, 2008.

Penereiro, F. M. "Sistemas agroflorestais dirigidos pela sucessão natural: um estudo de caso." 138p. (Master Thesis in Forestry Science) – Escola Superior de Agricultura "Luiz de Queiroz" (ESALQ), Universidade de São Paulo (USP), Piracicaba, 1999.

"Relatório De Atividades: Estação Florescer." Brasília: Manuscript of the Associação Novo Encanto de Desenvolvimento Ecológico. 39p., julho, 2006.

Silva, P. P. V. "Sistemas agroflorestais para recuperação de matas ciliares em Piracicaba, SP." 98p. (Master Thesis in Forestry Science) – Escola Superior de Agricultura "Luiz de Queiroz" (ESALQ), Universidade de São Paulo (USP), Piracicaba, 2002.

Singer, P. "Economia solidária: entrevista com Paul Singer." Estudos Avançados, São Paulo, v. 22, n. 62, p. 288-314, 2008.

Soares, A. L. J. "Conceitos básicos sobre permacultura." Brasília: MA/SDR/CENAGRI Preservação da Memória Agrícola Nacional. 53p., 1998.

Sites: www.udv.org.br and www.novoencanto.org.br (last visited 9/2013)

About the Authors

Antônio Alves – journalist, official orator of the *Centro de Iluminação Cristã Luz Universal (Ciclu – Alto Santo)* (Universal Light Christian Center of Illumination – CICLU – High Spirit).

Carmen Palet – licensed in physical education from the University of Brasilia, prenatal yoga instructor, doula, adjunct secretary (2003-2006), official orator (2006-2009), and currently the vice-director of the Department of Beneficence of the CEBUDV.

Charles S. Grob – medical doctor, professor of psychiatry and pediatrics at the University of California at Los Angeles (UCLA) Medical School, director of the Children and Adolescent Psychiatry Division at the Harbor Medical Center at UCLA.

Cristina Patriota de Moura – Doctor of Anthropology from the National Museum of the Federal University of Rio de Janeiro, adjunct professor of the anthropology department of the University of Brasilia, collaborator with the coordination of Institutional Relations of the CEBUDV.

Cristiane Tacla – psychologist, Master of Psychiatry and Medical Psychology from the Federal University of São Paulo, researcher for the Clinical Hospital of the medical school at the University of São Paulo.

Dartiu Xavier da Silveira – medical doctor, Doctor of Psychiatry and Medical Psychology from the Federal University of São Paulo, currently an associate professor of the Federal University of São Paulo, consultant for the Ministry of Health.

Edison Saraiva Neves – medical doctor, general clinical nutrologist, has previously occupied the following offices: president of the General Directorate, president of the Center of Medical Studies of the CEBUDV, director of the Department of Beneficence, and member of the Deliberative Council of the Novo Encanto Association for Ecological Development.

Edson Lodi Campos Soares – journalist, author of the books *Estrela da Minha Vida* (Star of My Life) (published by *Editora Entrefolhas*), *Travessia* (Crossing) (published by *Editora Thesaurus*) and *Relicário – Imagens do Sertão* (Reliquary – Images of the Brazilian Backcountry) (published by *Editora Pedra Nova*). Campos Soares previously held the offices of president of the General Directorate and member of the Deliberative Council of the Novo Encanto Association for Ecological Development, currently the coordinator of Institutional Relations of the CEBUDV.

Enrique Lopez – Doctor of Clinical Psychology, assistant clinical professor of the psychiatry and behavioral sciences department of the David Geffen Medical School of the University of California at Los Angeles.

Evelyn Doering-Silveira – neuropsychologist, Master of Psychiatry and Medical Psychology from the Federal University of São Paulo.

Flávio Gordon – architect and urbanist of the University of São Paulo, specialist in geosciences from the University of Campinas, previously president of the Novo Encanto Association for Ecological Development (2006-2009).

Flavio Mesquita da Silva – current president of the CEBUDV (2009-2012).

Francisco Hipólito de Araújo Neto – president of the *Centro Espírita e Culto de Oração "Casa de Jesus – Fonte de Luz"* (*Barquinha*) ("House of Jesus – Source of Light" Spiritist Center and Prayer Worship (Little Boat).

Iára Reinke Soares Castro – agronomist engineer, regional coordinator of the Novo Encanto Association for Ecological Development in the South Region (2006-2009).

Itiro Shirakawa – Doctor of Psychiatry, professor of the psychiatry department of the Federal University of São Paulo.

Jace C. Callaway – Doctor of Neuroscience, professor of the pharmacology and toxicology department of the University of Kuopio, Finland.

Jair Araújo Facundes – federal judge of the judiciary section, state of Acre, Brazil, member of the GMT – Multidisciplinary Study Group of the Brazilian Anti-Drug Council.

James Allen Paranayba – journalist, president of the General Directorate of the CEBUDV (2006-2008).

Jeffrey Bronfman – Representative Mestre of the UDV in the United States of America and responsible for the supervision of the works in that country during the lawsuit for the defense of religious freedom for the UDV before the United States Government (1999-2008), currently president of the CEBUDV in the United States.

Joaze Bernardino-Costa – Doctor of Sociology from the University of Brasilia, professor of the sociology department of the University of Brasilia, currently the secretary of the Scientific Commission of the CEBUDV.

John Boyd – Doctor of Common Law, senior partner of the Freedman, Boyd and Hollander Law Firm, specialist and professor in the area of civil rights, considered one of the best attorneys in the US by "Best Lawyers in the US."

José Beethoven Figueiredo Barbosa – Doctor of Forest Engineering from the Federal University of Paraná, adjunct professor of the Federal University of Roraima.

José Henrique Cattânio – Doctor of Agronomy from the University of Goettingen (Germany), adjunct professor of the Federal University of Pará.

José Roberto Campos de Souza – medical doctor from the Federal University of Paraná, specialist in homeopathy, director of the Medical Scientific Department of the CEBUDV 2006 through May 2010.

José Vicente Marín Prades – law degree, board member of the Novo Encanto Association for Ecological Development (2005 to 2009).

Júlia M. Casulari Motta – psychologist, Doctor of Collective Health from the University of Campinas, with a post-doctorate degree in Social Psychology from PUC-SP.

Lúcia R. B. Gentil – geographer and social scientist from the University of Campinas, specialist in education.

Luiza B. Nunes Alonso – Doctor of Education from Harvard University, professor, researcher and coordinator of the master's program in Knowledge Management and Information Technology at the Catholic University of Brasilia.

Luís Felipe Belmonte dos Santos – attorney, worked on the process of the legalization of Hoasca Tea with CONFEN (Brazilian Federal Narcotics Council), among other offices in the UDV he held the post of General Representative Mestre.

Luiz Fernando Milanez – Doctor of Mechanical Engineering from the University of Campinas, with a post-doctorate from Iowa State University, professor of the College of Mechanical Engineering at the University of Campinas, current coordinator of the Scientific Commission of the UDV.

Maria Alice Corrêa – Master of Botany from the Biosciences Institute of the University of São Paulo (USP).

Marisa Mendes Machado – law degree, general coordinator of the legal department of the CEBUDV from 1982-1998.

Marlene Dobkin de Rios – Doctor of Medical Anthropology and associate clinical professor of the psychiatry and human behavior department, University of California at Irvine.

Mário Tedeschi – production engineer, post-graduate degree in business administration, specialist in strategy and management, university professor.

Maurício Hoffmann – agronomy engineer from the University of Brasilia.

Milton M. Villas Boas Jr. – veterinary hygienist, post-graduate degree in health monitoring, specialist in urban pest entomology from the State University of São Paulo and the Biological Institute of São Paulo.

Otávio Castello de Campos Pereira – medical doctor, Doctor of Geriatrics from the University of São Paulo, member of the medical scientific department of the CEBUDV, logistics coordinator for the fieldwork phase of the Hoasca in Adolescence project.

Patrícia Lúcia Cantuária Marín – Doctor of Law from the University of Nottingham (Great Britain) and law professor for the Ensino Unificado Association of the Federal District.

Paulo Afonso Amato Condé – Master of Agro-ecosystems from the Federal University of Santa Catarina, agronomy engineer for INCRA/SC.

Paulo H. Bertulocci – Doctor of Neurology from the Federal University of São Paulo, professor of the Federal University of São Paulo Medical School.

Perpétua Almeida – Congresswoman (PCB – Acre), supporter (2008) of the project Ayahuasca as Immaterial Heritage of Brazilian Culture, with IPHAN.

Raimundo Monteiro de Souza – Mestre of the Council of the Recordation of the Teachings of Mestre Gabriel, has held the post of General Representative Mestre several times, having occupied this place from 2006-2009, the period during which the 2nd International Hoasca Congress took place.

Sara da Silva Abes – biologist, Doctor of Environmental Sciences from Maringá/PR State University, university professor and environmental analyst in São Paulo/SP, regional coordinator of the Novo Encanto Association for Ecological Development (2006-2009).

Tânia Maria Batista de Lima – Doctor of Brazilian Education from the Federal University of Ceará, adjunct professor of the Education College of the Federal University of Ceará, director of the Department of Beneficence of the UDV from 2008 to present.

TRANSLATOR

Celina Bennett – Has resided in the U.S. for 38 years, graduated from the University of Massachusetts, Amherst, and currently is a master degree candidate and teaching assistant at the University of New Mexico, Spanish & Portuguese Literature department.

www.ingramcontent.com/pod-product-compliance
Lightning Source LLC
Chambersburg PA
CBHW050103170426
43198CB00014B/2436